PRAISE FOR *SUNSET AT THE ZOO*

"This is probably the best book ever written on the zoo business. It provides an insider's view and makes real the day-to-day challenges any ethical zoo director or professional has to confront in managing wild animals in captivity."

Charles Hammond
Executive Director
Detroit Zoological Society, 1985-1997

"There is a lot to like in the book, beginning with its most human story and a life both challenging and adventurous and, yes, meaningful . . . What I like most, besides the basic story, is the integrity throughout."

David Lawrence, Jr.
Publisher, Detroit Free Press, 1985-1989
Publisher, Miami Herald, 1989-1999
Currently chair of The Children's Movement of Florida

"Great to read through your book – fascinating and in many ways courageous."

Norman Arlott
World-renowned wildlife illustrator and author

"As a nationally important zoo director at a time of conflict and change in American zoo management [Graham's] conversational voice is particularly welcoming ... The most attractive part for me was the anecdotes about zoos and animals."

Kurt Luedtke
Executive Editor, *Detroit Free Press*, 1972-1977
Screenwriter
Absence of Malice, Out of Africa, Random Hearts

SUNSET AT THE ZOO

SUNSET AT THE ZOO

THE ZOO YOU DON'T KNOW

STEVE GRAHAM

Copyright 2016 – Steve Graham

All rights reserved. This book is protected by the copyright laws of the United States of America. This book may not be copied or reprinted or commercial gain or profit. The use of short quotations or occasional page copying for personal use is permitted and encouraged. Permission will be granted upon request.

Drawbaugh Publishing Group
444 Allen Drive
Chambersburg, PA 17202

Hardcover 978-1-941746-26-4

Paperback ISBN: 978-1-941746-27-1

eBook ISBN: 978-1-941746-28-8

For worldwide Distribution, Printed in the United States.

1 2 3 4 5 6 7 8 9 10 / 19 18 17 16

*To my longtime friend Norman Arlott who introduced me
to the wonder of African birds . . .
To my companion Amy . . . Hilary, Brianna and Rae Lynn*

Contents

Chapter 1	An Elephant Story	1
Chapter 2	To Zoo, or Not To Zoo? That is the Question	15
Chapter 3	My Animal Family	27
Chapter 4	Angst and Angels – Finding My Way	55
Chapter 5	Salisbury Zoo (1972-1977) – My Career Begins	85
Chapter 6	Baltimore Zoo (1978-1982) – Moving on up	133
Chapter 7	Safaris – Another World	175
Chapter 8	Detroit Zoo (1982-1991) – Storms of Controversy	193
Chapter 9	Leaving the Zoo Behind (1991 – present)	269
Chapter 10	Corruption in the Exotic Animal World	285
Chapter 11	Coming Home	331
Appendix - Steve Graham's Credentials		341

Acknowledgments

Many fine people have been my support in a variety of ways in making this book possible. I hope it will touch the hearts of readers and help them to understand the challenges zoos continue to face.

Doris Applebaum, Lisa and Kim Arlott, Dr. William Barkley, Susan Basford, Marie Lanser Beck, Maxine Beck, Tom and Jane Bollinger, Charles and Eleanor Bounds, Kenton Broyles, Mitch Bush, Kathy Latinen Don Carlos, Joyce and the Honorable Avern Cohn, Dr. Roger Conant, Wib and Ruth Davis, Craig Dinsmore, Andy Eyster, Diz Freeman, Glen Frey, Don Fry, Jo Fritz, Jane Goodall, Harry and Helen Graham, Virginia Steck Graham, Emmanuel Greene, Charles Hammond, Jack Hathaway, Barney Hill, Tracy Holiday, Ed Hovis, Russ Irving, Melissa Graham Johns, Bobby Johnson, Eldon Joiner, Msgr. Robert Kline, David Lawrence, Jr., James and Louise Leaman, Brian Lefley, Bill Levick, Ida Linton, Tommy Linton, Joan Lister, John Luoma, Kurt and Eleanor Luedtke, Sen. Charles "Mac" Mathias, Tom and Yvonne MacBride, Charles McCleary, Alice Steck Jones McCoy, Laura McCray, Otho and Violet Mears, Charley Mentzer, Leroy Maxwell, Sr., Ed Miller, Kathy Moats, Cynthia Moss, Gary Muir, Miss Armatha Newman, Diane Nickel, Omari, Sidney Pollack, Dr. Jeanne Rauch, Dr. Ted Reed, Nancy and Paul Rendine, Renfrew Institute, Woody Ritz,

Gov. William Donald Schaefer, Alan Schwartz, Dr. Ulysses Seal, Alma Graham Bercaw Senkbeil, Mike Scherer, Pete Seeger, Dr. William Standaert, H.L. and Henrietta Steck, Doug Tawney, Vic Vollkomer, Dr. Frans de Waal, Pete Waldmeir, Robert O. Wagner, Miss Marcella Waltz, Lem Ward, Blanche and Charles Washington, Dedra Watts, Leon Werdebaugh, Oprah Winfrey, Dr. Richard Wrangham, Mayor Coleman A. Young, Bob and Sarah Zimmerman

CHAPTER 1

An Elephant Story

My first encounter with Kita was immediately significant, but little did I know how much. Our relationship would later prove to be a crucial turning point in my life.

Kita was a magnificent, four-ton Asian elephant, and I was the director of the Detroit Zoo. The year was 1990.

Although Kita was six years younger than me, she was clearly the veteran member of the zoo. She had arrived May 20, 1954, a mere one-year-old deprived of her usual three-year weaning from her mother.

I can only imagine the details of what an ordeal this was for Kita based on the typical protocol at the time. While being bottle-fed a formula of cow's milk rather than the sweet rich milk of her mother, ground grain and, perhaps, mashed bananas for flavor, she would have been hauled by truck from her natural habitat after a horrific capture and endured the long ocean passage on a freighter only to be loaded into another rig to travel halfway across the United States. Two or more other young elephants were probably traveling with her but had not survived either the voyage or the transition to captivity resulting in a failure to thrive. Perhaps they were the lucky ones.

I first met Kita on my arrival as the new director at the Detroit Zoo in 1990. I stood passively on the opposite side of the heavy steel bar enclosure while her roommate, Ruth, examined me with her trunk through the foot-wide gap. She and Kita were the same age and shared similar backgrounds but Ruth had been the first elephant resident of the zoo and *always* played the dominant role. She consistently had her fill of food before Kita could eat, no matter how the keepers tried to orchestrate the feeding. When Ruth stepped back from inspecting me, Kita moved in and took her turn. I knew to stand still. Elephants can use the 1,000 muscles in their trunks to transform the large lips on the tips into powerful cups with tremendous suction that can inflict real injury at any provocation. Giving me a final sniff and sideways glance, Kita moved back into the woefully limited enclosure. Apparently I had passed inspection.

The facility at the zoo was entirely too small for Ruth and Kita. In the winter, the harsh Michigan weather dictated that they be kept inside for weeks at a time, and in the summer, they were outside for more than six hours daily exposed to the sun without adequate shade. Additionally, the outside enclosure was surrounded by a dry moat several feet deep separating the elephants from the public. Apparently the *girls* had a spat one day and Ruth pushed Kita into the moat. Thankfully she wasn't seriously hurt, but the close call prompted staff to add an electric fence to prevent a repeat performance. However, Ruth was not to be outdone. She soon perfected a move to push Kita into the electric fence and zap her, but Ruth stepped back quickly enough to avoid any ill effects herself.

As is the case with most zoos, such limited space creates the worst possible conditions especially for the elephants' feet and joints, the most sensitive parts of their anatomy. The soles of their feet are actually sense organs able to detect rumbles of other elephants even miles away unheard by human ears. Complications of severe foot infections are the leading cause of death for captive pachyderms.

Earlier in my career, I had been privileged to work with Al Perry, chief elephant keeper at the National Zoo in Washington, D.C. A short wiry man in contrast the animals he knew so well, he shared his vast knowledge with me. Unique elastic muscles surround the bones in elephants' feet allowing them to spread when needed to support their immense weight. In the wild they spend many hours roaming over surfaces that are natural abrasives that keep their feet smooth. However, in captivity, elephants usually stand for prolonged periods on hard surfaces causing thick calluses to develop on the bottoms of their feet that severely limit the natural elasticity. As a result, their hard thickened foot pads crack forming large fissures that trap dirt and can cause anything from minimal discomfort to serious infection that can become systemic spreading to their other joints and more. Al taught me how to be aggressive in cleaning these fissures and trimming their pads – much like a manicure, relatively painless, but effective. I passed these methods on to the Detroit elephant keepers along with instructions to tend to their feet on a regular basis.

Elephant keepers are the elite of the animal keeper ranks. They need to be accepted as part of the herd to be able to care for them. Many elephant handlers are injured by their charges, not as a result of deliberate attacks, but by what the elephants consider to be gentle *reminders* exchanged between fellow elephants but what are actually significant assaults to humans, such as stunning trunk slaps. When I suggested that the elephants be removed from their enclosure and walked around the zoo grounds before opening hours the keepers were, to say the least, skeptical, but felt they would be able to keep Ruth and Kita under control and return them safely to the enclosure.

The typical training tool for elephants is an ankh, a four-foot long wooden pole with a two-pronged metal hook on the end.

Good trainers/keepers only touch their elephants gently with the hooks to achieve results, but the ankh can become a torture device in the wrong hands. The recent popular novel and film *Water for Elephants* vividly illustrates this abuse. To my knowledge, such was not the case with any elephants under my charge. I pray I'm right.

Despite the Detroit elephant keepers' "what ifs," we gave the morning zoo walks a go. Ruth and Kita's first response was fear – wide eyes, nervous trembling, low rumbling and (as anticipated) defecation. Early morning hours were pretty serene; the public wouldn't arrive for hours. Two keepers, the curator of mammals and I were the only witnesses to the initial outing. All the other staff members were warned to stay in their buildings and make no loud noises as the elephants inched away from their enclosure taking in all of the new smells and textures within reach of their trunks. They immediately snared each available green leaf, bush or stand of grass and stuffed them into their mouths. The horticultural staff cringed, but the greenery recovered.

It didn't take long for the trepidation of the new venture to transform into a scene from Disney's *Fantasia*. Ruth and Kita became light-footed dancers exchanging deep-throated chirps of happiness as they shuffled about smelling and exploring the landscape. The strolls soon became a pleasurable bi-weekly event for the animals and the handlers, weather permitting. Along with an improved diet assigned by the zoo's new nutrition-trained veterinarian, all seemed well for the girls.

About a year later, I was at my desk working when the zoo veterinarian called me on my radio. Her somber tone foretold the bad news. All was not well with Kita. This was not a surprise because I had noticed Kita days earlier when I did my usual end-of-the day round of the zoo grounds. The top bar of the elephant exhibit was about a foot higher than Kita's eyes, yet she had raised herself up enough to rest her chin on it. This was totally out of character, as was her occasionally sleeping on her side. Most elephants sleep standing. I left word for the keepers to check on her.

When the vet told me Kita's feet were in such deplorable condition that she might have to be euthanized, I was furious. Even knowing that the staff (as with all zoos) was understaffed and overworked – this was a case of benign neglect, not deliberate abuse – my emotions got the better of me. My self-control only deteriorated when I examined Kita. Her feet looked and smelled like raw meat. The vet and keeper and I were a very somber group when we convened later in my office to determine how to undo the damage *we* had done; how to keep our Kita comfortable. We all knew her odds were slim, but the word "euthanize" still stuck in my throat.

We began intense treatment and kept a close watch hoping for signs of improvement that never developed. I checked in several times a day.

During evening rounds on December 23, 1990 I arrived at the elephant house to the news that her condition had worsened, so I was very careful when greeting her. Experience had taught me that the gentlest, most effective way was to take her lower triangular lip in my hand and press my thumb against her tongue. Elephants don't see very well, but quickly recognize the taste of your hand. They'll remember it for years.

I was alarmed to find her mouth was like velvet, completely dry. I got so frustrated that I started throwing things as I searched for a clean bucket for water and sponge to hydrate her. My vet tried to explain that they hadn't given her any water because they were afraid she might have to be anesthetized for surgery. If she had anything, even water, in her stomach, she could regurgitate and then aspirate into her lungs causing foreign-body pneumonia. "That's no reason not to at least keep her mouth moist," I fumed.

I was standing by her head, facing away from her getting things ready, when Kita startled – like a person who starts falling asleep at the wheel of a car and then jerks awake. She flung her head blindly against me throwing me nearly ten feet into a brick wall that I hit soundly nearly nine feet above the ground with my left shoulder. Dr. Barbiers, the vet who was standing nearby, remembers hearing the sound when I hit the wall, like twin rifle cracks, that immediately indicated to her that both of my rotator cuffs were crushed. The impact on the left shoulder transferred across my clavicles to my right shoulder and caused even greater damage to the shoulder furthest from the wall. Then as I fell away from the wall, I turned and hit the ground with my left shoulder yet again.

The poor creature had no idea what she had done. Before I managed to get to my feet, she was chirping and touching me all over gently with her trunk because she had never seen me lying down before and sensed something was wrong.

I left the emergency room that night with both arms in slings and orders to do nothing with either. Kita and I were now both playing painful waiting games.

Within less than 12 hours of my injury Kita collapsed onto her hindquarters and couldn't get back up. Her caregivers tried repeatedly to raise her using mechanical devices but failed, at which point the curator, two veterinarians, the elephant-keeping staff and I agreed that the only proper solution was humane euthanasia. In hindsight, the kinder scenario may well have been to spare her the pain of extreme measures by doing this earlier. It is never an easy call.

My injuries prevented me from being present at Kita's death. I'm sure the process was similar to the elephant euthanization I had witnessed years earlier. The elephant must be lying down and an IV is placed in the tender, vein-rich hide behind an ear. Most animals are accustomed to frequent exams and generally passive to such procedures. Then the vet begins a slow sedation drip that depresses breathing until death occurs within fifteen to twenty minutes.

As traumatic as this is, especially for the keepers who have been so close to their charge, disposing of the body is torturous, emotionally and physically. No crematorium is large enough to accommodate most megafauna. The deadweight and huge mass of these animals make them nearly impossible to move without dismembering them. Add to that grizzly duty the unceremonious grinding of the backhoe needed to dig a cavernous grave, and the magnitude of horror of the process becomes clear.

Every zoo has a cemetery area full of unmarked graves and a busy crematorium for smaller species. Most zoogoers give little if any thought to this unpleasant but necessary part of the zoo scene.

Graham with Kita before the 1990 accident (Steve Graham)

Following zoo protocol, after Kita's death we performed a complete necropsy and took appropriate tissue samples to help determine future treatment in similar cases. Then we buried her as quietly as possible. I couldn't bring myself to contact the press as usual protocol would dictate. Maybe I wanted to save her from the spectacle of it all – allow her to rest in peace.

Kita had lived 35 of her 36 years in Detroit. Just when her situation was beginning to improve, if even a little, she was struck down.

Perhaps the one who suffered her loss the most was Ruth. Kita had been her constant companion for nearly all of her life. In the months that followed, I would linger with her during my evening rounds to jointly grieve.

Such a sad story all the way around should prompt general sympathy from the public and press – one would think. However, accusations hit the *Detroit Free Press* within the week because the zoo (more specifically, the director) hadn't informed the press that Kita had died. Reporter Michael Betzold's article, written without giving me sufficient time to be consulted on the issue, was full of inaccurate criticism and not-so-subtle implications. For example, on January 4, 1990, he wrote:

> *For more than 30 years, Kita the elephant swung her gray trunk, stomped her huge feet and delighted thousands of visitors at the Detroit Zoo.*
>
> *On Dec. 23 [24], Kita died. The zoo issued no announcement.*
>
> *Asian elephants are rare and their carcasses much in demand among researchers. But Kita was buried quietly behind the giraffe exhibit, zoo keepers said...*
>
> *On that day, Graham was in her exhibit and Kita swatted Graham with her trunk and threw him against a wall, injuring his arm, workers said.*
>
> *None of the seven current zoo employees who were interviewed for this story would allow their names to be used, saying they feared reprisals from Graham...*
>
> *Jeheskel (Hezy) Shoshani of Bloomfield Hills, an internationally known elephant expert, was surprised to find from a reporter that Kita had died... 'I almost feel like saying it's a crime,' he said of the burial. 'On the other hand, I know this is their business and no*

one can tell them what to do. But when an elephant dies, one should share as much of the information as possible ... I hope it's an isolated incident, that's all I can say.'

In truth, no employee who told the truth needed to worry and I had little respect for Shoshani's elephant expertise.

Some other comments went further implying that I ordered her to be put down and secretly buried out of revenge for the injury she had caused me. I discovered later in an article in the *Detroit Free Press* that the reporter who had suggested this had been arrested for solicitation. In truth, all the relevant information about Kita's condition was gathered before she was buried and later shared with anyone who legitimately requested the results.

My response to Betzold's January 4 article was printed in the editorial section of the *Detroit Free Press* on January 9. I made no mention of my injury as an attempt at sympathy, but wanted to set the record as straight as I could in regard to *many* of the inaccuracies in their earlier article. It read, in part:

> *The article [Jan. 4] implied that the zoo refused to comment. The only phone call I received from the Free Press was at 4:36 p.m. on Jan. 3 with a request to respond before 6 p.m. Due to another commitment, I could not respond by 6 p.m. This, however, hardly constitutes a refusal to comment ...*
>
> *Your article indicated concern that we made no announcement of this death. I did give some thought to a press release about the elephant's death, but decided against it. Animal rights activists have often accused zoos of 'speciesism,' that is, being more concerned about big, glamorous species than with other less glamorous ones. I agree that 'speciesism' is wrong, so we did no press release.*

However, just following *my* letter, the newspaper also printed three responses from general public, none of them zoo professionals, very critical of my decision.

My response hadn't been empty rhetoric. I truly believe that every animal that dies is equally important. The same day Kita died, the zoo also lost two rabbits and the same week we lost three snails, reducing the *entire world population* of that species to just eleven individuals, a story that the newspaper never deemed worthy of coverage.

More importantly, Kita had died. Why couldn't the press mourn and honor her. The spotlight should have been on her – not me.

I was making rounds some days after Kita's death. As I passed one of the zoo greenhouses I saw a lone, potted amaryllis that was blooming. On impulse, I took it out and put it on Kita's grave. Unfortunately, someone saw the flower and called the press giving them the opportunity for one last hurrah calling it an act of attrition instead of grief because I had so mishandled the situation. Oh, well.

Happily, not all the press was so negative. Keith Crain, owner and publisher of *Crain's Detroit Business Week*, came through for me in his column writing, "But poor Steve Graham has to continue to do what he thinks is right and run into one buzz saw after another. I hope he keeps his sense of humor as well as his perspective. If it was any of us, we probably would have taken a walk a long time ago. And no one would blame us." I must admit there were days that I truly felt splintered and battered.

My shoulders were never right after the injury. About the time they started to heal somewhat, I would react to some situation at the zoo that reinjured them. First, was the tragic drowning of a female chimp in the exhibit moat. I helped Dr. Robyn Barbiers pull her carcass out of the water. Bad idea. Then a few months later, I was by myself when I discovered a kudu, a large species of antelope that had her head entangled in the bars of her night quarters. She was still struggling, near death, as I tried to free her. By the time I managed to lift her out, she had died and so had my shoulder, again.

Artificial shoulder replacements weren't available in 1991 and it took 13 hours of surgery to repair my right shoulder with Gore-Tex, a waterproof/breathable fabric membrane material. As a result, my shoulder was warm, but not very usable. Because the rotator cuff had basically exploded on impact into tiny pieces that had to be removed, the procedure was almost useless. I spent eight weeks in a cast that felt like I was heaving around a six-pack of beer all day with very little improvement to show for it. After this fiasco, the doctors declared my left shoulder inoperable. Continuing in my role at the zoo in this limited capacity was in the best interest of no one – an act of perpetual frustration.

I tendered my resignation to Mayor Coleman Young in January 1992 to be effective May 1.

Twenty years of pain later, technology had finally advanced enough so that I had both shoulders replaced.

Incidentally, the first dog I got after my retirement I named Kita.

Little has changed to improve the situation for elephants in zoos two decades since Kita died. How could it when, in the wild, these magnificent creatures live in matriarchal herds where they spend sometimes 18 hours a day traveling up to 30 miles in search of fresh foliage and rivers for bathing? No facility can replicate this. Consequently these captive 8,000-pound proboscideans continue to be plagued by muscular-skeletal ailments, reproductive problems and psychological distress as evidenced by continual swaying, head-bobbing and pacing. Many zoos are investing millions of dollars to expand their enclosures, but to what end? Portland Zoo will spend $53 million to expand their enclosure from 1 ½ to 6 ¼ acres, but this still won't be adequate for their eight Asian elephants. Additionally, captive elephant populations are shrinking because of unsuccessful breeding and artificially short life spans.

More than nine years ago, in 2004, Ron Kagan, Director of the Detroit Zoo, made the controversial decision to send the zoo's two Asian elephants to a one hundred acre sanctuary in San Andreas,

California. This caused quite a stir because they were one of the zoo's most popular attractions. Kagan's defense was that despite their best efforts, the zoo was essentially ruining the elephants' lives. In 2008, Winky, age 56, was euthanized at the California facility, but as of 2009, Wanda was doing well. Kagan's decision reflected the growing shift in the zoo industry away from maintaining caged animals for entertainment and toward educating the public about preserving the natural world when we can.

For ten years, In Defense of Animals, an international animal protection organization that favors removing elephants from zoos, has released a list of "Ten Worst Zoos For Elephants." The appearance of the Toronto Zoo on the list in 2009 prompted a campaign that eventually closed their exhibit in 2013 bringing the total number of zoos with no elephants to 26. But, where did all of the elephants go? As positive as the sanctuary alternative sounds for the elephants, what would happen if a significant number of the many facilities holding elephants rejected them?

However, some voices in the crowd defend the condition of the zoo elephants and the benefits of keeping them there. Peter Leimgruber, an expert on wild Asian elephants at the National Zoo in Washington, D.C. claims, "The problem is the topic is very emotionally driven ... You can play the numbers different ways to make your point." I suspect the zoo officials had a lot to do with the scripting of his statement.

The National Zoo is obviously determined to continue to successfully house elephants. Their herd of Asian elephants now numbers seven, ages 66 (Ambika) to 13 (Shanti). Bozie, 39, arrived in May 2013 from a zoo in Baton Rouge followed by three more in 2014 from the zoo in Calgary, Alberta. They inhabit a new $56 million facility that is also a center for research into the mega fauna.

On Jan. 12, 2015 *The Washington Post* featured an article documenting the extensive efforts taken to treat Bozie for a life-threatening gastrointestinal disorder – everything from a colonoscopy conducted with hoses and a vacuum cleaner-like extension rod to a shoulder-deep rectal exam. Keepers stayed with her 24/7 as veterinarians conducted test after test and administered numerous drugs to cure her. Fortunately, she survived though no clear diagnosis was ever made.

Given that none of the zoo's collection was taken from the wild, these seven have probably found a preferable situation at the National Zoo with a staff extremely dedicated to their well-being. Hopefully zoogoers will respect these animals equally and appreciate the lengths taken and sacrifices made to allow such impressive close up encounters with these magnificent pachyderms.

Robert Wiese, director of collections at the San Diego Zoo and Wild Animal Park doesn't trust negative assessments based on conditions in the past because recent conditions at many zoos have improved. The seven Asian elephants at his zoo are all in their late 40s and 50s – past their life expectancy of approximately forty-two years. Also, seven of their eight African elephants were imported from Swaziland where they would probably have been culled due to overpopulation. Weise also argues that zoo visitors who see wild animals up close make personal connections that encourage them to donate time and money to conservations efforts.

Bill Conway, former director of the Bronx Zoo and currently a senior conservationist at the Wildlife Conservation Society, agrees. "It's very different to see an animal live, to make that emotional connection, to look it in the eye and have it look back at you."

The elephant conundrum is just one in a long list of controversial issues facing today's zoos. Though I was a party to the fray as a zoo director in my tenure (1972 to 1992), the list was no shorter then and very few of the topics have changed significantly.

My unfortunate accident with Kita may have marked the end of my professional working career, but it in no way diminished the respect and concern for the animals I had developed over those 20-plus years.

Chapter 2

To Zoo, or Not to Zoo? That is the Question

Had fate not led me to my unique connection with animals – often some of the most magnificent and astounding creatures on the planet – I literally may not have survived. They successfully filled a deep void created by my long undiagnosed manic depression that crippled me much of my early life. As it happened, I was privileged to enjoy/endure over two decades as a zoo director, and I've arrived at my senior years with an abundance of memories, both touching and tragic. The zoo granted me a special life I can never repay.

My professional venue as a zoo director occurred at a time of critical transition in the zoo community that was coming under increased public scrutiny. My early associations with large, prestigious zoos in the United States put me at the epicenter of controversial issues, especially during my tenure at Detroit (1982-92), and I've never been one to mince words or easily compromise what I feel are vital issues. The voice that never seems to stay quiet in me had many ears across the nation.

Challenges that threaten zoos, then as now, need the light of day and compassionate hearts to try to resolve them. The best of intentions are often at odds with each other and opinions are widely varied as to how to deal with the multiple issues threatening today's zoos and, more importantly, the animals they house. Although the years have altered some situations, many remain the same. Zoos are still struggling to arrive at some sound practical solutions to often overwhelming ethical and economic dilemmas.

Mankind's fascination with exotic animals is as old as time. From the earliest private collections of extraordinarily wealthy world rulers, to the wide-eyed children at the viewing tank of an aquarium's shark exhibit, we continue to be held captive by our curiosity and desire to connect as closely as we can with the other species of our globe. Over the centuries, we have become quite adept at capturing many them and bringing them to our world – be it to a zoo or a private home. Unfortunately, the animals have often paid a high price for our efforts.

However much we may *love* non-domesticated animals, all of our hugs and accommodations will never compensate for the loss of their natural environment.

Zoos have entered the current decade ripe with the challenges of a new age. Contradictions abound. Attendance and support for zoos continue to grow, (More than 175 million people enjoy visiting zoos annually.) but so does the criticism of their inability to provide humanely for their animals. The lists of pros and cons of zoos can be equally justified to most minds, but real solutions to commonly acknowledged problems still escape us. The logistics of providing adequately for species, especially the more massive ones, often referred to as megafauna, outside of their environment are Herculean but unavoidable. They are the proverbial, if you'll excuse the pun, 'elephant in the middle of the room' that no one talks about. The fact is the elephant is really there and not going away. It has no place to go – none that is at all convenient or suitable.

The 300-acre Givskud Zoo in southern Denmark is undergoing a vast reconfiguration to allow the public to view the animals unobserved by the animals. Various sorts of hovercrafts and windowed in-ground bunkers and passageways take zoogoers closer to the animals, but are less intrusive. This extensive effort to spare the animals our presence is arguably positive for the animals, but the bottom line still remains – they are captive wild creatures. As Charles Siebert writes in *The New York Times Magazine,* Nov. 2014, "... whatever thrill is to be derived from staring at a captive tiger is quickly dispelled by the animal's predicament. Awe gives way to abashment ... over being the only beast that does this to another."

The Association of Zoos and Aquariums (AZA – formerly AAZPA) was founded in 1924 as an affiliate of the American Institute of Park Executives as a non-profit organization to oversee public zoos and aquariums and grant accreditation to those facilities meeting standards established to ensure humane treatment of animals and promote conservation, education, science and recreation in the zoo industry. Chartered as an independent organization in January 1972, it has become the most significant group in the United States governing accredited facilities regarding the enforcement of legal standards established for animal care. As of February 2007, the United States Department of Agriculture (USDA) provided licensing for approximately 2,400 animals exhibits (surprisingly, they considered only mammals), but fewer that 10 percent met the accreditation standards of AZA.

The United States alone has 216 AZA (Association of Zoos and Aquariums) accredited zoos managing animal populations of all sizes and configurations under a wide variety of circumstances, climates, etc. The most severe critics of zoos would see them all discontinued, but what's to be done with the zoos' existing animals should that happen?

However, a strong case is still being made in favor of zoos by both the public that enjoys viewing and studying the animals with their family and friends (especially their children) and by animal professionals who recognize the role of the zoo (among other things) to serve as an ark for species that would otherwise become extinct because their natural environment has nearly disappeared.

In a recent online blog, a young mother who had spent the day at a small animal park with her son debated the issue. Although her family had a wonderful time, she also recognized the detriment to the animals. After some cursory research she shared a list of pros and cons. In their favor, she wrote, zoos promoted conservation efforts, rehabilitated injured animal, sought to preserve endangered species, and helped educate and support local communities. To their discredit, zoos violated animal rights, caused animals all degrees of suffering, and sold animals to undesirable third parties. She quickly concluded, "Wow, this is an issue where neither side is completely right or wrong. Zoos can do great things for animals, but they can also do bad things for animals." Simply said, but also simply accurate.

The general public, though often genuinely concerned, sees only the tip of the iceberg. Behind the scenes, zoos are a tangled web of funding, politics, battling egos, head butting, corner cutting, emotional extremes, and more. The not-so-pleasant aspects of everything from manure management to the disposal of huge carcasses of deceased animals are hidden from view, but dealt with every day by often overworked zoo staffers and generous well-intentioned board members and volunteers.

What are the *right* answers? Often such philosophical questions don't lend themselves to absolutes. The many shades of gray over such issues as euthanasia and captive breeding create emotional maelstroms that often paralyze any real progress toward compromise or solution. Humans do battle while animals continue to suffer. In spite of this, the clearly *wrong* thing to do is to do nothing.

As the public wanders the winding paths to the zoo menageries, they give little thought to the vast extent of what needs to happen behind the scenes to make their experience with the animals possible. Consider the issues under just one category of zoo management – animal care. They include daily cleaning and feeding, veterinary care, nutrition, behavioral management, population control, accurate record keeping, surplus and aging animals, reintroduction and rehabilitation programs, inadequate space, animal exchange and transport, enrichment activities, quarantine procedures, escape protocols, effective antivenin indexes – even bioterrorism preparedness. Then compound this many times over with each additional zoo issue including the responsibility to provide public education programs, conservation efforts, research and more all of which require substantial funding gained primarily by tax dollars and admission fees of visitors who want to be entertained, as well as enlightened.

Complicate the situation even further by acknowledging the intense emotional connection animals have with people and the immense sense of responsibility shouldered by those whose multifaceted decisions directly affect the quality of life of these helpless captive animals.

Finally, infuse widely opposing opinions about how to address all of these concerns. Clashes are inevitable between individuals and groups who are passionate about achieving what they think is right – who believe they are justified in spinning the facts or equivocating their responses to achieve their righteous goals. No wonder the public is confused. No wonder the path of progress is slow.

Controversial Issues

What interest should be served first, entertainment or education? Zoos, despite their evolution beyond showcasing exotic species for curious spectators, are still viewed as a source of entertainment with the animals playing the main role. But, who says education can't be entertaining?

The first transitions by zoos from concrete and iron cages to expansive natural enclosures pleased the animals, but not the public who paid admission to see the animals that took advantage of new places to hide. However, experience and better planning led to improved exhibits that draw animals into the open using natural lures such as strategically located streams or release of prey. Better to observe bears lolling on heated rocks and catching live fish from a viewable stream or cheetahs chasing some prey across a broad expanse on a pulley than to laugh at chimpanzees dressed as kids riding bicycles. Many things are changing for the better, but at a snail's pace. Humans are not noted for their patience.

Recent evidence (though possibly biased in an attempt to improve public perception) suggests that a relatively small number of zoos are succeeding in their efforts to improve. A 2009 survey of more than 5,000 zoogoers conducted by AZA reported that 57% said their zoo visit strengthened their connection with nature, 54% said zoos and aquariums prompted them to reconsider their role in environmental problems, and 61% talked to others about what they had learned. Although the source may be somewhat biased, it's reassuring to consider that perhaps zoos aren't so bad after all.

Aquariums have not escaped recent scrutiny either. The dark underbelly of such highly popular and lucrative attractions as Sea World has been brought to light by the documentary *Blackfish*, first released at the 2013 Sundance Film Festival. A significant part of this film examined the tale of Tilikum, a captive orca that fatally attacked handlers in 2010 at Sealand of the Pacific. The film sought to vindicate the abused orca and condemn the facilities' treatment of its animals that very likely contributed to the tragic incident.

SeaWorld Entertainment calls the film propaganda rather than a documentary, but the ensuing drop in attendance at their various facilities – a startling loss of half its market value in one year –

will likely prompt improvement in conditions for their animal populations.

On a different front, the film industry has victimized hosts of animals in the name of entertainment. The number of individual animals sacrificed for even one feature film is shocking. Happily, technology has advanced enough to provide strikingly lifelike alternatives to the *real* thing. With evermore sophisticated animatronics and digital animation, movies such as *Happy Feet* and the new *King Kong* can be successful without ruining the lives of innocent creatures. Sadly, many other world cultures haven't kept pace with monitoring destructive or degrading animal acts.

Other issues are more difficult to address, especially the challenge of maintaining a healthy population of animals in a severely limited amount of space that many zoo advocates refer to as "the ark" – the last hope for animals with no viable homes left in the natural environment.

The basic necessities of providing the animals with adequate food, shelter, cleanliness and veterinary care are, by themselves, daunting both physically and fiscally. A recent estimate cited a cost of approximately $10,000 annually to maintain one adult tiger in captivity. But animal management extends far beyond these efforts to ensure a healthy, *happy* zoo population given very limited money and space.

All animals, captive or in the wild, should remain the first responsibility of zoos and wildlife exhibitors. In an effort to avoid removing species from their natural habitat, zoos employ captive breeding of in-house species aimed at replenishing their aging and declining populations from within. Here, controversy abounds. The obvious problem is inbreeding which weakens the species. Advanced technology has allowed very sophisticated means to achieve positive matches by identifying suitable unrelated partners from different zoos. This has been for the most part successful except for some emotionally tough calls that sometimes prompt public outcry such as the euthanizing of a young male giraffe, Marius, by the Copenhagen Zoo in Denmark in 2013. Overpopulation necessitated reducing the herd and no suitable alternative placement was available. Marius was chosen because his genetic markers were overrepresented for successful captive breeding needs. Although the zoo officials took great pains to explain their actions to the public, much of the press undermined the cause by reporting the action as "butchering" rather than selective culling.

What many zoos *want* to do falls far short of what they are *able* to do principally because of limited funds. Zoo officials have to spend countless hours raising funds to support their facilities' very existence – hours that otherwise might be spent meeting the immediate needs of zoo. Most zoos receive public monies. That translates to political involvement that is often a zoo unto itself.

The plight of captive exotic species extends far beyond zoos. More tragic is the fate of many animals populating unaccredited roadside zoos, hunting ranches, or less-than-ethical research facilities. Equally sad is the growing exotic pet trade that almost inevitably results in private owners seeking to abandon the cute baby chimp or ring-tailed lemur that has become unmanageable. Venomous snakes and larger predatory animals continue to escape their would-be protectors and endanger themselves and innocent victims. Exotic imports are also the hapless victims of the drug trade, often used as means of illicitly transporting dangerous substances inside their bodies or as money laundering exchange.

Zoos can play a vital role in helping to alleviate such situations by continuing to build positive relationships between their animals and people like you and me who hold the future of such creatures in our hands. Positive personal connections with our exotic cousins created by the physical proximity and eye contact zoos can provide may inspire us to rise to the challenge to honor and protect them. If you've never come eye to eye with an exotic animal, I encourage you to visit an accredited zoo and give it a try. You won't regret it – and neither will the orangutans or leopards you meet.

If you prefer the comfort of your home, Microsoft Studios has begun offering an alternative. Working with the AZA, the computer giant has adapted its popular game "Zoo Tycoon" to allow viewers to build their own virtual zoo and contribute to real-life wildlife conservation at the same time. Jorg Neumann, studio manager, said, "... we aimed to capture the essence of what you would experience when at a real zoo ... We worked with the AZA to ensure the scientific accuracy [of the animals]." Players additionally learn about what it takes to run a responsible zoo with high standards and vote for their favorite conservation project as endorsed by the AZA Species Survival Plan (SSP) Programs. Microsoft will respond by donating $10,000 to each project helping to protect endangered animals and their habitats.

The AZA surely recognizes that Zoo Tycoon may offer an alternative to actually going to a zoo, but the organization must also be confident that attendance numbers won't drop. Nothing can replace the face-to-face zoos provide, but the benefits to be gained by working with Microsoft and similar opportunities can't be denied and would be foolish to spurn out of unfounded jealously or fear of competition. Bottom line, as long as the animals win, everyone wins.

My past career with zoos grants me some basis for my prejudice in favor of zoos. I spent the most productive years of my life trying very hard to improve them as much as time and circumstances would allow. In the 70s when I took my first position as director at the small struggling zoo in Salisbury, Maryland, the accreditation process by the AZA (then AAZPA – American Association of Zoological Parks and Aquariums) had just begun. All three zoos I subsequently directed, from the 18-acre Salisbury Zoo to the sprawling 260-acre Detroit Zoo, required extensive upgrades to finally achieve that status, but my priorities were always the same:

1 – Caring for the animal collection
2 – Conducting ongoing staff development
3 – Fixing USDA violations
4 – Enhancing educational programming
5 – Renovating and constructing new exhibits and grounds
6 – Working with AAZPA and other national affiliations

A competent support staff was key to success in all of these areas, but often difficult to maintain.

Salisbury was small and so was the number or people on staff. As director there from 1972 through 1977, I not only coordinated services to maintain the general welfare of the animals and management of the facility, I also handled the finances and budget, assisted keepers with hands-on animal care, gained extensive knowledge of *every* species at the zoo, made many public speaking appearances, mowed the lawn and took trash to the dump on a regular basis.

At The Baltimore Zoo (1978 – 82) [renamed The Maryland Zoo in Baltimore in 2004] and Detroit Zoo (1982-1991), the workforce expanded considerably to meet the vast demands of the much larger facilities. My highly competent assistant directors, skilled secretaries, horticulturists, and host of curators (who ranged from fabulous to farcical) in charge of various species were invaluable. Operations took on the new complexities of dealing with workers' unions and powerful city councils/mayors who were my immediate superiors. Fundraising demanded many compulsory benefit events and handshaking (my personal bane), but also afforded me the opportunity to attend priceless African safaris with many high-profile zoo supporters and animal enthusiasts. Additionally, the press was an omnipresent blessing/curse conundrum as were the full range of – welcome and not-so-welcome – animal rights groups

As I will detail later, the most important of the personnel I worked with were the animal keepers. Theirs is a backbreaking, dirty job, but they have the most intimacy day-to-day with the animals themselves. The relationships they build and the observations they make are invaluable to the animals' wellbeing. As with most rank-and-file positions, animal keepers are the invisible backbone of the system. I feel I owe much of my effectiveness as a director to my having been a keeper myself for a significant time. In truth, a zoo can function without a director for months – maybe even years – but a zoo cannot survive for a single day without the keepers.

There are perhaps 7,000 jobs in the accredited zoo industry in the United States – total. After I became a zoo director I had folks with PhDs applying for entry-level minimum-wage positions just to get their foot in the door. I still marvel when I consider the chain of events that led me to the zoo. I marvel and count myself blessed.

Chapter 3

My Animal Family

"Steve, grab Stinky!" Susan yelled as I stepped through the front door into the hallway of our long, narrow, *economy* apartment after a very long day of work in the fall of 1970.

Malcolm, our black mostly Lab-mix, raced past me in a blur with Stinky, our young baboon, latched onto his back like a Brahma-bull rider. Trailing just behind them – gravity driven by the undeniable slope of the creaky floorboards - was the stream of Malcolm's urine, clear evidence of his hysterical dislike of Stinky's brand of fun.

I skirted the mess, scooped Stinky from Malcolm's back up onto my shoulders and patted Goofy on the head as he welcomed me, his tail wagging at warp speed behind him. The stray dog had joined the chaos of our Emmitsburg, Maryland, second-floor apartment some weeks earlier after following our car home from work at the Cambridge Rubber Factory. Susan was frantically gathering her second graders' homework papers together on the cluttered kitchen table, including one with the oversized scrawl of a seven-year-old across the top reading "[Tow] Little Rabbits" on the top of the heap. The only vestige of calm was the three snakes in the aquarium on the bookcase.

Susan and I were living our early months of marriage on a very thin shoestring. She was teaching in nearby Taneytown and I was attending classes at Mount Saint Mary's College three days and earning what I was able to in a nearby rubber factory two days a week. Obviously, we both loved animals, a preference that has endured. We both went on to very successful careers as zoo directors, though our marriage ended in less than two years.

Although I have a real aptitude for sabotaging my personal relationships, fate was kind in directing my career path to my first zoo directorship by 1972. I was born in 1945 in Waynesboro, a small town in south central Pennsylvania, to Virginia and Don Graham, an unlikely match, who named me, their first son, Stefan (an old world vestige I abhor in preference to Steve). For unfathomable reasons I have been blessed with many, many angels who managed to save me from my own choices that were destined to lead me nowhere quickly. I've always had a love of books and an unquenchable thirst for knowledge, but little tolerance for the conventional means by which to acquire them. Throughout my life and to this day, I've never been one to censor myself or worry about the consequences of speaking what I believe or know to be true. This has been both a blessing and a curse. Thank goodness my angels were there to bail me out time after time. What can I say? I was a true child of the 60s.

After a very twisted road and countless missteps, I eventually embarked on a very eventful 20-year career as a zoo director, first at Salisbury, Maryland, and later at the Baltimore and then the Detroit zoos. This challenging profession ended prematurely after my 1991 encounter with Kita. The long and painful recovery prevented me from continuing to do either the things I *wanted* to do or the things I *didn't want* to but *should* do. So I retired – first to the Eastern Shore of Virginia and finally to Sabillasville, Maryland, just about 20 minutes from my hometown of Waynesboro.

I had been a very hands-on director, but after retirement I maintained very little contact with many of my former zoo colleagues and organizations. However, my concerns about abuses and wrongful practices in the zoo community that existed during my tenure and continue to negatively affect the creatures I honor have never allowed me to rest easy.

The 2014 controversy about The Copenhagen Zoo in Denmark euthanizing a young giraffe spurred me on to write this book. Many of the necessary changes that zoos should be making are still being sidetracked by emotional and inflammatory responses from an uneducated, misdirected public – sometimes even by the zoos themselves. Often times, zoos are the only viable refuge for species whose native habitat is swiftly disappearing. Hence, a zoo's role is vital and must be done well.

Bad Boy in a Small Town

First years are formative years – years of childhood memories we cherish and those we would like to forget. The fact that I returned to my hometown for my more 'mature' post-retirement years suggests something positive about my early experiences. These early years were most certainly a conglomeration of good and bad. Most critical to my decision to come back to the Waynesboro area was my desire to care for my remaining elderly relatives and Blanche Washington, who had been such an important part of my youth.

My mother's family members, the Stecks, were well-educated for the most part, especially for the 1950s. She graduated from a two-year course at Drexel, taught school for two years in Washington Township, Pennsylvania, and was a legal secretary, court stenographer and society editor for the local newspaper, *The Record Herald*. Her uncle, Dr. James Steck, the family's first PhD, was head of the English Department at Shippensburg University. Renowned poet Archibald (A.H.) Rutledge, a professor at Mercersburg Academy, was one of my mother's 'heroes.' Ironically,

I recently purchased a small book *In the Pines* at a local auction for $2 that turned out to be Rutledge's first book of poems and is assessed at $4,000 - $6,000. I've loved going to auctions for as long as I can remember, sometimes perched on my father's shoulders, and great finds like this keep me coming back for more.

My grandfather, Howard L. Steck, was treasurer of the Landis Machine Company in Waynesboro for nearly 50 years. He started as a cost accountant and worked his way up. He was respected for his work ethic but felt somewhat ostracized by his peers in the community, he believed, because he was a staunch Democrat amid so many Republicans.

One of the toughest duties I had in grade school was to show my report card to Grandfather Steck. I had notoriously poor grades – a sign of early rebellion, I suppose. He just sat in his overstuffed chair and stared at the brief report for longer than necessary, glancing at me a few times without lifting his head. Then he bowed his head even further as he handed it back to me with a sigh. I had so much respect for him that I was totally devastated. As one of his seven grandchildren, this was pretty heady competition, and he had high expectations for all of us.

On the other hand, I was the *only* grandchild on my father's side until my sister was born ten years after me. Grandfather Graham used to pick me up every Saturday morning to run errands with him. I had a much warmer relationship with him than with my father.

I recently donated my collection of early farm tools and household implements to our local Renfrew Museum and Park. The tools are in honor of both of my grandfathers, both fine craftsmen in their own right, and the household items are in honor of my grandmothers. It is identified as the Steck-Graham Collection and Library.

Of perhaps more interest regarding the Steck side of my family is that my maternal great-grandfather, Luther Martin Steck, was married five times. Maybe I should claim a genetic predisposition to account for my own four marriages. Maybe not. More likely, just stupidity. Martin was a buggy maker in Welsh Run, Pennsylvania, a small community about 30 miles north of Waynesboro. Local history claims that "Steck was to buggies as Ford was to automobiles."

The Stecks held in their minds an unspoken higher 'status' in the community than my father's family, the Grahams. My grandfather Harry Graham was raised at Quincy Orphanage just outside of Waynesboro and was the third student to leave there. He used to deliver bread for the orphanage's bakery – the cheapest bread available locally and wrapped in wax-paper. The story goes that he and LeRoy Maxwell, Sr.'s father walked together nearly 140 miles from Coatesville, Pennsylvania, their original home where they worked for Lukens Steel, to Waynesboro. My Grandfather Graham ended up working for Frick Company his entire life and lived in an apartment in a large building on Grant Street that also housed the Junior OUAM (Junior Order of United American Mechanics) and various other fraternal organizations, including the Ku Klux Klan in its early years.

Harry Graham returned to Coatesville to marry Helen Vanderslice. They then ventured back to Waynesboro and set up housekeeping in various apartments ending eventually on Grant Street where they raised their two children, Alma and Don (my father). My grandparents remained there after the children had married until Helen passed away.

Grandmother Helen Graham was a sweet lady and wonderful cook. My birthday always included one of her chocolate cakes with peanut butter icing. She had diabetes and unfortunately loved the sweets that my grandfather constantly tried to monitor despite the stashes she kept around the apartment. On weekdays when she took me to the movies at The Arcade, we always bought Caramellows at Newberry's first where they cost less. On the walk to the theatre she often complained about her sore feet. Small wonder because she always battled her weight and vainly wore her shoes many sizes too small.

Her three medicines of choice were ST-37 for topical use (like iodine, but it didn't sting), Alka Seltzer and Doc Connor's Liver Pills (the concoction of a local physician). One day she called my father at Frick Company in a panic. "The Russians have taken over and I think they've killed me!" she explained. (Paranoia about a Soviet takeover was not uncommon in the 50s and Grandma Graham had it bad.)

"What, Mother?"

"The Russians have taken over the M&M factory and poisoned the candy. I just ate one that tasted terrible. I think I'm going to die!"

After some quick investigation my father figured out that one of Doc Connor's Liver Pills had gotten into her candy stash without her knowing. When the dark M&M tasted bitter, she immediately deduced the Russian takeover scenario.

Grandfather Graham loved new gadgets and splurged on one of the first televisions in Waynesboro. Grandmother Graham loved to watch 'professional' wrestling, particularly the midget wrestling. She'd yell at the screen and take punch after punch at the air during the bouts.

I'll never forget the day she died. I had just helped her and Grandfather Graham carry groceries up to their second floor home. She sat down at the top of the stairs looking just awful. "Go get me some Alka Seltzer, Steve. Quick," she said. She drank the fizzy medicine and knitted her brow, confused because it didn't work. Then her head dropped to her chest and she was gone. I stayed with my grandfather and heard him sobbing all that night. Ironically, it was Thanksgiving Day. My Grandfather Steck would later die on another Thanksgiving Day as well.

My father, Don, never graduated from high school. With money being short in the Great Depression years, he went to a CCC

(Civilian Conservation Corps) Camp along with other 'poor' kids in the area and around the country at that time. He was always embarrassed about that.

His first serious job was at Frick Company, then Grove Manufacturing (now Manitowoc Industries) in nearby Shady Grove and finally at Landis Tool Company (now Fives Landis Corporation) where he was a self-made civil engineer, quite a feat for a high school dropout. He earned a respected place in the community, but I think he was never quite able to overcome a feeling of inadequacy around my mother's more 'sophisticated' family and friends.

I tried working a drill press at Grove Manufacturing one summer. My job was to drill a hole into short lengths of pipe and then machine-tool screw threads onto the ends – a mindless task. I broke so many tooling machine tap-heads that I finally walked out – a real embarrassment for my father who was still working there.

He and my mother, Virginia Steck, must have met at one of the infamous Pen Mar dances. Pen Mar Park was a very popular attraction in the Blue Ridge Mountains about ten miles east of Waynesboro that offered a large dance pavilion and wonderful music on many weekends in season. Don and Virginia both loved to 'trip the light fantastic.' Donald Graham was a handsome, ambitious young man, but certainly not appealing to my mother's parents, especially her father. Their marriage endured, but despite my father's success, the social gap never really closed.

Our family moved every ten years at my mother's insistence. In my younger days, we lived at 25 West Second Street and every day after dinner we would drive to my Grandparent Steck's house on nearby East Second Street – *every* day. But, we had much less contact with the Grahams, whom my mother considered 'lower class.'

I still continue to keep a close watch over the Steck cemetery, God's Acre, at Welsh Run, my mother's family's home place.

The family has been granted eternal access to its location in the middle of a farmer's field by decree from the builder of God's Acre manifested in the deed. The oldest stone is dated circa 1808 – Philip Steck, a Revolutionary War veteran.

My mother and I were close and I truly cherish her memory. But I always struggled with my relationship with my father.

Truth be told, raising me was not an easy job. I was a chronically poor student, late and lazy, making every stop I could along the slow walk to Waynesboro Senior High School and sleeping for the most part after I got there. One of my best teachers, Jack Hathaway, once asked me, "Steve, you're the smartest one in this class. Why don't you apply yourself?" My reply, full of attitude as always back then, caused me to repeat my senior year.

Childhoods and childrearing were different in the 1950s. The local truant officer, Les Bohn, was also an auctioneer, and I always loved auctions. One day Mr. Bohn spotted me in the auction crowd when I should have been in school. He just shook his head and told the crowd, "I can't be an auctioneer and keep him in school, too. I give up." He pretty much left me alone after that.

Dealing with a son like me had to be difficult. My father's method was to take me to one end of the long, narrow basement of our Grant Street home and start hitting me with a length of board until I was able make my way to the opposite end of the room and touch the wall. As harsh as that sounds, I believe that kind of discipline was much more common in those years. And, yes, I did deserve some sort of punishment.

Not until after my father died in 2002 did I come to *understand* him and forgive him. Expressing warmth wasn't as much a part of the father-son equation in the 50s. Without placing blame, we were never on the same wavelength – never able to connect emotionally. The only together time I can recall spending with him was when my mother asked him to take me along to get gas at Floyd Eyler's on Clayton Avenue – a very short trip.

My mother died nearly a decade before my father of hepatitis she contracted from a postsurgical blood transfusion at Johns Hopkins Hospital. My father then moved to an apartment on Second Street directly across from Grove Funeral Home. I used to joke with him that he chose that complex to avoid pickup charges after he died.

Despite our difficulties, my father was well liked by nearly everyone he met and known for his good humor. After his funeral our Presbyterian minister, Rev. Charles B. Jessen, told me that many folks admired him. My Aunt Alma blanched at my response: "Yes, if they weren't related to him." (I've always spoken my mind, if sometimes inappropriately.)

I'm the first to admit that I was a very difficult child for my parents, especially in a small town where everyone knew everyone else's business. Years later, after I did well in my work at the Salisbury Zoo, Wib Davis, a local reporter, wrote about me for my hometown newspaper, *The Record Herald*. I saved the tissue-papery carbon copy of a letter of thanks I sent to him on Oct. 7, 1975. Part of it reads:

> *"I just wanted to thank you for the nice column concerning myself at the zoo which was printed in the newspaper. I was grateful for your time and interest and was particularly grateful for my mother who unfortunately had to put up with some adverse publicity with me at one time or another. I think this has balanced the ledger for her."*

With both of my parents working fulltime in my early childhood, I was destined to meet my first guardian angels, Charles and Blanche Washington, the black couple hired to mind me in my parents' absence. I've always contended that I grew up with two families – one white and one black. In my infant and preschool/elementary years, Blanche came to our home to watch me. She was the main source of genuine warmth for me, not the more formal affection I got from my mother (I dared not call her "Mom.") I dearly loved them both.

My mother once cautioned me, "Don't you ever say anything about Blanche being a different skin color than us."

"She is not!" I yelled back. I was shocked. To my mind, Blanch wasn't different. Her darker skin was never obvious or relevant in either my young or adult mind.

A lot of my early years were spent on The Hill, the designated black section of Waynesboro, with Blanche, Charles, Miss Marcella Waltz and Miss Armatha Newman. The black community always prefaced their first names with 'Miss' or 'Mister.' The Hill was the closest-knit society I've ever been a part of. No one went hungry unless everyone went hungry. Many leftovers found their way to The Hill households from the homes of various employers and were shared by all. Charles Washington taught me to tell time at their kitchen table and I also have an old 78 rpm record jacket from their home with the shaky, scrawled letters of my first attempts to write my name.

I truly regret that the history of The Hill hasn't been recorded. I would dearly love to see that happen, but doubt that it will. Miss Marcella has most of the details in her head but she's in her fragile but feisty 90s.

When I came back to town in later years, I made it a point to visit Blanche and Charles on The Hill at every opportunity. In fact, I went to see my black family *before* I went home. My mother somehow knew of my earlier visit by the time I finally arrived at her door. Word-of-mouth traveled faster than I did. This truly displeased my mother and vexed my father, who was very prejudiced. He even accused Blanche of stealing one time and tried to fire her. Mother and I both knew she would never do that, so Blanche stayed with us. He made it a point to warn the neighbors who were selling their homes not to sell it to any "n%*#*s." Ironically, he eventually sold our Grant Street house to the first black family to move into the neighborhood. His wallet was more important than his racist beliefs.

✦ ✦ ✦

In my lifetime I've probably written at least 100 letters to the editor. It's just what I do. I feel obliged to do my small part to combat the injustice I see in this world.

The first letter I recall writing to the local *Record Herald* had to do with a car that buzzed past me going obviously over the speed limit on Main Street in Waynesboro. I followed it and discovered the passenger being dropped off was none other than Chief of Police Don Pryor. It was his ride home from work. I guess maybe he was hungry; hence the rush, but that didn't make it right for him to speed, but not for the rest of us.

Another letter dealt with a much more serious issue. Miss Marcella Waltz from The Hill lost her husband Floyd when a gas line exploded in their home. They had reported the problem, but the gas company hadn't responded to fix it. To my mind, if the Waltzes hadn't lived on The Hill, the gas company would have been prosecuted, or at least paid damages or compensation. As it was, the Waltzes received very little help from those responsible.

I can only remember one letter I submitted that wasn't printed. *The Record Herald* sponsored a 'Beautiful Baby' Contest. People voted by giving money for their favorite child – money the contest advertised that went to the local Easter Seal Society. The baby receiving the most 'votes' was deemed the most beautiful. That was a little iffy, but not really a problem. Now, call me a skeptic, but I checked it out and discovered that only $350 had made its way to Easter Seals. I alone had donated $300, so something was definitely wrong. I really wasn't surprised that *The Record Herald* wouldn't publish my letter to the editor, but *The Herald Mail* in Hagerstown refused as well.

I was often lonely as a child at home. We lived on West Second Street until I was ten, and there were very few children in the neighborhood. My best, most constant friends were books, an obsession that has never left me. When I moved in 1994 my book collection weighed in at 3 ½ tons.

When we lived on Second Street I spent some time at the Dietrich home next to the Lutheran church on Church Street with their twin sons Daniel and David. The 7 p.m. church bells reminded me that it was time to go home. Don 'Herb' Ankerbrand was also a friend through Cub Scouts. I spent considerable time at his home, too, making Chef Boyardee pizza from a box and playing. I'm not really clear about why, but my friends never came to my house. I always went to theirs.

I had a kind of 'Dennis the Menace/Mr. Wilson' relationship with Marlin Poe who ran the funeral home on the corner of Second and Church. I loved watching him shoot pigeons from the Lutheran and Methodist Churches that flanked the funeral home. One time he had a little too much of my company, so he tied me up and put me on the front porch of my house – all in fun, of course.

I also enjoyed helping our neighbor George Royer who was always outside in his huge garden in the spring and summer months. His wife Mamie made delicious cookies that she brought out to me when I was on the back porch.

When I was ten years old, my sister Melissa was born and we moved to our new house on Grant Street. That's when I ceased to exist for my parents – especially my father. That may sound more than a little harsh and most certainly prejudiced, but I've had friends of my parents agree with me for the most part. My father even told my sister and me tales about each other that perpetuated a distance between us. She's married with two daughters and lives in Pittsburgh. Happily, we've managed to recover a caring relationship in our later years.

By the time my family moved to Grant Street, I hated being at home. That's when I got my first job at Leaman's Seed Store and

Pet Shop at 209 West Main, just a block away from where we lived. Perhaps that's where my love of animals began. We had no pets at home, though my parents would later become 'dog people.' My new job was also the start of my close relationship with Jim Leaman and his family. I spent my time after school and every weekend either at the store or with the Leamans at their farm on Price's Church Road.

I never played sports because I was always working. I also got a part-time job at Carl's Market. Part of the reason I worked was because I had to buy most of my own clothes. My parents provided some basics, but my father contended that he had worked to pay for his clothes, so I should, too.

When I was about 14 years old I had advanced from Cub Scout to Boy Scout and was patrol leader for a group of five tenderfoot campers at Camp Sinoquipe near Mercersburg. The large gathering included around 25 patrol groups competing for honors at the end of the week based on daily inspections by camp officials. Since none of my group had ever been camping before, my goal was to not to embarrass our troop too badly. As the winners were announced in reverse order from lowest to highest, I was at first relieved that we were not among the first called and totally elated when we were actually the last one named – first place honors. Walking up to get the winning ribbon was one of the highlights of my young life.

Moderation was a concept that exceeded my grasp for many years. My obsessive, addictive personality was apparent early on with my compulsive reading and hoarding food when my mother felt I was eating too much. I was always kind of a 'fat kid.' She'd find stashes everywhere.

Tobacco, alcohol/drugs and women quickly followed on the list of things I indulged in to excess for too many years. I was married and divorced four times – a very expensive hobby I needed to give up. I've often lamented the multitude of hours I lost feeding these habits that I might have spent more positively. One obsession that I continue to indulge in is going to auctions, but nothing gets hurt except my wallet, and I donate many of my purchases to local museums and historical societies.

Hindsight is most certainly 20/20 but I try to avoid pointless regret and remorse and use my past as a lesson not to repeat the same faults. Redirecting my compulsive nature gave me the energy to keep pushing to make the zoos I managed the best they could possibly be and inspired me to help others around me. Maybe it has helped me to add some balance to the scale for all the undeserved help that so often came my way.

I was an alcoholic by age 15 and was hospitalized at Brook Lane Psychiatric Center with delirium tremens by 20. I drank anything I could get hold of that had alcohol in it – from vanilla extract to the pure wood alcohol squeezed out of the wax base of Sterno. The smell of Mennen Skin Bracer still sickens me. I'm not sure if that's because I drank so much of it or because my father always wore it.

My very first taste of alcohol was unintentional. I was about 11 years old when a friend and neighbor, Mark Florence, and I were hanging out in the large backyard at his house on Main Street while our parents shared drinks on the porch. At one point I ran up and gulped my mother's drink that looked just like water but was really gin. It was a shock, but I must have enjoyed the effect.

In high school, I hung out with the 'tough crowd' at Zook's Bowling Alley and Roller Rink because that's where I could get my booze. One of the better students in my class spotted me walking there one night and asked, "So when are you picking up your whore?" I've never forgotten the small-mindedness of that remark.

Like most teens, I loved cars. Mine was a '49 red Ford coupe, nosed and decked (hood and trunk ornaments removed). Weekends when I could swing it, I took it to drag races in Hagerstown, Maryland, about 15 miles south of Waynesboro.

Local showdowns were thrown together like a scene right out of *Grease* with spectator cars parked at an angle along both sides of the road with their headlights on and lookouts for cops at both ends (Midvale Road in Pennsylvania and Ringgold intersection in Maryland). Sometimes I was the flag man who stood between the competing cars to signal the start, not very safe as the takeoff often involved major fishtailing. My friend George White had a bucket of metal teeth from repairing my transmission at least a half dozen times.

One evening Steve Leaman and I were headed down Frick Hill west of town about 70 miles per hour when my car hood, damaged by a minor accident, flew up just as we were nearing the narrow Memorial Bridge. I tried to lean out the side of the car to see around, but Steve Leaman kept pulling on my other arm yelling that the hood had popped up. Like I didn't know! How we survived that one is still a mystery.

Maybe more amazing is the smash-up high school pal Wally Hannah and I survived after we rammed into the building at Shank's Mill on a sharp curve just outside of town. We crawled out of the car that had the front half of the chassis buried in the wall. Both of us were drunk and started laughing so hard that we had to lie down. We were still doubled over when the police arrived. Years later I was Wally's best man at Mercersburg Academy. We both arrived at the ceremony late and intoxicated.

One of the more positive things I did in my youth in Waynesboro was to participate with about 15 other teenagers in the Proud Piper's Car Club. We often got together in the garage behind Bobby Barnhart's house on South Clayton Avenue where he had this great Coke machine that was stocked with beer. His stepfather, Paul Doub, was a borough engineer who had hired me to work summers for the borough.

One evening Ed Hovis, the club vice-president, was drag racing his '52 Chevy truck against me in my '49 Ford down Clayton Avenue, one of the town's main roads bordered by some of the largest, wealthiest homes in the area. As we crested the rise in the road just before the intersection with Fifth Street and State Hill, we almost ran head-on into Abe Sanders in his police cruiser coming from the other direction and barely managed to split around him on either side and avoid a collision. Abe just shook his head, smiled and kept going.

Our formal club meetings were at Vic Hughes' house who was our advisor. We met weekly via a 'pickup parade' whereby one car would begin at the far end of town and cruise past various locations where other members waited in their customized hotrods to jump onto the end of the line and make our way down Clayton Avenue as a group to our destination. At one of our major event/fundraiser, the Jingle Bell Rock Christmas Dance at the local armory, Danny and the Juniors actually played.

Bob Couch, our president, was in a terrible car accident returning from Florida. His parents were killed, and Bob and his younger brother John were horribly injured. I was totally shocked, not only by the tragedy of the accident, but by Vic Hughes recommending me as president to replace Bob. I was probably the last choice of the members of the group, but Vic chose me anyway. I was really touched by his confidence in me.

Bill Levick and Diz Freeman were co-owners of a service station on South Potomac Street where I bought my gas and spent a lot of time. They had bought an African green monkey on a lark from a man in nearby Gettysburg. Daisy lived in a cage at the station where she was eventually buried. When she got loose and headed for nearby Park Street, as often happened, I'd chase her down for Diz.

Like just about everyone in town, Bill and Diz knew about my drinking problem. To keep me off the road after a binge, they gave me a key to the ladies' room that had an outside entrance. (The Men's Room entrance was inside the station.) I could make my way there late on cold winter nights and have a heated place to sleep it off. One night I passed out before getting out of the car and fell on the horn. The blaring alerted the police, and when a young officer opened the car door, I fell onto the ground and came up swinging. Luckily, his partner Charlie Mentzer, an older cop and another of my angels whom I respected, stopped him from possibly shooting the gun he had pulled on me in self-defense.

On Church Street just up from the service station lived local legend Dutch Shaffer and his wife. A former star welterweight boxer, he had snow-white hair and a wonderfully gregarious personality. Everyone in Waynesboro knew and liked him. His wife had the first unofficial humane society at their home in town, housing a variety of strays where I often contributed four-legged residents.

The local police knew me all too well – so well that I had my own cell, the last one back in the row of three at the Waynesboro Police Station on Main Street. Just like Otis in Andy Griffith's Mayberry, I'd park my car in front of the police station, stumble in, empty my pockets on the night desk, wander back to my cell and pass out. They even moved my car so I wouldn't be ticketed for blocking the street sweeper.

Most of my friends in my teen years were generally three to four years older than me, among them Andy Bitner, Rod Fitz, Tony Haugh, Jed Benchoff, Jim Cradler, Roger Kauffman, Ed Hovis and more. But I'll always remember one memorable event with Leroy "Tiger" Watts. He had enlisted in the Army, returning home for the first time one late-summer day with a fifth of tequila for me. In return, I offered my Ford to cruise around the borough. By early evening we were pretty well wasted when we drove past his former girlfriend's house only to discover her on the front porch with her new beau. Tiger was draped in the front seat with his feet propped on the dash.

Wild comments started flying between the two would-be boyfriends. The girl's father appeared on the scene and I said to Tiger, "Let's go. We need to get outta here." Just then Tiger took a wild swing at the new gentleman caller, smashed the passenger side window with his fist and responded to the pain in his hand by shattering the windshield with his booted foot.

I took off while the gettin' was good and we immediately burst out laughing so hard I could barely drive. I made my way to Tiger's house where we both rolled out of the car onto the ground laughing uncontrollably. His distraught mother came running and asked, "What have you boys done?" She left shaking her head when we couldn't catch our breath enough to answer her.

Hours later, about midnight, I was asleep with my sister and parents on the sleeping porch of our Grant Street home when the phone rang. I winced knowing what was probably coming. I overheard my father saying, "Don't you say that about my son." He hung up and barked at me, "Get dressed. We're going to the police station."

"Let's take your car," I suggested picturing mine parked nearby behind Leaman's Seed Store and Pet Shop on Main Street so my father wouldn't see the broken windows.

"We'll just go get yours and park it at home when we come back," he insisted.

I was too groggy to come up with a counterargument and steeled myself for what was to follow. When he finally got a look at my car he growled, "What the hell happened to your windows?"

With nothing to lose I suggested weakly, "Wow! It looks like someone tried to break in and then broke out again."

Dad gave me a look before he opened the car door and stuck his head inside to investigate. "This car smells like a French whorehouse."

Knowing I was dead in the water anyway, I risked digging myself in deeper. "I don't know. I've never been in one."

Then, with perfect timing, the empty tequila bottle I'd stowed under the front seat rolled out and dropped on my father's foot.

The two-block ride to the police station was a *long* trip. Luckily the girl's father who lodged the complaint was such a jerk when we got there that my father focused more on him than me. I just sat on the familiar wooden bench and watched the show as Officer Don Fry tried to keep them apart. What my father considered my just desserts would come soon enough.

I have bad memories of most of my late-adolescent Christmases. The Christmas Eve after we moved to 515 Clayton Avenue, I left my house late afternoon en route to a bar. As I passed my father shoveling snow he stopped and said, "Well, there goes my son, the fruit of my loins, out to get drunk again." That set me off into the storm – or gave me an excuse – to really tie one on. Very late that night my father woke up sensing something was wrong. He checked the front steps and saw my signature Frey boot sticking out of a snowdrift. He managed to get me into bed where I woke up soaking wet and shivering hours later – but alive. I often heard my father retell the story to friends adding, "I've always had second thoughts about why I brought him in."

I understand why he said that. I admit I might even have deserved to die in a snowdrift. But to this day, what he said still hurts.

Understandably, I barely managed to graduate from high school. My counselor, Helen Hoover Hoffman, worked a unique situation for me the year after my class graduated without me. The next school year I was allowed to attend school in the morning to earn my diploma and work in the afternoon as produce manager at Carl's Market on West Main Street.

When I was about 18, I got my first illegal bartending job at Werdebaugh's Tavern near Pen Mar Park. Everyone called it "Water Balls." The management served anyone, and the cops all looked the other way. One afternoon Leon, the owner, saw me sitting on the front step of the tavern and stopped.

"Steve, what are you doing?"

"Waiting for you to open," I said.

"But it's Sunday," he said.

"It's not Thursday?" I questioned.

He shook his head. "Go home, Steve."

I had lost four days.

After I had graduated from high school, I was still drinking and getting nowhere fast. I might have continued to spin my wheels destructively had it not been for a family friend and another of my early angels, Eldon Joiner, golf pro at the Waynesboro Country Club. His wife, Jeanette, was good friends with my mother. Mr. Joiner was a very special mentor to many boys whom he knew either as caddies or as family friends. He shared his amazing insight and wisdom with those who needed it most. He was the first adult to acknowledge to me the sibling rivalry in my family that had plagued my life since my sister's birth. That confirmation of my difficult situation from a man I respected was invaluable to my floundering self-esteem.

As Eldon so often did with young teens coming of age, he asked me what I was going to do with my life now that I had graduated. When I told him that I had applied to Mount Saint Mary's College in nearby Emmitsburg, Maryland, but had been rejected, that was unacceptable to him. He didn't care what a 'challenged' student I had been; he believed, based on the time he had spent with me, that I was potential college material. He went directly to Dr. Jack Dillon, then president of Mount Saint Mary's, who played a lot of golf at the club. Dr. Dillon told him I hadn't graduated from high school, so was ineligible for admission.

Eldon promptly went to the high school to investigate. My official record had no indication of my second senior semester. Duplicate copies were kept on file for all students, but mine was missing. Luckily for me, Helen Hoover Hoffman, my guidance counselor, had her copy that included the second semester – proof that I had graduated. Mr. Joiner and I were convinced that high school principal had deliberately mislaid my file. Eldon was furious and harangued him about it even though the principal was in the hospital recovering from an appendectomy. Weeks later I received my college acceptance.

Jim Leaman

As mentioned earlier, I began working at Leaman's Feed Store when I was ten years old. In addition to garden items, the shop carried dogs, cats, tropical fish, parrots, snakes and even squirrel monkeys. Jim Leaman must have sold nearly 50 monkeys to people in the area. In retrospect, I'm sure most of them didn't live much more than six months, but Jim didn't really know any better back then.

Jim Leaman became like a father to me. Looking back, I know my father was actually jealous of our relationship.

In early spring, around Easter, the front store window was crammed with scads of brightly dyed peeps and yellow ducklings. Most had very short life expectancies, but were always popular with the customers. Every morning it was my job to remove those that had died overnight. I still remember the gruesome sight of the little down-covered bodies as they swirled down the toilet in the back room. As necessary as it was, I hated that job.

One day I was helping a little, elderly lady who had come into the shop to buy some fertilizer. When I showed her the pile of large bags stacked along the wall, I noticed the black snake that had escaped its cage earlier sticking its head out of the display. Anticipating her reaction, I stepped between her and the snake to hide it from view. It promptly bit me on the back of the leg and then several times on my hand as I tried to grab it behind my back without alerting the customer. The bites felt like sharp bee stings or fishhooks, but I kept smiling at the oblivious lady until I finally got hold of the critter.

"Excuse me, ma'am," I said. "I need to step into the office a minute. I'll be right back."

She nodded as I backed away, snake tucked behind my back, and gave it to Jim in the office. Then I returned and finished the sale.

**Graham on the Jim Leaman farm circa 1955,
taken by H.L. Steck (Steve Graham)**

Some of the happiest years of my life were spent with the Leaman family at their 13-acre farm on Price's Church Road. I suppose the strained relationship with my own family sent me in search of a replacement. I ate with the Leamans on a pretty regular basis. We always had lunch at 11 a.m. because the store was busy over the noon hour. After every meal, Linda (the youngest daughter), their son Steve and I would wash up the floor on our hands and knees. 'Sis,' Jim's wife, insisted on that. I'll never forget how she served her vegetables – all of them. After she steamed or boiled them, she poured milk over them. They were delicious.

I connected with many of their farm animals, too. Among them most memorable was a cow being raised for slaughter. I became quite fond of her and brought her old produce from my second job at Carl's Market. I told Jim I didn't want to be there when he shot her.

"I'm not going to shoot her," he said.

"You're not?" I replied hopefully.

"No. *You* are," he said.

"I don't want to do that."

"It's all part of the process. You need to learn that," he explained.

So I did it. I didn't like it, but Jim told me to do it, so I did. Hell, I'd probably have shot his wife if he asked me. I loved the man.

Jim's father, Clayton, ran a store in Lancaster where he was a Mennonite bishop. When he came to live in Waynesboro, he made a strong impression on me. He adored his first wife Fanny and never stopped mourning her death, but his second wife was a real shrew, so Clayton visited Jim's house quite often. He always wore plain garb and stood very erect. His presence filled the room. There was one matter really bizarre about him. After he finished his meal, while he was still at the table with everyone, he would pop out his glass eye, put it in his mouth and roll it around – I supposed to clean it – and then pop it back in. He, no doubt, got some pleasure out of the effect it had on us, but he never let on.

Jim Leaman had the strongest spirit of anyone I've ever known. He had a distinct hobble to his walk caused by his earlier bout with polio. He always wore wide suspenders and flew around the feed store at a clip with his elbows hiking up and down from his huge shoulders to balance his gait, a lot like the character actor Walter Brennan. It was nothing for him to heave up a 100-pound seed bag under each arm and carry them. I worked like crazy to match him on that count – and finally did. One of my most cherished compliments was his comment to my father that "He [meaning me] was never afraid of hard work."

Jim Leaman was always close to the land and kept a tremendous garden. He liked to tell the story of how he sold asparagus to Al VanSandt who had a market across from the local post office. Al would ask Jim to replace it daily, so he simply took it back, cut off the browned stems and gave the same asparagus back to Al the next day. Jim couldn't help but grin when he told the story claiming that Al never knew.

Jim had to keep up his strength to keep up with his women – four wives and some 'extracurricular' ladies. He and his first wife Louise (Sis) had three children – Doris, Steve and Linda. They were like siblings to me.

Doris served as a WAC and married Skip McCrea, her second marriage. They lived with their five children in nearby Cascade, Maryland. Unfortunately, she inherited her mother's love of alcohol and died from complications of a hip replacement. Steve is an honor graduate of the U.S. Naval Academy and very successful businessman owning a large fleet of tugboats in Norfolk, Virginia. He's married with no children. Linda married a local boy, Sam Stevenson. They live on Fish and Game Road in Waynesboro and have three grown children.

Jim's first marriage was a turbulent match. Sis enjoyed more than the occasional drink – actually about two cases of Old German beer every week. She always had one with her when she was at home. She cut off the whole top with a can opener and drank it warm. Even at the height of my drinking, I could never abide the thought of warm beer.

Jim didn't drink much except for anisette liqueur, his weakness. I bought him a bottle every Christmas.

Jim and Sis were both rumored to have some dalliances while they were married. After they divorced, their farm on Price's Church Road was sold. Sis moved to Bingaman's Trailer Court in nearby Zullinger, Pennsylvania, and Jim proceeded to his next three relationships.

Jim once had a long-term affair with the wife of a local eye doctor. They actually took a cruise together at one point. But his later affair with Dorothy Pugh, who eventually became his second wife, finally ended his first marriage. Dorothy's son, Steve, was a Waynesboro casualty of the Vietnam War. Dorothy owned a farm on Cider Press Road off of Iron Bridges Road south of Waynesboro. When she died, there was a court case over the inheritance, but Jim retained the property.

Being reared in a Mennonite home, Jim, like most of his siblings, decided after his Rumspringa experience when he was 16, not to join the order. This is an acceptable choice within the Mennonite community – far better than choosing to join and then leaving. However, it seems that some of the rites associated with the belief surfaced as part of Jim's experiences with his own children.

Jim gave his eldest daughter money to leave her abusive husband, but instead she got pregnant again. After that Jim refused to talk to her or her children for many, many years – similar to the shunning practice of some Mennonite and Amish sects.

Years later, Jim was jailed for nonpayment of alimony to Sis. He was incarcerated for 17 days before his lawyer managed to get him out. Neither his son Steve nor his younger daughter Linda had done anything to accomplish his release. Jim vowed that for every day he was in prison, he would shun his children for a year. Seventeen years after his release, to the day, he called Linda to come visit him. When she and her husband, who worked as a welder, showed up, Jim's first words after 17 years were, "Good to see you, Sam. I've got some things here I'd like you to weld for me." After all those years, Jim acted as if nothing had happened.

While Jim was still married to Dorothy Pugh, he was cared for by Jaretta Rosenberger whose husband I was working for at Rosie's Bar on East Main Street. She might have been Jim's third wife after he divorced Dorothy, but things changed and that didn't happen. So Jim, being *newly* single, sat down at his 'new' computer in search of a 'new' companion.

Jim found his third wife, Jeannie, online. She showed up at his door with a dozen roses and he was so impressed that he married her almost immediately. They divorced almost as quickly.

Jim's fourth wife, Geraldine "Gerry" Rogers, owned a small restaurant that used to be in the small block building located on the Leitersburg Pike just before the Leitersburg Cinemas. He would often stop there for lunch when he was working at his new shop just down the highway. He had relocated from the Main Street site in Waynesboro. Gerry also operated a nursing home on her farm just behind the restaurant. One day she called Jim to see if he would board her 20-plus cats at his farm.

One thing led to another and Gerry was evicted. She and her cats moved in with Jim on Cider Press Road while his third wife was still there along with her adult son who was suffering from cancer and had moved into the basement. The son continued to live there with Jim and Gerry even after Jim divorced his mother. I perpetually teased Jim that his divorce decree from his third wife and his marriage license to his fourth wife appeared in the local newspaper on the same day. I was Jim's best man at that wedding.

Jim kept his indomitable spirit until the very end. He loaded his wheelchair into the back of his van with the adapted lift and drove out into their large garden. Then he lay down on the floor of the van and reached over the side to plant onions, as always, before St. Patrick's Day.

After I began my erratic studies at Mount Saint Mary's, I spent my time in Waynesboro either on the job or drunk – or both, so the situation with my 'replacement' family pretty much dissolved, though I'll always have a warm spot in my heart for the love and guidance Jim Leaman gave me.

Jim's daughter Linda called me when Jim was in his final hours at the Washington County Hospital in Hagerstown, Maryland. I was retired and living on the Eastern Shore of Maryland at the time. I made the trip as fast as I could and relieved Linda at his bedside as she looked worn out when I arrived. I talked to Jim most of the night as he lay unconscious, but I believe he heard me. After he passed, his son Steve said something that I'll always treasure. "There's no doubt he considered you another son." That meant everything. Jim had been a father to me.

Geraldine was wonderfully devoted to Jim until his death. She still lives in the house on Cider Press Road with countless cats.

Chapter 4

Angst and Angels – Finding My Way

Mount Saint Mary's (1964-1971)

Although I was grateful that Eldon Joiner managed to get me into Mount Saint Mary's College, I didn't do much to improve my student performance. I became the second seven-year student to graduate from the college following in the steps of Slick Murray from New York. In fact, my college nickname was Baggit because of my repeatedly cutting class saying, "I'm just gonna bag it."

At one point, basketball star Fred "Mad Dog" Carter was my roommate. Coach at The Mount, Jim Phelan (still one of the most successful coaches in college basketball), had meager funding compared to The Mount's athletic competitors. Consequently, he had recruited Fred from the industrial leagues in Philadelphia.

Fred was only the second black student enrolled at The Mount at the time and the other black student lived locally off campus. Prejudice was a more prevalent and 'accepted' practice back then, so Fred's welcome was at times lukewarm. My early relationships with The Hill group in Waynesboro made his race irrelevant to me and we got along famously. We both shared an equal disinterest in many of our classes despite our abilities, but had no problem excelling in those often less academic ones that we enjoyed.

Even though I was one of the most notoriously challenged students to graduate from Mount Saint Mary's, I came to be honored years later as one of their outstanding alumni. In the fall of 1987, while I was Director at the Baltimore Zoo, I was interviewed for an article in the school's bimonthly magazine publication, *Mountaineer Briefing*, said to be the longest write-up of an alumnus to date. In it I recounted my years as a student deeply involved with SNCC (Student Non-violent Coordinating Committee) and SDS (Students for a Democratic Society) – a real 60s radical. I was so deeply involved with the Civil Rights movement that Martin Luther King, Jr's death hurled me into a deep, long-lasting depression. A black sock pinned to my sleeve as an arm band marked my sign of solidarity in mourning his passing. I don't think the Civil Rights movement ever really recovered from the loss of its most influential voice of this century.

Graham as featured in *Mountaineer Briefing*, fall 1987 (Steve Graham)

It was a far cry from my high school association with guidance counselor Kenton "Kempy" Broyles, a staunch Republican and another of my early mentor/angels.

In the 60s college was often a way to dodge the reinstated military draft spurred by the Vietnam War. At first student deferments were granted. Undergraduate seniors were very conscientious about grooming professors who could recommend them for graduate school and keep them out of the service for a few more years.

Back then colleges offered Saturday morning classes – not the most popular to post-Friday-night-party students for obvious reasons. I routinely fell asleep during my Saturday morning history class whose professor had warned us, "Don't ask me for a recommendation if I don't know who you are." One morning I actually fell out of my desk onto the floor. Fully awake now, I discovered the professor staring down at me. "Mr. Graham, I will never forget you," he said. I dropped history as a major as quickly as I could.

Monsignor Robert Kline led me through the required nine-hour curriculum in Catholic philosophy I had dreaded. As far as I knew, I was the only non-Catholic of the 1,800 students at the time. On the first day of class I mostly dozed in boredom, as usual. At the beginning of class on the second day the Monsignor jolted me to reality saying, "Mr. Graham, can you synopsize yesterday's lecture?" I nearly fell out of my chair. Well aware of my dilemma, the Monsignor then led me through the entire previous day's lecture.

Each day after that, Msgr. Kline made it my job to review the previous lecture for the class, so I quickly learned to listen and be prepared. He'd often look at me and say, "Steve, I like the way your mind works. See if you can make the class understand this concept."

More than anyone or anything else in my college career, he gave me a new, positive self-confidence I might never have had otherwise. I emerged from his classes feeling I was capable of being much more than a poor student. But it didn't stop there. He was also responsible for convincing me to stop smoking marijuana.

One evening he invited me to his room. This was unusual, but I respected and trusted him, so I went. "Steve," he said. "I know you like to walk on the mountain behind The Grotto up to the old reservoir. Have you ever been there at sunset?"

"Yes," I said. "It's absolutely beautiful."

"Probably even more dazzling when you're high, right?"

I had to agree.

"The problem with that," he explained, "is that you set yourself up to be disappointed by what it looks like when you're sober."

"That's true, too."

"If you want to be able to cope with real life, you can't keep doing that."

He didn't berate me or make the mandatory dire predictions I had heard so often, but I couldn't shake the obvious point he had made. So, I quit.

He was one of the most respected men I've known.

Another colorful figure at The Mount was Dick Etchison, my History of Art professor. He was brilliant and flamboyantly bisexual. He had the whole campus buzzing the day after renowned political theorist Johanna "Hannah" Arendt had spoken and he appeared the next morning wearing her earring. He truly wanted to live in the 18th century. His immaculate house had a woodstove and no hot water or central heat.

He announced that his final exam would consist of ten questions taken from his lectures. One day he shared an interesting fact about American artist Grant Wood's famous painting titled *American Gothic* of an older farm couple standing stoically in front of their home, the husband holding a pitchfork. Professor Etchison told the class that the models for the painting were the artist's sister and his dentist. He also said that that information wouldn't be on the exam. I immediately circled it in my notes and sarcastically labeled it "definite test question." When all of the other students missed the question that appeared, as I had predicted, on the final, I was able to produce my notes to Professor Etchison and get the rest of the class a reprieve on their grades.

Father Coad lived in the infirmary. He was more than 100 years old, but he had a TV that many students would stop by to watch. His family had been killed in the Johnstown Flood, and in his less lucid moments he announced, "Think I'll hitch up my team and go to Johnstown." He was often stubborn, saying "I only take orders from the Holy Father." Then he'd look at us and add, "You all think I'm crazy."

We'd say, "What makes you say that."

He'd smile. "Well, we're all here together, so we must *all* be crazy then."

The nuns' convent above the infirmary was presided over by Sister Miriam Gertrude. She was over six feet tall and wore a white habit, so she was dubbed "the white whale." When she came down the long flight of the infirmary stairs in her hobnailed boots it shook the whole building. Sometimes the pre-med students who had night duty called her to handle Father Coad if he really got on a roll.

I was notorious for checking into the infirmary claiming serious migraine headaches in the winter around final exam time. I was familiar with the symptoms as my mother often suffered from them legitimately. Sister Miriam Gertrude strongly doubted my claim, but still let me sleep in when she woke the other patients early in the morning. I'd find a glass of orange juice cooling on ice beside my bed when I woke up, so she must have liked me for some unknown reason.

During my seven years at Mount Saint Mary's, I was often given mandated 'vacations.' I was booted out on numerous occasions for either poor grades or anti-war demonstrations. At Saint Joseph's College nearby, SNCC had hosted activist Dick Gregory as a speaker. Not a wise move for a somewhat conservative college, but quite an inspiration for me at the time.

I always seemed to be rebelling. When I did something stupid like drive drunk and wreck the family car, my mother would say, "What will the neighbors think?" I'd say, "I don't give a damn what they think. I'm not saying what I did was right, but what they think doesn't really matter to me at all."

When I was 18, I dated a 40-year-old divorcee who was also dating a local married man. We met at the Anthony Wayne Hotel, an impressive, stately four-story structure on East Main Street with a notorious bar, Anthony Wayne's Cellar. I was living there at the time after my parents kicked me out of the house. She and I were both working at the hotel bar. I made no attempt to hide the relationship. As far as I was concerned, it was nobody else's business anyway.

There were some actual celebrities at Waynesboro's Anthony Wayne Hotel. One was Secretary of State under Dwight Eisenhower, Dean Acheson. He was quite dapper looking with an impressive mustache and often came to town from nearby Washington, D.C. to visit his sister.

The sister of one of the town's most successful business executives lived at the hotel and was somewhat of a local heavy drinker. One of her favorite bar orders was a "Creamy deMenthe" and for some reason her nicknames for me were "horsefly" and "dog biscuit."

What didn't help my drinking problem at college was that many of the priest/teachers at The Mount were also pretty heavy drinkers. Someone once suggested that this was because most priest/teachers were in charge of classrooms because they couldn't cut it as parish priests. Anyway . . .

One of the Mount's priests was an infamous sociology teacher who lived on my dorm floor as supervisor. He had chicken arms and a dumpy pear-shaped torso and we harassed him unmercifully. I can still picture him one evening in a drunken stupor leaning into his room door with his head to keep from falling down. He was fumbling with his key to unlock the door and repeating, "Please, God – please, God." We had Super-Glued the mechanism.

Despite our pranks, he welcomed our company – he was a lonely man. One night he invited three or four of us to Fitzgerald's (now The Shamrock) for a nice dinner – more upscale than our usual fare. What we didn't know until after the meal and drinks was that the restaurant wouldn't accept his check – his reputation preceded him – and they weren't going to let him leave until the bill was paid. So two of us drove back to the dorm, collected change in coffee cans from our dorm mates and went back to bail him out.

I was even able to convince the befuddled priest/professor that a disgruntled ex-girlfriend had burned the Catholic Instruction paper I needed to turn in to save my grade in his class. "Women!" he said. "Don't you just hate em?" He shook his head. "Don't worry about the paper. It's not your fault." I knew he was not just a drinker, but also gay – a much tougher thing back then. I'm not proud that I used it to my advantage.

One winter day he was fighting a headwind walking his little rat terrier back from the dining hall with his long cloak billowing out behind him. I hollered, "Drunk as a loon. He looks like a tugboat pulling the *Queen Mary*." He really didn't appreciate the remark. Times were different then, but I still wish I hadn't said it, even though it got a lot of laughs from my buddies.

As I mentioned earlier, my actions often granted me 'non-participation' status at The Mount. During one of my extended times off, I worked for Frederick County under the old Office of Equal Opportunity (O.E.O.) as a community organizer (not unlike President Barack Obama) covering the destitute Appalachia area near Emmitsburg. The extreme poverty and cultural ignorance I saw there left a lasting impression on me.

My friends on The Hill in Waynesboro were strapped financially, but not to this extreme. One impoverished mother lamented to me that she knew the nuns who visited them from time to time meant well when they gave her children candy saying they loved them, but she was afraid her children thought she *didn't* love them because she *couldn't* give them candy herself. She watched their tiny TV and said, "Those lives can't be true. No one lives like that."

As part of the program, we started a preschool presided over by a Catholic nun. The activity that dominated the day the school opened was repeated flushing of the toilets because many of the kids had never seen them before. The building is still standing across from the former Saint Joseph's College site.

I was in Frederick next to the courthouse one afternoon sometime in 1965 and ran into a sidewalk salesman, the kind who keeps his goods in a briefcase that opened up into a small table. He was selling necklaces with metal peace symbols. The one I purchased that day has been a permanent fixture around my neck ever since. In some ways I'll always be a child of the 60s.

Nancy Blank was my supervisor at the Frederick Community Action Agency, a part of the O.E.O. still remaining today. She was married to a black man and their home had been fire-bombed several times, but she was a wonderful lady. She knew I was involved in anti-war protests that would have made me ineligible for my job because of the Hatch Act that barred all government employees from being involved in any political activities. Consequently, every Friday after work I'd leave my written resignation on her desk. If I avoided arrest at any demonstrations I attended over the weekend, I'd show up for work Monday and she'd 'lose' my resignation until the following Friday when we'd replay the whole scenario.

One time the agency workers were invited to Hood College for a reception honoring their President, Dr. Randall Elliot. Nancy told me, "You know, you don't have to go."

"But I'd like to," I said.

"No," she went on. "What I'm saying is, 'you can't go.' I know how you are. You can't keep your mouth shut. I can't trust you."

"I'll behave," I promised with my fingers crossed.

I wore my signature polo shirt and peace symbol necklace. President Elliot and his family sat at the dais in the same dining hall shared by the college students. No one was allowed to take a bite until President Elliot did, regardless of how cold the food got. He was that kind of guy.

President Elliot approached me after the meal and asked, "Young man, just what do you do?"

"I work in the Appalachia district near Emmitsburg and try to help out Lenny Green with 'the cause.'" I smiled. (Green was the Eldridge Clever of Frederick.)

"Oh, yes," he said. "Nigras. We have some of them working in our very kitchen."

I looked him in the eye. "Touch your food, do they?"

The blood drained from his face and he moved away. Nancy came up and kicked me really hard in the shin. "I can't believe you said that to him!"

"What?" I said. "You think he's upset because of what I said? No. It's because he just figured out that they actually *do* touch his food."

I returned to school after that experience but would never have managed to graduate on my own. It took still more angels to get me through.

The summer after my sophomore year I had fallen out with my parents yet again and was living and working as bartender at the Anthony Wayne Hotel. Things were not looking at all good financially for my tuition and transportation to The Mount to continue my education in the fall as my parents had given up on me. Desperate, I went to see Eldon Joiner about my plight.

"I'd really like to help you, Steve," he said, "but I'm pretty strapped with house payments and other responsibilities right now. Just give me a day or two and I'll see what I can do."

I thanked him and said I'd wait to hear from him. Good, as always, to his word, he called me a few days later and told me I was to meet with Glen Frey, a very successful local businessman who owned Bonded Applicators, a roofing company. My only familiarity with Mr. Frey was as a customer at the Anthony Wayne bar prior to his Lion's Club meetings there. No one ever tipped back then, but he would always flip me a quarter after he finished his pre-meeting drink. That's all I knew about him. I doubt that he knew my name.

His office in the basement of his business building on East Main Street was one of the darkest, dingiest places I've ever been. I sat down across from him and he said, "Eldon tells me you need some money for college."

"Yes, sir," I said. "I'm afraid if I don't go back now, I never will."

"Well, son, I'll be willing to help you out on two conditions. First, if you get any grade lower than a C, you'll come to work for me for $1.75 an hour until you pay me back." I winced inside when he said this because I'm deathly afraid of heights and his company did roofing work. "Second," he continued, "you need to stop seeing that divorcee now! What do you say?"

I reached out my hand. "I say 'thank you, sir.' That's very generous and more than fair."

He picked up the phone and called Fred Terry, President of Citizen's Bank. "Steve Graham's coming down to pick up a check for . . ." Then he looked at me to fill in an amount. He hadn't asked about that earlier.

"$1,500," I said.

"$1,500," he continued. "I'll co-sign for the loan." Then he listened for a bit, "Good, Fred. Thanks," and hung up. He smiled at me. "Fred says you cut his grass. He'll have a check by the time you get to the bank."

And he did.

You would think this much caring and generosity would make me reconsider my poor choices, but that didn't happen. I fell right back into my old patterns, most of them dictated by my alcoholism. One time after an all-night bout with dry heaves I couldn't talk. I went to Dr. William Barkley's office on Roadside Avenue in Waynesboro and he examined my throat. "Looks like you've damaged your vocal cords. You might never speak again. The best you can do now is not talk for at least a month." Luckily my voice slowly came back. You'd think that would shake me up enough to stop drinking, especially considering the tremendous respect I had for Dr. Barkley, but I wasn't thinking straight at that point.

Having nowhere else to go at Christmas break, I was given permission to stay at The Mount. On Christmas Eve, with no one else around, I decided to walk from school into Emmitsburg to The Palms, a small bar/restaurant on Main Street, to get drunk. It started snowing as heavily as I was drinking and I got lost in the weather trying to make my way back to the dorm. The Assistant Dean of Students found me walking the yellow line on Route 15 in the middle of the storm. He picked me up and took me back to the school. I have anonymous angels to thank for saving me from death during this adventure.

Dr. Morningstar was the physician at The Mount. A handsome, dapper man in his 40s with lots of children and a beautiful Corvette, I'm not sure what brought him to the school. I was a familiar sight to him, especially for my 'winter rest' around exam time when I would show up at the infirmary with stomach complaints. One day he broke the usual pattern of checking me in at the infirmary. When I showed up 'sick,' he said, "Meet me at my car (the Corvette) in half an hour."

When I got there he was waiting. "What's going on?" I asked.

"We're going to the Gettysburg Hospital, Steve. I'm checking you in to dry out. If you don't stay sober soon, you're going to become a stomach cripple."

I'd never heard that term before, but it didn't sound good. I did my compulsory time in the hospital and was released only to resume my former binge drinking. Finally Dr. Morningstar and Dr. Barkley from Waynesboro co-signed to have me admitted to the Gettysburg Hospital to dry out more thoroughly. I remember having the DTs so bad that they had to strap me to the bed. My roommate was Kenny, a long-term alcoholic. I think I was put with him deliberately to wake me up to my future if I didn't get it together to quit drinking. He died while I was there, but I chose to ignore the obvious dangers.

I continued to drink and take drugs. Valium and Librium were my tranquilizers of choice, and I still considered Mary Jane (marijuana) to be a friend.

I managed the first semester my junior year – barely. Heading into second semester I got a job at Mountain Manor Motel to stay somewhat solvent, but discovered near the end of the semester that I was definitely was getting a D – no way around it. So I put on a suit and headed to the guidance office to talk to Mike Scherer, my guidance counselor. I told him I was ready to "hit Route 15" and wanted to say goodbye. That meant I was leaving, headed for Florida, the popular plan at the time for Mount students who dropped out of school and needed to get out of town, as I did. There was no way I could handle the heights of Glen Frey's roofing business, as per our earlier agreement about my not getting any grade lower than a C.

Mr. Scherer said, "Just give me a week. I'll see what I can do to keep you here."

Another angel was destined to throw me yet another line.

A few days later I was called to the guidance office to meet Barney Hill, a relatively nondescript typical low-level bureaucrat from the Office of Rehabilitation for the State of Maryland. I was stunned to hear his offer – the first alcoholic rehabilitation scholarship ever given by the state of Maryland. It would pay off my debts for the last year and give me money for my senior year provided I quit the job I had cooking at Mountain Manor Motel so I could concentrate on my studies. They also provided books and spending money. Crazy thing was, they didn't require that I sign up for any recovery programs or report to anyone about my sobriety.

Within a pretty short time, the promised check arrived from the State of Maryland.

Now anyone with half a brain would have thanked his lucky stars and run to the college to deposit that check, but I had much less than half a brain back then. Instead, I went to the college business office and asked them to cash it. Then my buddies and I went on an extended bender for a couple of weeks. Our activity of choice was golf at some of the local municipal courses with just a five iron and half a gallon of wine in the golf bags.

When I got back to The Mount, I ordered the most expensive class ring they had to offer – 18kt white gold with a star sapphire.

Over my student career, my addiction to alcohol, marijuana and tranquilizers repeatedly undid all the efforts of help that came my way. I had stolen my hometown doctor's prescription pad to get drugs, although Dr. Barkley had been a good, supportive friend. If I couldn't get the drugs, I'd buy an over-the-counter product called Miles Nervine and wash down the tablet form with the liquid form.

After those not-so-brilliant moves, I was back to working my way through school again, and maybe, starting to come to my senses a little. The toll my long-term drinking and drug abuse was taking was too much for even me to ignore anymore.

Although I had regained a finger hold on my student status, alcohol was still in charge of my life.

After my last class at 3:00 p.m., I'd get in my car and head west. First stop was the Blue Duck Inn, a small roadside bar just past the Emmitsburg town limits. As one of the earliest customers for the day, I'd drink some Rolling Rocks and play pool with the owner, a feisty old soul named Timer.

Then I'd push on down the highway to the top of Blue Ridge Summit about six miles east of Waynesboro to my next watering hole, the not-so-fashionable two-story Monterey Tea House. It sounds much more elegant than it was, but the beer was always cold.

I'd finally arrive at Rosie's Bar and Grill in downtown Waynesboro around 5:30, a half hour before my official check-in as bartender at 6 p.m. There were usually a few regular early customers willing to buy me a couple, thinking I'd be heavy-handed with the booze in the drinks I'd be mixing later, or 'forget' to ring up a couple of their drafts. As I worked, I always had my own beer at hand topped off with a double shot of Calvert Whiskey every half-hour.

At midnight I'd clock out and move to the other side of the bar for some more free drinks from my grateful patrons before heading east on Main Street a few blocks to the Anthony Wayne Hotel. At 1:00 a.m. I stumbled to my car for the longer stretch back to the Blue Ridge Summit Monterey Tea House until closing at 2:00 a.m. I left there prepared for my last leg back to The Mount with a six-pack of Rolling Rock tucked under my arm. The passenger door of my car was so damaged from hitting guard rails that it no longer opened.

Students at Mount Saint Mary's had an 11:00 p.m. curfew, but I had special permission for late arrival because of my job. A security officer was stationed at the campus entrance and one night I ran into his guard shack trapping him behind a large blue plastic barrel. Another very late night/early morning I made it past the check-in but proceeded to drive on the sidewalk to my dorm where I hopped out of the car while it was still running before slowing to a stop a few feet ahead.

It's small wonder that I was again corralled into treatment by people insistent on my survival – go figure.

I had a recovery stint at Brook Lane Psychiatric Hospital in Leitersburg, Maryland. That was time wasted. Being low security, the incentive to keep us on site was to take our shoes, but that didn't stop another resident and me from walking in our stocking feet into town to the Leitersburg Hotel to drink. By the time we returned to the hospital, the soles of our socks were nothing but shreds. The psychiatrist warned me at my exit interview, "You'll never get off the bottle if you go back to tending bar."

I told him, "I'll either quit drinking on my own or be a drunk for the rest of my life, but I won't spend the rest of my life looking over my shoulder to see whose coming." They gave my father Antabuse pills and told him to make sure I took them every day. It turned alcohol into ammonia in my stomach making me deathly sick. I drank anyway and got violently ill most every night.

After somehow managing to make it through that semester, I started to realize the clock of my life was running out. I needed to get a grip and get it together, so I called Glen Frey to tell him that I'd found money for the next semester and would pay him back at the end of the summer. Then Susan Basford, my girlfriend, and I moved to her grandmother's vacation home in Stone Harbor for the summer. I got a job as a cook at an eatery in Wildwood, New Jersey. My schedule was to work 7 a.m. until 2 p.m., go back to the house and jump in the ocean, and work from 4 p.m. until 9 p.m. seven days a week. By the end of the season I had earned enough to repay Mr. Frey.

I was beginning to turn things around, but it was a one-day-at-a-time proposition.

Having floundered in various major courses of study from history to sociology, I finally took a stab at psychology. Professor Emanuel Greene, a psychology instructor and orthodox Jew, told me, "I'm going to find a way to graduate you." Part of his approach included an independent study project at nearby Catoctin Mountain Zoo, a small roadside zoo, where I soon discovered that once I'd been in zoo work, it was almost impossiblefor me to think about doing anything else. My turnaround was still holding its own and I was amazingly on the Dean's List.

My independent study at Catoctin involved an imprinting study. In early developmental stages, baby animals separated from their birth mothers will imprint or connect with a member of another species as a substitute. My work compared four young chicks given very different imprinting environments. I kept one alone, one with another chick, one with an adult rabbit and one alone with a mirror. The lone one was generally confused, the two chicks together imprinted with each other, the third imprinted with the rabbit and the fourth one with a mirror demonstrated my theory of self-imprinting by acting much like the two chicks that I had kept together. My findings were actually published in *International Zoo News*.

In the last semester of my senior year, I married Susan Basford and we moved to Emmitsburg. She was originally from Haddon Heights, New Jersey, but she had graduated from Hood College in Frederick. Mount Saint Mary's men said back then, "You date girls from Hood, but marry girls from St. Joseph's." I didn't follow many rules back then. This had been a good one to avoid. She took a job teaching second grade in Taneytown while I continued my last year of study in addition to working for a wage. I refer you back to the beginning of Chapter 3 recounting our household menagerie – Stinky the Hamadryas baboon rejected by his mother at Catoctin, Malcolm the black Labrador, Goofy the stray mutt and our trio of snakes.

Three days a week I went to classes and two days I worked at the Cambridge Rubber Factory in Taneytown where they manufactured rubber boots. The conditions were atrocious. Liquid rubber was poured into the molds, the excess was then poured out to recycle and a second treatment was given. Later down the line, my job was to dip the boot molds into an acid bath to remove excess rubber. I had to wear heavy rubber gloves that reached nearly to my armpits, but often the acid still managed to leak in.

We were so poor that all we had in our refrigerator was bread, mayonnaise and A1 Steak Sauce. I made two sandwiches of that for lunch on my first days of work. After I got my first paycheck, we made a beeline for the little butcher shop across the street from our apartment, bought a couple pounds of hamburger, cooked it and ate until we got sick. Andy Eyster, one of the finest men I've ever known, allowed me to get seven months behind in my rent, trusting me to eventually pay him. And I did!

For a short time in the early 70s, Susan and I were house parents for the Methodist Board of Childcare, a sort of court-placement reform school in Reisterstown, Maryland. Each of five cottages housed around 15 displaced youths and/or teens who attended the nearby public schools, but lived the rest of the time in the incompetently managed facility.

Each cottage had two pairs of house parents to handle the 24-hour shifts with a four-days-on/three-days-off cycle. The screening process for employees was less than adequate. On one occasion we saw the 'father' from the cottage next door chasing his wife at a dead run past our window. Seems he had discovered her sleeping with one of their seven-year-old charges. The clueless chief administrator who lived off site, delegated the day-to-day management to an absolute idiot who had a residence on the grounds.

Jack was one of the most challenging of the 15- to 17-year-olds living in our cottage. He had an explosive personality as a result of his violent, broken home situation. Susan and I could see the tension building in him until it threatened to boil over. I tried to make it a point to have a one-on-one with him at least once a week to defuse his predictable buildup of anger. We would actually push each other around in his room, sharing a few decent blows, but it worked.

However, one evening at the dinner table Jack dropped the F-bomb, a flagrant violation of the rules we had established to keep a modicum of order. The other boys got very quiet anticipating my response to his uttering the dreaded four-letter word.

I stared at him. "Leave the table. Throw the rest of your food in the sink and leave the cottage." I said this with authority – not his favorite thing – but held my breath hoping he wouldn't seriously challenge me.

He paused, but then pushed away from the table and took his plate into the kitchen. This was followed by a clatter of dishes and utensils on the other side of the door. I went to investigate. Jack was shoveling food into his mouth as fast as he could when he heard me come in. He turned from the sink with a butcher knife in his hand and a dark expression on his face.

"What are you going to do, Jack?" I asked. "Make a decision. Either stab me or lay the knife down, but for once in your life make a decision."

I'm not sure what angel (or other divine intervention) saved me that time, but he put the knife down and pushed past me to go outside. I had no choice but to report the knife incident. The director's feckless assistant called Jack and me into his office. He yelled at Jack, "Are you trying to get me fired?" and then continued with his series of threats. He had no sympathy for Jack or what might have motivated his actions. It was all about himself.

A far better memory of our experience with the boys involved a short, slightly built teen named Paul. He loved the outdoors and wandered in the nearby woods whenever he got a chance. His first love was reptiles – an interest we shared. What he wanted more than anything was a boa constrictor. I told him there was obviously no way I could approve of that.

One day he discovered an endangered Muhlenberg turtle in the woods. He knew it was a very important find, so he immediately took it to the local pet store to ask about trading it for a boa constrictor that a sympathetic schoolteacher said he could keep at school. When I discovered his plan, instead of punishing him, we talked, mostly about conservation and the turtle's value in the wild to sustain the species. When we finished, he took the turtle back to the very spot he had found it. Now Paul owned almost nothing. Having a boa constrictor meant the world to him. I was truly moved that I touched him enough to inspire him to pass up the opportunity to have the snake and return the turtle to the wild. He had an integrity that I could never have managed at his age.

The experience as house parents was short-lived for Susan and me, but in many ways rewarding. I still remember how much the boys enjoyed my French toast for breakfast – simply dip the slices of bread in a mixture of a few eggs, sugar, a lot of milk and a little vanilla and fry until golden brown – comfort food.

After seven years of ups and downs, finally graduating from Mount Saint Mary's was more of a relief than a celebration, so I decided not to attend the ceremony. The Dean of Students apparently wasn't pleased about my choice. As I heard later, he threw my diploma into the trash and a friend, Registrar Guy Baker, retrieved it for me. I never managed to pass the required course in Logic, but I suppose they were tired of seeing my name on the rolls, although for the final semesters I had become a Dean's List student, for the most part. Guy Baker confided in me later that only three students had ever graduated from Mount Saint Mary's without passing Logic – himself, Father Grace the Dean of Men, and me. Anyway, I was more than ready to move on.

Catoctin Mountain Zoo

In the 1970s the Catoctin Mountain Zoo, comprising about 20 to 30 acres in Thurmont, Maryland, developed and maintained only five of the acres. It's known today as the Catoctin Wildlife Preserve and Zoo and has expanded its developed area. During my time there the bulk of the land was still wild forest. It was a typical roadside zoo, which is a derogatory term in the zoo business, as the low profit margins often necessitate tough choices for the animals and there are almost no accreditation standards.

As rough as the zoo was, after my independent study there, I really wanted to pursue my connection with the zoo experience. I had finally graduated and needed a real job, so I went there cold hoping to get hired.

The first owner, when it was still called Jungleland, was Gordon Gaver. He was an alcoholic with a love of venomous snakes. He often got drunk and released the cobras in a room to spar with him. One time he was finally bitten and died.

My interview was with the next co-owner, Rick Hahn. Wayne Drda was his partner. Rick has a strong German background; I always picture him slapping a riding quirt against his leg. Anyway, we got into a discussion about the endangered Pennsylvania Muhlenberg turtle. He was so impressed that I knew something about the subject that he hired me on the spot as an animal keeper.

My initiation happened the first day on the job during my training for cage cleaning. The zoo setup had rows of consecutive cages with gates between them. Rick locked us into the first cage and released Jackie, a very large male chimp from the adjoining cage. Then Rick told me to turn around and face him as he instructed Jackie to jump on my back without any warning. Now chimps are generally three times as strong as comparably sized humans, so this was a pretty major shock for me. When I managed to stay relatively calm with this huge chimp clinging to my back, Rick smiled and said I had passed the test.

Jackie escaped years later and had to be shot because he badly injured a young man who worked at the park.

Escapes often ended badly.

Rick knew Karl Mogenson, a former state trooper from upstate New York who had opened a small zoo business of his own that eventually burned down, probably with the help of a competitor. Karl stood over six feet tall and was strongly built like a weightlifter. He was en route to the National Zoo to deliver a pair of tapirs and decided to stop on the way at Catoctin with his wife and kids. Tapirs are the size of large boars but have a prehensile nose, like a small trunk. While the Mogensons were visiting, the female tapir escaped from the trailer and ran into the large expanse of woods surrounding the zoo.

We chased her around for nearly half a day. The last time I spotted her she was in one of the natural ponds on the property with just the tip of her snout sticking above the surface of the water. We finally gave up and poor Karl was left with the far less valuable male to deliver.

The next spring I stopped at a local market for breakfast when I overheard a report coming over the scanner about a cow hit on the highway, but it wasn't a cow. I knew immediately it was the tapir and went to the scene to recover the body. When we performed the necropsy (animal autopsy), a routine protocol when any exotic animal dies, we discovered lots of fat in her body. Further investigation revealed evidence that she'd been living in an old fruit cellar in Catoctin State Park and feeding on the local windfall apples.

Sunday was cobra-catching day at Catoctin. Rick Hahn would have the crowd gather around and release a big king cobra. Then he'd wave his hand to keep its attention while either Mary Anne, his wife, or I narrated the action. She was much better at building the drama than me with her "Oh, watch out, Rick!" and such. Rick was an expert at grabbing the snake at just the right section high enough to prevent the snake from reaching back to bite, but not so high as to get bitten on the initial grab.

The Reptile House was a small, dark block building. Behind the semicircular plywood wall displaying a series of covered glass aquariums full of venomous snakes, was the hot room. We went there to gain access to clean and feed the snakes. One afternoon I had taken just one step inside when I caught sight of some movement lurking at eyelevel. It was an Egyptian cobra. I fell backwards on the floor and rolled out of the room, slamming the door shut with my foot.

Unfortunately Rick was in the hospital recovering from hernia surgery. I had a loose venomous snake. They didn't pay me enough to even consider attempting to catch the snake, and I was worried Rick would be moving slowly when he returned later that afternoon, so I called John Groves, Assistant Reptile Curator at the Baltimore Zoo. When I explained what happened, he wasted no time in coming to help. Rick was white-hot mad when he got back and found out John was on the way. He shouted, "No one does anything in my zoo but me! You get to that gate and turn him around. *I'll* catch the snake." And he did.

Rick and Mary Anne rarely took time off together. On one such rare occasion I was left in charge, which really kept me hopping. Early one morning I was just about to open the front gate when I noticed a pile of fresh lion dung just on the other side. The lion enclosure was out of view toward the very back of the park. Though I kept trying to reassure myself that one couldn't escape, I didn't have the luxury of confirming it with my own eyes. With really no one to call at hand, I drew a deep breath and went inside, closing the gate behind me and made my way toward the lion cages with my eyes peeled for any unusual movement. When the lions' area came into view I counted very carefully and found them all accounted for. With a sigh of relief, I decided the pile at the front gate must have fallen from a wheelbarrow load during cage cleaning the evening before. Still, those earlier uncertain moments were some of the most frightening I can recall.

Rick got his first chimps from Charlotte Hunt Levine whose family-owned Hunt Brothers' Circus, one of the cleanest shows of its kind in the country. Charlotte was a real character – a high-wire performer and animal trainer who continued to work in her tutu until she was in her 80s. She was married to Harry Levine. He always stressed the long "I" because he didn't want people to think he was Jewish. They worked the circus up and down the East Coast and wintered at their quarters in Florence, New Jersey.

After the circus disbanded, Charlotte and Harry needed to find somewhere for their chimps to live. Keeping them at their home wasn't an option.

Most chimps only cooperate with handlers until they're five or six years old. Then they get very aggressive and take orders from no one. Since chimps can live to be 50 or 60 years old, many are sold to research facilities and often euthanized. Charlotte and Harry loved their chimps, especially Mia, and wanted a better situation for them. She gave Rick Hahn money for his first chimp house at Catoctin and all of her chimps – except Mia, an especially docile young female, who stayed with the Levines.

Years later when I was working at the Detroit Zoo, I got a call from Charlotte who was finally looking for another home for Mia. Sadly, we had no room, so I suggested that they place her with a friend of mine, Jo Fritz, at the Primate Foundation of Arizona. It was the best option.

The chimps at Catoctin Mountain Zoo could really raise a ruckus when something disturbed them. Everyone for miles around knew when the group was unhappy.

One female chimp that was very special to me was Marlena. Charlotte Levine had named her after Marlene Dietrich because her ears stuck out. The other chimps determined that she was low chimp on the totem pole at the zoo and were often less than kind to her. When things got bad, she would scream. No matter where I was on the grounds, I always recognized her voice. When I went to the rescue she would motion to me with her upturned hand and roll her fingers for me to hold her hand and give her a kiss to comfort her.

The entire chimp population at Catoctin eventually died due to some strange virus. Marlena was the last to succumb. She had a special fondness for green peppers and sweet potatoes. When she got sick, I cooked some to soften them, delivered them after work and spent hours trying to get her to eat. When she passed (I don't often use that word with animals, but she was more than just a chimp to me) I was given the job to deliver her to Johns Hopkins for a necropsy. The attendant there said, "Just put her in that trash can."

"Like hell I will," I said.

Marlena – Catoctin Mountain Zoo circa 1971 (Steve Graham)

The vet overheard the exchange and stepped in. He gently carried her directly to surgery. I went along. It reminded me of the barebones surgical units on the TV show *M.A.S.H.* with loud rock 'n roll blaring. The compassionate vet was Mitch Bush, who would later become a wonderful friend and chief vet at the National Zoo.

Often on Fridays Catoctin would get a large delivery of rats and mice from the nearby National Institutes of Health (NIH) that were used for research. It was cheaper for the NIH to euthanize them than to pay someone to care for them over the weekend. Rick welcomed them because they were good food for the many reptiles at the zoo. I'm pretty sure the arrangement was an illegal deaccession. The government never gives things away, at least not without a ton of paperwork.

There were too many rodents for the zoo's reptiles to eat immediately, so it became my job to kill the leftovers – hundreds of them. I found the easiest, most humane way to accomplish this was to grab them by the tail and whack their heads against the edge of a tabletop to break their necks. Then I'd bag them in lots of 25 and freeze them for later. Not a pleasant duty. A gaboon viper nearly got me one day when I offered him a thawed dead rat. The snake rarely moved, but that day it was like lightning. After that, I was much more careful.

Catoctin Mountain Zoo was also on the road-kill list of the state police. When they delivered dead deer or other highway victims, Rick and I butchered them with a chainsaw – very messy.

On another occasion a local woman called reporting a snake she believed to be a copperhead. She wanted confirmation. According to zoo policy, we didn't identify dead snakes that looked like snake burger delivered on site. I arrived at her home to discover that she had already beheaded it with a shovel. Even more unfortunate, the victim was a rare albino black snake, not a copperhead. I told her the zoo probably would have offered her up to $1,000 for the snake had it lived. Judging by her reaction, that's the last snake she ever killed.

A far more positive situation involved some of the neighboring farmers. They would periodically call us with animal emergencies when a vet couldn't be reached or was too expensive to consider. I recall one problematic calf birthing where we actually used a cable and pickup truck for the delivery and managed to save both the cow and the calf.

Around 1971 the Hershey Zoo that had been founded by Milton Hershey closed down to upgrade to what would become Zoo America. Rick bought all of their animals for the Catoctin Mountain Zoo. They had a colony of 30 or so rare gray mangabeys and a pair of Alaskan sled dogs, among other breeds – a strange mix, as many small zoos come by their collections through various unpredictable situations. These species were good additions to Rick's collection. Those he didn't want he resold, many of them to research or other buyers, although that was definitely *not* the impression he had given the officials at the Hershey Zoo.

Rick often dealt with Warren Buck, an animal dealer in New Jersey at the time who associated with the dregs of the animal kingdom – one-eyed llamas and three-legged coyotes. For reasons like this, and some I will discuss later, I tried to close Catoctin Mountain Zoo many years later when I had the means. Sadly for the animals there, I was unsuccessful.

Hershey Zoo had been one of the first to prohibit the public from feeding the animals. Such uncontrolled feeding entertained the crowd, but was never a good idea for the animals. There were many jokes about "messy Mondays" for the zoo vets who were always busy treating diarrhea caused by the treats the animals had gotten over the weekend. The only exception to public feeding was made by Milton Hershey who posted signs that read "Do not feed the animals – *except* for Hershey chocolate which is good food." Rick had gotten the old signs along with the animals.

I made careful note of this example and decided that I would never allow public feeding at any zoo I was associated with – especially not chocolate.

My relatively short association with Catoctin Mountain Zoo offered me a number of unique opportunities that would later shape my attitudes about the animals in my charge. For example, caring for young exotic animals can be rewarding and fun for a time, but the early imprinting the baby makes with humans isolates it from its natural species. This isn't good. I learned a lot about this and more working with the drill baboons at Catoctin. This is a rare species of baboon, even uglier and scarier than the more familiar species, especially the males.

We had two – one male and one female. They bred successfully and the young female had her first baby. I've become convinced over my many years of experience with wild animal births that for many the first birth is a kind of trial run. That was crystal clear in this case. After the delivery, the mother looked wide-eyed in shock at the baby and retreated to the corner of the cage. I tried to urge her closer to the baby by pushing it gently towards her with a broom. She finally touched it, but jumped and ran away when it moved. I kept repeating my attempts to make her bond with the newborn and was finally able to lay it on her chest. The baby immediately grabbed hold, but the mother shoved it away. It took many hours of repeated placements, but the bonding finally happened.

My love for the zoo business was sparked and took flame thanks to my job at Catoctin, so I owe Rick that debt, but I spent years afterwards trying to shut his operation down. As I mentioned before, too many things there were obviously wrong, even to my inexperienced eyes and I couldn't let them go.

I realized that money was always in short supply for housing and feeding the animals. That was Rick's reason for considering the dollars before the animals, but I couldn't help but think there had to be a better way. All of the carnivores were fed raw chicken necks often coated with maggots. Rick bred and sold exotic animals like wolf pups and mountain lion cubs as pets to the public, knowing the eventual outcome – animal abandonment. He also accepted exotic animals/pets that had become violent or otherwise unmanageable, promising to care for them, and then promptly sold them to researchers.

An especially sad story involved a call to Catoctin asking if we would accept a pet spider monkey that had become unmanageable. The caller said the spider monkey was very special because it had no tail. This seemed highly unlikely to me because spider monkeys use their long tails like a fifth hand regularly to hang from limbs or pick things up. I suggested that the monkey might be a stump-tailed macaque that has a vestigial tail. "No," she assured me, "It's a spider monkey. My vet removed her tail because it wouldn't fit in the diaper." Thirty years later, this story still makes me sick to my stomach.

One morning Rick got a call from Roger, a pet shop owner he often did business with in D.C. Someone had boarded a chimp with him and not paid the bill, so he was looking for someone who would come pick up the chimp. Rick accepted and then promptly gave me the pickup duty. So I headed for downtown D.C. alone with no sense of direction or GPS in the decrepit old Jungleland van.

I arrived at the pet shop to find a very unhappy chimp in a cage approximately four-feet square. The animal's owner was a male ballet dancer who had beaten her with electrical cords. There was no way to get a handhold on the cage to load it in the van without her grabbing us. I sat down to think about an option and lit up a cigarette. The chimp shook her hand at me. She obviously wanted a smoke. I lit another and passed it to her and we finished our cigarettes together. Roger smiled and said the owner had sent some whiskey with her, too but it was all gone.

Then I noticed a hardware store next door and sent Roger after two eight-foot sections of pipe while I went to get a pint of alcohol. We threaded the pipes through the cage, lifted it by the protruding ends and loaded it into the van. I gave the chimp the pint that she quickly drained and we shared another cigarette before starting out, figuring that would hold her for the two hours it took to get back to Catoctin.

Two hours later I had circled the White House numerous times and was hopelessly lost. My passenger had sobered up and discovered she could reach the inside handle of the van's side door. Every time I had to stop she threw the door open, hitting whatever was in its path. The neighborhood looked very foreign and unfriendly, so getting out wasn't an option. While the van was moving the air flow kept the door closed, but she did a good bit of damage every time I stopped before we finally 'made it out of Dodge.'

Rick made it a habit of taking anything that was free. One such animal was a half-grown lioness that he put in one of the circular corncrib wire cages when she arrived. Often relocated animals do better with a 'stable mate' so Rick decided to put his German shepherd in with her. We both held our breath not sure of what would happen, but they hit it off well.

Cleaning the cages meant going inside, so I became very close to the animals while I was a keeper. After a time the lioness liked to rub up against me and play, sometimes jumping up on me from behind with her front paws on my shoulders. This was fine until she decided to take a bite-hold just above my right kidney. I couldn't chance struggling because that would make her bite harder and deeper. Finally the dog distracted her and she let go. I went to the office with four puncture wounds in my lower back. Rick poured some peroxide on them and sent me back to work. The marks are almost gone now.

My only other scar came from a lemur bite on my right wrist that I got while changing its water bowl. That one sliced a good-sized vein, so I drove to a local physician to get it stitched up.

It became increasingly hard to believe Rick cared about animals. His sister had moved to Germany with her husband who was in the service and they had taken their Great Dane, Ule, with them. The situation didn't work out so she asked Rick to take it.

I was relegated to pick up Ule at National Airport in Washington, D.C. in the decrepit Jungleland van. When I arrived at 2:00 a.m.

to pick her up, the official at the desk said the USDA vet who had to sign for the dog wouldn't be in for another six hours. "Can *any* vet sign?" I asked.

"Sure, I guess," he said.

"Well, I'm a vet. I'll sign," I said with a straight face. He passed the forms to me and I wrote "Steve Graham, DVM." He studied the signature for a second and then went to get Ule. As it turned out later, I almost wish I hadn't gotten her.

After the huge but very docile dog arrived at Catoctin, Rick kept it on a very short chain attached to an outside doghouse. She howled all day; it was horrible. I asked Rick repeatedly to give her to someone else or even put her out of her misery, but he refused saying he couldn't do that to his sister's dog that he had promised to keep. If she had known how he kept his promise, she would have been as appalled as I was.

I started to look in earnest for new employment.

During my job search prior to being hired at Salisbury Zoo, I also worked as a telemarketer for the Frederick sheriff's office promoting their big Western show starring Jack Greene and Jeannie Sealy – pretty big names in the industry. I was pretty persuasive on the phone and made high sales and good money. Greene and Sealy wanted to hire me as a permanent promoter, but I didn't take it. Good choice, as the Salisbury Zoo offer soon followed.

Susan found time to work part time in the gift shop of the Catoctin facility in addition to her other jobs, but we were both eager to move on. When I got wind of an opening at Salisbury Zoo south of us, I went for it.

CHAPTER 5

Salisbury Zoo (1972-77) – My Career Begins

By 1972 I had spent some time working at the Catoctin Mountain Zoo when they could afford to hire the help they needed. I actually had the title of Assistant Director, though that was more about the words than the money or real credentials. My wife Susan and I had been bouncing around to various jobs trying to get our careers jumpstarted when I heard through the grapevine that the Salisbury Zoo, on the Eastern Shore of Maryland, had an opening for zoo director. Having little or nothing to lose, I called cold, no introduction, to apply for the position. Pete Cooper, head of engineering and Director of Public Works for the city, told me on the phone that they had pretty much decided on their hire, but if I could be in Salisbury by the next morning, they would grant me an interview. I hit the road.

After an interview at lunch the next day, the head of the zoo commission asked me, "Would you accept the offer if we were to extend it?"

"How soon would you need to know?" I asked as the waitress served the dessert.

"Before the check comes," he said without hesitation.

I said yes and, at 26 years old, became the youngest zoo director in the country.

When Susan and I arrived in Salisbury, the landlord of the apartment we thought we had rented changed his mind because he discovered I was the new zoo director. He didn't want "all of those animals in the place." We finally found a sad little house and I started work.

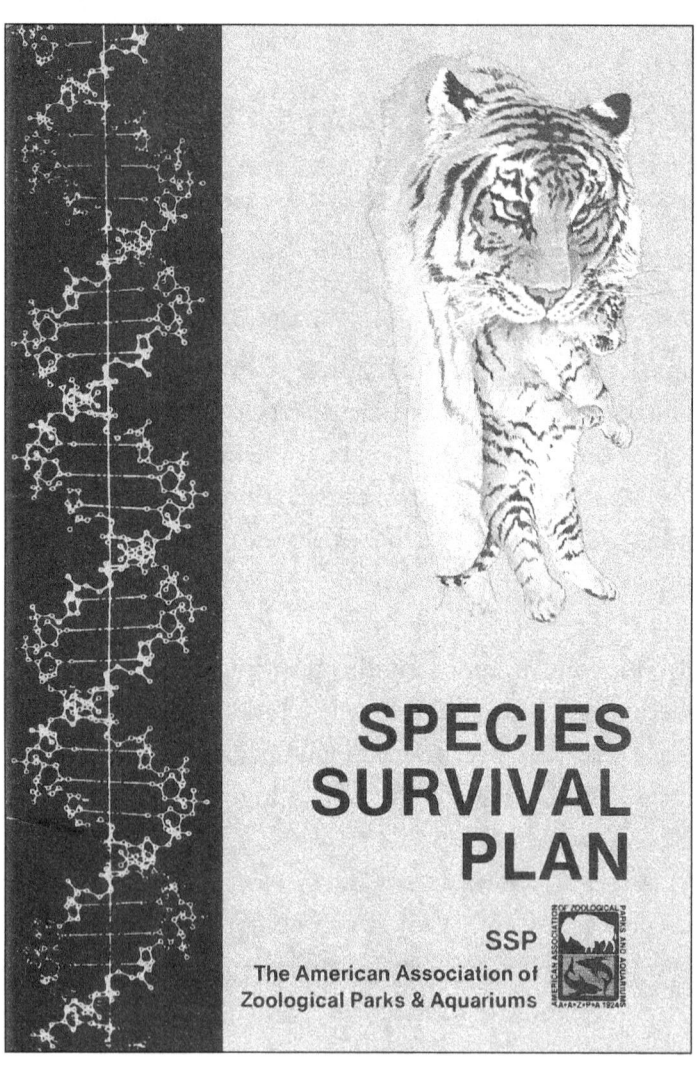

Once I had the title of zoo director, I was in 'the club.' I had the opportunity to work with directors of the largest zoos in the country. Prior to my hiring in 1972, Robert O. (Bob) Wagner in Jackson, Mississippi, was the youngest zoo director in the country. I came to have the utmost respect for Bob. He later became the second Executive Director of American Association of Zoological Parks and Aquariums (AAZPA) – now American Zoo Association (AZA). He served in that position for more than 20 years at Oglebay Park in Wheeling, West Virginia. As part of that office, he oversaw the original accreditation of zoos in the United States, the Species Survival Plan (SSP), the International Species Information System (ISIS) and many other innovations. He was always a close and valued friend.

As the accreditation process was a new program in the '70s, no zoos had been accredited previously. It was a slow transition. In fact, even the Baltimore Zoo wasn't accredited until after I was hired as associate director there in 1977.

The accreditation process began shortly after I started working for Salisbury Zoo in 1972. The zoo board didn't want to apply for accreditation because they were afraid the zoo wouldn't meet the standards and coming into compliance would be too expensive. However, I really wanted to give it a try to prove that a zoo didn't have to be *big* to participate and gain the accreditation – Salisbury Zoo was approximately only 13 acres. I count it as one of my more successful coups that it became the *tenth* zoo accredited in the nation – and the *first* small zoo. This proved that any zoo could achieve accreditation, regardless of size. No animal-keeping facility could use their size as an excuse not to be accredited.

I served at Salisbury for nearly six years from 1972 until 1977. The need for cleanup was monumental. Most of my 20 years in the zoo world was spent cleaning up dirty little – and big – zoos. Although a relatively small zoo, we had more than 300 species including 60 birds. For the first three years I was there I worked seven days a week and took only three days off. I gave *all* of my employees off every Christmas. If I worked straight through that day I could just manage to cover what needed to be done without them.

I also served as vice-president and then president of the Salisbury Humane Society during my years there. I had to investigate any reports of animal abuse or abandonment. Some of the places this required me to go were not the most desirable and folks weren't always happy to see me. Judge Robert Dallas, a unique, aging man who should have retired from his office years earlier, called me aside at a party one evening and told me to report to his office the next week. When I showed up as requested he looked at me and said, "What are you doing here?"

"Well, Your Honor," I said. "You asked me to stop by – at the party last weekend?"

"Oh, yes, right," he stuttered. "I was thinking you should be deputized." When I responded with a confused expression, he went on, "If you go and get yourself shot on one of your Humane Society calls, you ought to be covered – for insurance, you know."

So I became Deputy Graham, to be employed as needed.

What the badge didn't protect me from was the task of euthanizing 20 dogs and cats nearly every week at the Humane Society shelter. The shelter's policy, as with many smaller humane societies, is to keep an animal for seven days and then put it down if there isn't sufficient room to keep it. It was a terrible learning experience in many ways, and one I never got accustomed to. Especially difficult were the dogs with young pups. I quickly learned that the bitch should be euthanized first so she doesn't have to witness the demise of the pups. Sadly, they continue to cling to her still-warm body. Tough stuff.

I had taken over the euthanizing duties because I discovered that the veterinarian in charge had delegated the job to a young kid who not surprisingly didn't have very good skills and the smaller animals often became pincushions.

The Humane Society could have become a hotbed of controversy over an agreement I made with the neighborhood Peninsula General Hospital that was pioneering the newest open-heart surgical procedures. I had taken over as president of the society when a doctor on the hospital staff approached me about providing larger dogs that were scheduled to be euthanized to be used instead for their research practice procedures. Since the dogs would not endure any additional pain and medical science could advance to help treat victims of heart disease, I said yes, but never went public. More tough stuff.

There were no systems in place at all at the Salisbury Zoo. For example, chickens were free ranging on the zoo grounds. I was afraid of their spreading disease and generally dirtying the area, so I promptly got rid of them. *Then* I found out they had been donated to the zoo by Frank Perdue and the Perdue chicken business was huge in Salisbury. When I later went looking for funding for the zoo, Frank Perdue reminded me every time I asked for a donation that I had "killed [his] damn chickens."

The zoo had come by a rare American white pelican that had shown up in the chicken yard of a lady from nearby Princess Anne who called the zoo about her strange visitor. The species was part of the Midwestern flyway and never should have been in our vicinity – an amazing find. It takes a large population to get them to breed, so I managed to persuade Perdue Foods to donate money to purchase ten more birds for $750. After two died, the 'money man' at Perdue asked for the money back for the dead ones.

Of course, I had also given the Perdue folks other reasons to take issue with me. They didn't appreciate my sharing with them that many residents of my small Pennsylvania hometown of Waynesboro had become millionaires because very successful local businesses allowed the citizens to purchase shares in their companies. In 1964, *Dun and Bradstreet* listed Waynesboro as having more millionaires than any other town by population in the United States. This generous business policy was something, I tactlessly suggested, that Perdue Foods had never done.

I also clashed with them over a machine they had devised to remove chickens from the chicken houses. It had long rubber fingers that picked the birds up and placed them on trucks. I *publicly* reminded the Perdue Company that chickens were "living things, not footballs."

Sometime later I got another call from a local resident who discovered a Tundra Swan in her yard that was injured and couldn't fly. When I arrived on the scene the bird was in very poor condition, but I carefully placed her on the back seat of my car and headed toward the zoo some miles away. As I was driving I began feeling something crawling on my arms and neck. Soon I was covered in inch-long bird lice. The swan had died and the wriggling vermin had moved to the nearest warm host – me! I pulled over and jumped out of the car brushing myself frantically with my hands. Fortunately they quickly realized I was not feathered and therefore unacceptable so they dropped off.

In addition to gaining accreditation for the zoo, I was able to raise our annual rating given by the Humane Society of the United States (HSUS) from 2 to 1. Sue Pressman was a key figure in granting the zoo standings, so I took her advice to heart and made the necessary changes to improve the facility for just a few thousand dollars.

By September 1975 *The Sun Magazine,* Sunday supplement to *The Sun* newspaper in Baltimore, printed a glowing article about the zoo that began by touting our title of "Best Zoo in Maryland" that the HUSU had bestowed.

The worthiness of the title followed as the piece went on to describe how I had acted on the philosophy I had explained to them. "There are three goals of any good zoo: (1) to educate, (2) to breed endangered species and (3) to provide recreation. If you do a good job, a visitor can't tell you which you are doing." Salisbury was living up to these goals. The zoo was close to successfully breeding rare Bald Eagles and had already bred spectacled bears, a critically endangered species. Attendance of school children had grown to over 14,000 annually from Maryland, Delaware and Virginia.

Complimentary article in The Sun newspaper in September 1975
(Steve Graham)

The quality of the students' visits improved markedly thanks to our outstanding docents. Previously, buses would drop the children and leave them unescorted at one end of the zoo to make their way to the other end where they would meet the buses and the teachers who had ridden there. Many of the rambunctious youngsters left to their own devices and in large numbers, attacked the zoo like little savages and learned next to nothing. We changed policy to require reservations from the groups that would then be escorted by our dedicated, well-trained volunteers who transformed the chaos of earlier years into a real learning experience for the students. Student groups who arrived without reservations were turned away rather than having us risk a return to bedlam. They soon learned the drill and had a much better zoo experience for the lesson.

The welfare of the animals was always my first concern. I sent the popular sea lions to Lincoln Park Zoo in Chicago to the salt-water pool they needed. In the fresh water that was all Salisbury Zoo could offer, they were plagued by eye problems and had to be kept on constant doses of drugs just to keep them alive – and many of them died anyway. I also refused the offer of a jaguar from Peter Batten, a former zoo director, because I wanted to properly house the animals we had before I accepted any more. Neither of these decisions was especially popular. This wasn't arrogance, but determinations based on my belief that, as animal experts, zoo directors should give the public what they *should* have, not what they *want*.

Sometimes I gave in a little. For example, I had a difficult time justifying keeping the monkeys with us since they could be available for the public only around four months a year. The nights were too cold for them the other eight months. I relented on this because they weren't really being harmed and they were one of the most popular attractions.

With only one heated building on the zoo grounds, the winter accommodation for the animals was crowded and far from adequate. I am a proponent of working to acclimate animals to the environment. If they are kept minimally warm and well fed, they should be healthier than having to readjust to artificial climate changes. As it turned out, this was successful for the most part at Salisbury. Small, three-sided boxes of black plywood with small heat lamps in the outside enclosures worked well for the macaws and Sun Conures. Their plumage actually brightened and they were healthier overall. The same was true of the small red brocket deer when provided simple, overgrown doghouses with heat lamps. The flamingos loved the additional access to the river and played in it except on the most severe days when we herded them into the barn.

One change that was unpopular initially was to stop all public feeding of the animals, but the public soon accepted it when they understood my motive was to improve the animals' nutrition and health. It brings to mind an amusing story involving a wonderful high school boy, Gary Muir, who was working with the zoo through the Federal Job Partnership Training Act (JPTA) program.

The zoo had acquired some ravens from the National Zoo. We initially clipped their feathers to temporarily keep them grounded, rather than pinion their wings by clipping off the bony tip which is permanent. Even after they regained flight, they stayed at the zoo. One day a woman came through carrying a large open bag of popcorn. A raven swooped down after the food, grabbed the corner section of the bag and pulled a strip, opening the entire side of the bag and dumping all of the popcorn to the ground. She was quite flustered until Gary, who had witnessed it, went to her and explained, "Sorry about that, Ma'am, but we have a no-feeding-the-animals policy at the zoo. The ravens here are trained to stop anyone who tries. Hope it didn't startle you too much." This was a total fabrication on his part but, to my mind, pretty quick thinking. She bought his story and was impressed with the raven's quick response to training.

On another occasion I told Gary to put a water bottle into the emus' enclosure. The male had been incubating some eggs during which time he would neither eat nor drink; however, a few of the chicks had hatched and needed water. I passed the cage later that day and saw no water. I asked Gary why he hadn't done what I asked, but he looked at me puzzled and said that he had. I then pointed out the *absence* of the half-gallon inverted drinking bottle which confused him even more.

Then it struck me. The plastic lid of the water bottle was nearly the same deep- green color as the emu eggs. I checked under the nesting bird and, sure enough, discovered the male emu had mistaken it for an escaped egg and added it to the nest. I apologized profusely to Gary, but we both got a good laugh over it.

Gary worked with us for two years until he graduated from high school. He then went to Salisbury State but soon decided college wasn't for him. After just a few weeks he returned to the zoo and has been there ever since.

We did the best we could with our limited budget, but some of my least favorite enclosures on the grounds were the large silo-shaped heavy wire cages with pointed tops. They were difficult to beautify. The best we could manage was to add a few plants and pile stones on either side of the base to disguise the line.

One large one where we housed the more valuable and colorful waterfowl, so they wouldn't escape via sky or the Salisbury River, had a concrete base with a six-inch lip that held water. We added some nutrias, a kind of overgrown muskrat, to the mix.

Now nutrias have an interesting history. They were imported from South America with the plan to use them for their fur. They were uniquely designed for this because their nipples are on the top of their bodies instead of their bellies where the fur is always superior; but, with other animals this belly fur is not usable because of the nipples. They were being raised near the Cambridge, Maryland, Natural Wildlife Refuge where they were released into the wild after they became unprofitable.

Once in the wild they 'went viral' and became very destructive to bay vegetation. Even with the trapping to use their fur and their meat – as food for minks up north, but for *any* species down south – nutrias became a scourge to the land. After intensive efforts they've been eradicated in the north, but they still teem in the bayous of Louisiana.

Many zoos, especially roadside operations, accept just about any animals offered – exotic pets that were *cute* when the owners got them but soon outgrew their homes, injured or abandoned wild animals and so forth. I very rarely followed this practice because too much time with humans almost always alienates such animals from their own species. They get caught up in a no-man's, or no-animal's, land, so to speak. Besides, unlike other animal facilities that made empty promises of a good home for the animals, I made a point of being honest about their probable far less rosy future.

I did bend a bit on the issue of Easter bunny pets that soon outgrew their owners' homes. We had so many requests to take them that I decided to say yes, but was careful not to promise anything specific about their fate. I simply pointed to the enclosure where the rabbits were kept but hedged a little in not saying for how long. I instructed the zoo staff to be sure there was always at least one of each basic color group – white, black and white, brown and white, gray, etc. Any former owner who visited the zoo would be able to find their bunny in the mix. The actual *surplus* rabbits were good food for the carnivores at the zoo.

Another exception I made involved two eight-day-old Osprey chicks brought to us by the Fish and Wildlife Service. Linda Prestillio, zoo dietician, became their primary caregiver. As they outgrew hand-feeding, Linda had to swim to the middle of the river and I threw the Ospreys to her as I sat in an old tennis umpire's chair on the bank until they learned to fly. Then we had to drop them on top of fish to teach them how to feed on their own. One left at migration time while the other broke a wing and became a permanent resident of the zoo. That was a lot of time to invest in one or two animals when so many needed attention as well.

Unfortunately, most endings aren't as happy as the Ospreys' for orphaned wildlife that are adopted. Years earlier at Catoctin I had hand-raised a baby baboon. It was rewarding and fun for me until he got older and became hyperactive. I attempted to introduce him to other baboons, but the dominant males attacked him. He ended up at a roadside zoo where he later died in a fire.

As I've said, our budget was very limited. When I arrived, the veterinarian servicing the zoo was an alcoholic, often staggering, who had clearly passed the time he should have retired. He was also head of the state parole board, and one of the deals that worked in his favor as part of that position was the services of Jeff, a black inmate – a prison release agreement. He was basically, if you'll excuse the term, a 'slave' who was obliged to do all of the vet's bidding.

One of the last incidents that happened before the vet hired a younger vet to work with him involved the problematic delivery of a mouflon lamb. After the birth he said, "Where's my watch?" I had no idea, but when a search of the ground came up empty, he re-examined the ewe that had just delivered and found it inside of her. His young associate, Dr. Ronnie Fulmer, was a definite improvement, but didn't stay long.

The zoo vet finally sold his practice to yet another vet who brought two brand new Mercedes with him – one as a *spare* from which he removed the tires and put up on blocks. He also inherited Jeff and was little, if any, improvement over his predecessor.

Jeff told me about the time a mother and her young child, obviously challenged economically, brought their ailing black Lab to the vet's office. Jeff knew it was dead when he carried it from the back of their car into the examining room. The vet was out at the time, so Jeff decided to let the doctor deliver the bad news. He told the lady and her child that the doctor would call them. What the vet told them later was that the dog had been extremely ill and required a lot of treatment, but eventually died. He was "so sorry." Not too sorry to bill them for the non-existent procedures.

Consequently, I inherited many of the vet jobs at the zoo, whether I was licensed to do them or not.

One of my earlier experiences with this involved one of the zoo's flamingos that simply collapsed near the end of the day. Now flamingos were always captured in the wild and difficult to age, so it's difficult to consider that in assessing their condition. I scooped it up, took it to my office and gave it an injection of azium, a pretty powerful stimulant that only medical people should administer. I saw no immediate reaction and had to leave for a speaking engagement. At one point I spoke to various groups three to four times a week for 21 straight weeks. When I returned to my office later that night the flamingo was standing on top of my desk pooping all over my papers. It lived for many years after that.

One of the speaking engagements I mentioned was for a local chapter of the Daughters of the American Revolution (DAR). As part of my presentations, I often put a hognose snake in my pocket. They're a very passive and colorful species that grabs the audience's attention and helps make my case for not killing every snake you see. All snakes are very useful, even if they're scary. Given the more mature, feminine profile of the DAR, I prefaced revealing the snake with, "Ladies, I was warned about introducing my next topic to a sensitive group of women, but I said, these are strong daughters of our brave forefathers. I believe they can handle it." So when I pulled out the snake, they took it very well. With that kind of lead-in, they could do no less.

Late rounds of the zoo were the prime time for emergency procedures. One windy night in a light snowfall, I came upon a female llama in distress with a difficult birth. When I stripped off my shirt and reached inside her to determine the cause, I realized that I had to turn the fetus completely around. Every time the mother had a contraction, it felt like my arm was in a vise, but we both persevered until the baby was safely born. My previous experience at Catoctin Mountain Zoo helping local farmers by delivering stubborn calves came in handy.

Fortunately, I had considerable help from some very experienced professionals in performing my various veterinary duties. The association with the AAZPA that blossomed with the accreditation of the zoo gained me an invaluable association with the National Zoo, specifically two of their veterinarians,

Dr. Mitch Bush and Dr. Clint Grey. They were always as close as a phone call when I needed their help. Their friendship lasted throughout my career.

On one of my visits to the National Zoo the Curator of Reptiles gave me an exhaustive tour of their amazing facility. Part of the extensive collection was a blood python that they were concerned about because they hadn't been able to get it to eat. The prominent backbone of the species had taken on a disturbingly unique triangular shape due to malnourishment and they were anxious to have it thrive. After telling me about the problem, the young curator paused a second and looked at me. "You know," he said, "you probably have more time to give this snake than I do right now. Would you consider taking it with you to Salisbury to see what you can do?"

I was a little shocked but felt honored that he'd ask. As soon as the python and I got back to Salisbury, I got busy researching how to get the snake to feed. I discovered that they prefer a moist warm habitat so I put the python in a large wet secured burlap bag and put it in the chick incubator.

It was the spring of the year and we were hatching some duck eggs from our collection. When I went to turn the incubating eggs I noticed a new mallard duckling – our mallard population was thriving. I also detected some movement in the snake's burlap bag. "Snake food?" I wondered. So, with nothing to lose but, hopefully, one of many mallard hatchlings, I placed the duckling in the bag with the snake and left. The next day I checked the bag and the bird was gone. This went on for around two months with the snake consuming a duckling every ten days or so.

Three months later when I returned the blood python the National Zoo, they couldn't believe it was the same snake. I like to think my stock went up considerably that day – teachers proud of their student.

My connections at the Baltimore Zoo were fruitful as well. Animals often needed to be anesthetized to be treated for injuries or inoculated or moved, etc. A vet from the Baltimore Zoo, Dr. Barbara Divers, gave me some M99 for this along with the antidote, M5050, to revive them. I couldn't risk keeping it on zoo grounds because it was a legally controlled substance, so I stored it in my car glove box. I hate to think of the repercussions if I had gotten pulled over and that was discovered.

Ollie

Animals can and will steal your heart. Such was the case with Ollie, the baby elephant I tried unsuccessfully to prevent from being delivered to the zoo because I felt that she was entirely too young to be separated from her mother. Ollie came anyway because the process that had started before my arrival had gone too far and was too popular to reverse. She was the gift of a local car dealership, Oliphant Chevrolet, hence the name Ollie.

When she arrived on July 9, 1972, she was only eight months old – at 36 inches tall and 325 pounds, one of the smallest baby elephants to come to the United States. Her backbone was lower than my belt buckle. I did extensive research in preparation for her arrival – what to feed her, how to house her. I called the best experts I could for advice.

The first night she was with us, I was too worried about her to sleep so I got up in the early morning hours to check on her. I had read disturbing stories about rats and mice gnawing on elephants' sensitive feet. When I got to her shelter she was lying on her side with the bottoms of her feet showing. For a sickening moment, I forgot that baby elephants' foot pads are pink and mistook the color of her feet for blood. Though that initial shock faded, I lay down beside her for the rest of the night, not a good one for me as we had lots of roaches and mice for company.

Ollie – eight months, 36", 325 pounds – one of the youngest elephants ever to come to the United States. (Steve Graham)

Needless to say, Ollie and I totally bonded. After closing, she would follow me around the zoo like a dog. When we passed by the enclosure of black bears she stayed to the far side of them and pushed me along from behind to hurry me. She was afraid of them. If anything startled her, she came charging at 20 miles an hour and knocked me about 10 feet – and I was 6 feet 4 inches tall and weighed over 200.

Most surprising were our games of hide-and-seek after the zoo closed for the day. I had read that elephants could do it, but was very skeptical. The first time I ducked behind a tree out of her sight she became agitated and began shuffling around and trumpeting loudly until I showed myself. I repeated this move for a few days until she seemed to get the hang of it. Then came the clincher. *She* moved behind a tree wide enough so that her close-set eyes couldn't see me ahead of her. She stopped and waited, convinced I couldn't see her since she couldn't see me. I gave her a few minutes before coming around the tree and acting surprised.

Susan, was a fantastic mother to Ollie, bottle feeding her four times a day with a large calf nurser. Her formula which Susan made up every day was a combination of cow's milk, raisins, oatmeal and vitamin supplements concocted by my good friend Roger Conant who was Curator of Reptiles at the Philadelphia Zoo. They worked with Penrose Research Laboratory, an excellent facility at the zoo that offered expert support. Susan was at the zoo with Ollie so much that Salisbury Zoo actually put her on salary of $1.00 a year to cover her insurance liability.

Susan was also the guardian angel who helped to keep me on the road to sobriety. Despite all of the well intended attempts by caring individuals earlier years to treat my addiction, I went voluntarily to only one AA meeting. Once I made up my mind that I was finished drinking, I simply quit. No doubt a satisfying profession and supportive wife were a significant part of that success. Not to say there weren't some tough days, but I've been for the most part sober ever since my early years of association with zoos.

Sadly Susan and I parted ways, she being the first of my four wives. She has just recently retired as Director of the Tuscon Sonora Desert Zoo. After she remarried, she began her zoo career as an animal keeper at the Bronx Zoo (AKA the New York Zoological Society), currently one of the top ten in the country. She had an outstanding ability to determine the sex of alligators because her fingers were tiny enough to enter the cloaca where the sex organs are located. Unfortunately, this outstanding zoo is also remembered for (1) Ota Benge – a human pygmy they displayed in a cage with the primates for years until he hanged himself and (2) importing 12 trees from China that brought with them the chestnut blight that decimated the United States chestnut tree population. The Bronx Zoo has long since redeemed itself, but bad news dies hard.

Raising Ollie at Salisbury was an amazing experience. We had a great time, but I couldn't give Ollie what she needed most, her identity. She was an elephant that had no idea what an elephant was. I turned for help, as I often did during my time at Salisbury, to friends and professionals at the National Zoo.

They were delighted to have her on loan. They had no baby elephants and she would charm the crowds. We hoped Ollie would eventually be delighted to discover her adult counterparts. Unfortunately she contracted a virus that added complications to some ulcers she had already developed. She became gravely ill before she could make any meaningful connections with the other elephants. I got the call from the National Zoo around noon and broke more than one speed limit getting to her.

In spite of her failing condition, she knew me immediately. A familiar look of recognition filled her eyes as I knelt beside her. She felt me tenderly with her trunk and trumpeted softly. That night I slept with my head on her chest so she would know I was with her. Two keepers and three of the best zoo veterinarians in the country who had done their best to save her were also present to say their farewells. I felt her breathing grow more and shallower until it finally, the next morning, it stopped.

The others were kind enough to leave Ollie and me alone so I could cry myself out. No animal's death before or since has affected me so deeply. I've never allowed myself to get that close to an animal again. Had I not learned this lesson, emotionally surviving the continued onslaught of animal deaths in a zoo may have been overwhelming.

I asked that they cremate her immediately following the necropsy. Two incidents made me grateful that they complied without question. First was a comment made by a young naval officer once stationed in Ceylon who had been called in as a consultant on the case. When he heard about Ollie's death he asked, "You think I could have that elephant's feet? They'd make great umbrella stands." National Zoo Director Ted Reed, a wonderful man, hustled him out of my sight before I could retaliate. Second was the almost immediate request of the mayor of Salisbury. "Could you possibly send the body back? We could have her stuffed and never have to lose her." I had actually anticipated *that* request, if not the first one. Thank goodness I couldn't comply.

Just a few weeks after Ollie arrived at Salisbury, I was called to participate in an exciting endangered animal rescue. In nearby Ocean City, Maryland, someone observed a rare Caretta caretta (otherwise known as loggerhead turtle) come ashore and deposit a large cache of eggs. The loggerheads were on the endangered species list and although there had been reported sightings of their nesting on Maryland beaches earlier, none had been officially recorded. This was first *recorded* nesting on a Maryland beach, so it was a very big deal and would be one of my proudest accomplishments.

I was dispatched by Harry Kelley, the larger-than-life mayor of Ocean City who had been made aware of the situation, to gather the eggs from this highly populated beach, where they would most likely be destroyed, and transfer them to a quieter location.

The Caretta caretta has long been on the endangered species list protected by the U.S. government. In previous years it was hunted to near extinction for its meat and eggs. Some countries still continue the practice, like Mexico where the precious eggs are considered to be an aphrodisiac. However, the greatest threats to its survival are its extremely low reproductive yield and injury from fishing gear.

The 133 eggs at Ocean City were extremely delicate. I contacted my longtime friend Dr. Roger Conant who had written *The First Field Guide to Reptiles and Amphibians*, a very prestigious highly referenced guide which lists all the reptiles east of the Mississippi. He was one of the finest, most thoughtful men I've ever had the privilege to work with. Our friendship endured for many years. He was an invaluable mentor to me.

Amanda Blake with her baby cheetahs circa 1975 (Steve Graham)

Following Roger's specific instructions, I placed the eggs as gently as possible in clay pots of moist sand being careful not to stack them or rotate them on their axis because they almost immediately attach inside the shell. Any slight movement could render them infertile. After around 60 days at 27 degrees Celsius and daily misting, on September 20 the excitement began. After ten days of hatching, the final tally was 103 infertile and 19 hatched, three of which died later. Twelve were taken to the National Zoo when they reached 200 grams, to be released at a later date from Little Cumberland Island, Georgia. Four stayed at Salisbury in my second-floor bedroom and were later released at the Assateague Wildlife Refuge near where they had hatched. Because I reported the births officially, the loggerhead was added to Maryland's endangered species list.

It was exciting to be a vital part of this process. Sarah's zoo story, unlike Ollie's, has a sweet ending. She was the zoo's jaguar acquired as a juvenile from a circus traveling through town. We needed to build a suitable exhibit area for her and pair her with a compatible male by the time she was grown.

Being short of the necessary monies, our "Save Sarah" campaign was launched and, to our delight, attracted some well-known celebrities including tennis star Jimmy Connors and Amanda Blake (Miss Kitty of TV's *Gunsmoke* fame). She heard about the zoo's campaign from Sue Pressman and already had a love of cats as evidenced by the cheetahs she was raising on her Arizona ranch. Her pet lion Kemo often used to accompany her on the *Gunsmoke* set.

Amanda and I would continue the close friendship we formed during the "Save Sarah" project for years to come. Thankfully, the zoo successfully raised the $50,000 needed to complete the work and Sarah was saved. I still have a 45 rpm record of a piece of verse I wrote and recorded as part of the PR.

Another successful fund-raising event for the Salisbury Zoo fell into my lap through a connection with Ted Roth, assistant director at the Baltimore Zoo. Having eliminated the black bears from the Salisbury Zoo, I was trying to replace them with spectacled bears which, if they bred, could be very lucrative because they were critically endangered. The only funds we had for animal purchases came from the sale of our surplus. The Baltimore Zoo was advertising some spectacled bears from the birth of twins. When I inquired, Ted quoted me $500 if they were two males, $2,000 for a pair, and $5,000 if they were two females.

A husband of one of the zoo docents managed to get the local Hecht Company where he worked to donate $500, so when word came the bears were both males I told Ted we would take them. However, when the cubs arrived, I suspected they were females. It is difficult to determine the sex that early, so I called my buddy Mitch Bush, vet at the National Zoo, to confirm my opinion. When he did I, albeit reluctantly, called Ted Roth to tell him. He flatly refused to admit his mistake, so the Salisbury Zoo got to keep the two females.

I promptly sold our female and bought a much less expensive male for a nice profit. Then the pair bred many times and we sold those cubs to other accredited zoos for still more profit. The monies from that fortunate exchange enabled us to purchase many animals and supplies we might have been unable to otherwise.

Another favorable profit came from the zoo boarding a number of exotic animals confiscated by the USDA from a private individual in Delaware. It was a win-win because I negotiated payment to the zoo from the USDA to pay for their care and the zoo got to properly treat the animals and bring them back to health. A lion cub they brought to us was suffering badly from hyperparathyroidism that resulted in severe bone deterioration caused by a lack of bone calcium in its diet. Too many amateur owners feed their large exotic cats raw meat or *people* food rather than the diet they require. This poor cub had compression fractures in both rear legs and couldn't stand. We started her on a new diet, and by the time she transitioned out of our care, she had almost totally recovered.

I'm not sure why, but I never had a fear of the animals I worked with. Clint Gray, the chief veterinarian from the National Zoo, pointed that out to me after the adventure we shared anesthetizing a number of bison purchased by Karl Mogenson from a very wealthy resident who had a huge property near Easton, Maryland. He kept a number of exotic animals on his property but had more bison than he wanted.

I called Clint Gray to help me with the transport. A cap-chur rifle or blowgun is normally used to administer the anesthetic. Clint shot the bison and I corralled them into the transport after he hit them and before they passed out. After we finished he shook his head and said, "Don't call me to do this again – you're nuts! You don't have *any* fear at all."

"Really?" I said. "I never thought about it before."

As you might suspect, escaped animals go with the territory of being associated with a zoo.

The ravens I mentioned earlier not only harassed ladies with popcorn, they also flocked around kids eating their lunch on field trips. They started marauding and frightening too often, so we had to capture them. Problem is, they are incredibly bright. One of them frequented a very tall loblolly pine. The power company brought in a cherry picker, but it couldn't get near enough to capture the raven. I decided the only option was to use a cap-chur blowgun to get it.

By then a crowd had gathered and the pressure was on for me to make a clean hit without killing the bird or chasing it away with a near miss. Luckily my aim was good and the raven started to sway before it flew. Unluckily, birds' feet contract when they go to sleep so they can roost safely at night. The raven ended up dangling upside down from the limb. My Assistant Director, Bob Reese, and I were both afraid of heights, but I got the job of going up in the cherry picker and he held the net below to catch the bird when it fell.

Just as I reached out shaking like a leaf to unclench the claws, the raven woke up and flew away. He did a deep swoop and ended up flying right into the waiting net, kind of like a *Bad News Bears* little leaguer's centerfield catch with his eyes closed. The crowd burst into applause at what looked like a practiced circus act.

I also did a solo capture act one afternoon when a coati, a member of the raccoon family with an elongated nose and long striped tail, escaped and climbed a tree on the other side of the Wicomico River across from the promenade. I was alone except for the lunch crowd of zoogoers out on a beautiful day who spied what was happening. I had to act quickly before the animal got beyond our reach, so I got a cap-chur gun and aimed. I guess an audience improves my aim, because I was fortunate again, making a clean hit – just like the raven. As the coati started swaying, I dropped the gun and grabbed the net just in time to catch him. Again, I got to take a bow.

It started to feel as though just about any animal emergency or need in the city of Salisbury landed in my lap. The chief electrician of the city called one spring asking what to do about a mound of swarming bees that had landed smack in the middle of a residential road. When I arrived it was clear that the queen bee must have become disoriented when trying to move her colony.

I asked for a large paper grocery bag and two stiff pieces of cardboard. Then I spied the queen in the pulsing pile of insects and gently scooped her up along with the bees surrounding her and put them carefully into the bag. I kept scooping and dumping until they were all in the bag, with a few of the stragglers following voluntarily. Once I secured the bag, I called a beekeeper who was very happy to claim the prize and relocate the bee colony. The grateful electrician was very impressed with my *bravery*. I told him, "It's all relative. I'm scared to death of electricity. I wouldn't go near some of the wires and transformers you work with all the time for all the money in the world." I wasn't stung at all even though I was wearing no special protection.

Around 11 p.m. one evening my phone rang. A very distraught lady on the line said, "My dog, he's sick." She went on with a list of symptoms ending with "What should I do?"

"Ma'am," I explained. "I really can't give you advice because I'm not a licensed vet. I think you should call the local veterinarian."

"I thought about that," she said, "but he don't like you to call after hours."

That helped to define the term 'public servant' in my mind. It is someone to call at night when you don't want to bother a professional. After all, public servants get their salary from the taxpayers.

Dr. Bill Standaert was a middle-aged, unassuming biology professor at Salisbury State. We'd become close friends so he asked me to take care of his only pet for two weeks while he was on vacation. It was a ten-year-old Colorado River toad the size of a dinner plate. I figured the large utility sink in my office was the perfect place for Toad, as Bill cleverly named him. The sink was rarely used and sufficiently deep with good access to water. Unfortunately, somehow a small bar of soap fell into the sink. Toad ate it and died. I put Toad in the freezer wondering how I was ever going to tell Bill what had happened. He came to claim the body with a large box fit for burial. I thought he would cry when he laid Toad to rest.

Bill Standaert forgave me, but I'm not so sure the avid hunters of Salisbury ever did after my stand on waterfowl during the Freeze of 1977. Record cold temperatures had frozen vast parts of the Chesapeake Bay so solid you could drive a car across some areas. Sparked by a concern for the survival of local waterfowl, the Ward Foundation put out a plea for money to buy feed for the wild ducks. The zoo board pledged $300, but I stopped payment as soon as I found out.

Understandably, the Ward Foundation people were not happy, nor was the zoo board. I explained that as harsh as the winter was, there had been and probably would be worse. The ducks had survived before and would do so again without our help. This was nature's way to cull the species and allow the strongest to survive. Helping the weaker ones to continue would eventually make the species weaker and more vulnerable. Additionally, the feeding sites would also attract the ducks' natural predators that would kill them and concentrating the population could spread disease. Finally, the public might not be pleased to discover local duck hunters, many associated with the Ward Foundation, camping out near the feeding sites in the spring to improve their chances – as deer hunters do after planting salt licks in the woods.

Of course, the entire situation attracted huge publicity in Salisbury. Dr. Standaert called me. "Steve, you'd better back off. People are beginning to think you're a real fool."

"Am I wrong?" I asked. That ended the conversation.

Salisbury Zoo Politics

A zoo director's main focus should be to care about the animals in his charge and learn as much as possible about their care, but dealing with the staffing and the politics associated with the position can't be ignored – as tempting as that can become at times.

Salisbury's Director of Public Works was instrumental in my hiring, but our positive association was fleeting. He lived in one of the large houses that surrounded most of the zoo grounds. Some folks referred to the zoo as "the public works director's front yard." I have to agree; he sometimes acted as if he owned it. His paid position somehow made him my boss. He had come to Salisbury after being dismissed as head engineer of a large bridge-building contract in Annapolis. He, to my mind, was an all-too-frequent visitor to the zoo and constantly tried to block my ideas. I soon realized the best way to get *my* ideas approved was to convince him they were *his* ideas in the first place. "Remember what you mentioned the last time you were here," I'd begin and then tack on my idea.

However, this adversary did come to my aid at one point. The zoo had a pair of black bears in a cage that was far too small. They bred on a regular basis but, due to the crowded conditions, the male promptly ate the newborn – often with the public watching as we had no idea when the birth would occur. There were no funds for a larger enclosure, so I made arrangements to send them to another zoo that guaranteed them a much better situation.

Problem was, not long after I sent the bears away, an officer from the Department of Natural Resources showed up at my office and served me with a subpoena. It seems that I needed a license to move them because they were considered a state endangered species. The fine was $500, which wasn't too prohibitive, but if I admitted guilt a felony conviction would be on my record. My boss okayed the city attorney to make sure this didn't happen.

Allow me to digress with a side note about an incident at Salisbury Zoo I can't resist sharing.

Not long after my arrival, I hired a new animal supervisor. Even though he had come highly recommended from The Catskill Game Farm, I had a bad feeling about him. As it turned out, my instincts were right on. Not long after his arrival, I was called into my boss's office to answer charges made against me by my new hire. I listened briefly and simply tossed my keys on the desk and said, "You two have your little talk. If you decide you want *me* to run the zoo instead of him, you bring me back my keys." Then I left. Later that day the new hire was fired and my boss returned my keys without one word. In fact, we continued to work together for three years after that without speaking at all.

The further background for the tale returns to The Catskill Game Farm in New York. The facility was an excellent private zoo started by Roland Lindemann, a German gentleman who had started the concept of savings and loans in the United Sates and invested much of the huge profit from that venture into establishing the site. His number-two man was Heinz Heck whose uncle, Lutz Heck, had operated a zoo in Poland that was sympathetic to Hitler. But Heinz was knowledgeable about animals, a good man and a close friend.

Roland Lindemann's daughter Kathy married Jurgen Schulz whose father was the largest exotic animal dealer in South Africa. As Director at Salisbury, I had some dealing with Jurgen and was invited to visit their zoo. Touring The Catskill Game Farm's collection of beautifully maintained exotic species with Heinz was a real treat. Being invited for dinner was a bit less tempting as they were noted for eating whatever had died in the park.

They had an especially fine group of a very rare horse breed. I was puzzled when I noticed a corral of common Shetland ponies among the mix. When I questioned Heinz about it he said, "Oh, they're pretty simple stock, but when properly prepared . . ."

Then there were the mayors of Salisbury. Dallas Truitt initiated me to the world of city councils and effective persuasion. He was a flamboyant wholesale food salesman with snow-white hair and a fire-and-brimstone attitude when it was needed. His business specialties were, as he called them, the "four whites" (flour, sugar, salt, and milk) and cracked crab claws. You couldn't help but like him in spite of some of the stuff he pulled while in office. He was stubborn but lovable and well liked in Salisbury.

Paul Martin was head of the City Council. He was an executive with the Acme Store Corporation and could be a steamroller if he wanted something. Luckily, we were in agreement most of the time.

One of the council members during Truitt's tenure was Sam Seidel, one of the few Jewish citizens of Salisbury. His son, Mike, is currently a regular on *The Weather Channel*. Sam approached me one day about getting a pet chimp for his children. It took some fast talking on my part, but I finally convinced him it wasn't a good idea, regardless of how much his kids thought they had to have one.

Sam was good friends with podiatrist Verdie Cantrell, another council member. I deeply respected him.

It was my habit to work from sunrise until sunset at the zoo with one of my evening duties being to mow the grass with a push power mower. The zoo looked better and I got some exercise. Susan and I had divorced and being single made such hours easier. I've often said that I've had four wives but one very demanding mistress, the zoo.

One night I heard some cheering and applause over the roar of the mower. Sam and Verdie had been passing by and stopped to cheer me on, obviously impressed with my work ethic. They afforded me a lot of respect from that time on. Sam left a considerable fortune to the city of Salisbury to fund a newly created foundation.

I discovered Assateague Island, Virginia, my place of blessed refuge from my rigorous zoo schedule, while I was at Salisbury. The wide pristine beach along the Atlantic Ocean stretches clear to the Maryland border where I spent every possible minute from early morning until *hard* dark walking the ten mile track past blankets of sun bathers and radios to the more secluded reaches where clothing optional sections often appeared. I made friendships with other regular visitors that lasted for years.

Later when I was at Baltimore and Detroit, I claimed the month of May for vacation after gearing up the zoo for spring and before the onset of post-school summer crowds. I always headed for Chincoteague, Virginia, an island just adjacent to Assateague, and stayed until June 1.

Most notably, while I was at Salisbury, I was honored to become associated with United States Senator Mac Mathias, to my mind the epitome of what a senator should be. I had met Senator Mathias and Henry Cabot Lodge on the square in Hagerstown years earlier when I shared a podium with them as President of The Franklin County Organization of Republican Students, via Kenton Broyles. I was only about 15 years old at the time, but it stuck with me.

I kept an autographed photo of Mac on the wall of my office while most of the other Eastern Shore city officials opted to display their photos of Maryland Senator Rogers C.B. Morton, a much more conservative Republican. My Democratic leanings were showing for sure. Salisbury Zoo had one eagle and Mac Mathias got us a second. That was just one of the favors he did for us.

More impressive was the coup he managed when we were having trouble shipping a pygmy hippo to Europe. The deal had been arranged through exotic animal broker, Fred Zeehandelaar, with the USDA in charge, as always, of shipping. Just after the hippo arrived at the airport, a government shutdown kicked in, leaving the animal stuck in the winter cold with no authorization to ship since the USDA official *didn't exist* until the dispute was settled. I quickly phoned Senator Mathias about the situation. His secretary said he was on a plane en route to North Carolina, but within an hour, in the era before cell phones, he returned my call. I'm not sure what strings he pulled, but the hippo shipped not long after that.

When he retired from office to return as head of a law firm in Washington, D.C., I sent him a long letter of congratulations and gratitude. To my shock, he sent me an equally long letter in return. I'll always treasure it.

Another of my staff members at the Salisbury Zoo was Don Zanghi. He dropped his studies at Buffalo State University before getting his degree in English and biology to become an animal keeper with us. He had visited the zoo previously and fallen in love with it.

The best anecdote about Don happened with our collection of guanacos, a wild form of the llama with large canine teeth unusual in hoofed stock. The males could be pretty aggressive, especially around the females. It was always required to take a rake along to fend them off when feeding or cleaning their area. One day the aggressive male got past Don and bit his bicep in two. Not that *that* was amusing, but as we rode to the hospital together in the ambulance he kept repeating, "I'm gonna pass out – I'm gonna pass out – I'm gonna pass out."

I finally lost it and said, "Don, just *do* it. Pass out, OK?" I'll never forget the look on his face, but he never lost consciousness.

The guanacos weren't always *my* friends either, in spite of the fact that I had built them a ten-foot mountain. They were climbers by nature, but there are no rocks – none at all – on the Eastern Shore of Maryland. One day I noticed a series of dump trucks passing by with loads of fill. When I asked, the drivers said they were just dumping it at another location to get rid of it. It didn't take much to convince them to unload the dirt in the middle of the guanaco compound, a strip of land on the far side of the Wicomico River that divided the zoo grounds.

As part of my learning curve with the guanaco males, I had discovered that part of their offensive moves involved rising up on their hind legs, hitting with their front knees and attempting to slash with their abnormally long canines. One of them decided to demonstrate this on me around noon on a pleasant day when the crowd that often shared lunch at the zoo was watching. They thought it was pretty amusing, so I played along as if it were part of a deliberate show. The guanaco knocked me to the ground pretty hard at least four or five times before I made it out of the enclosure.

Now I would never really hurt an animal, but this particular guanaco and I needed to works things out. After closing that day, I returned to the scene with piece of 2x4 and traded that male's repeated attacks on me with sharp smacks of the board. We fought for about ten minutes until he stopped, so I did, too. He stared me down to make it clear that he had accepted me as part of the herd, a rival perhaps, but not an enemy. We had a truce that we both honored after that.

As I mentioned earlier, I became close to many of the staff at the National Zoo while I was at Salisbury. They were an invaluable source of information and support. Clint Gray, senior veterinarian at the National Zoo, was about 20 years older than me, but a great guy and good friend. We had worked together years earlier with the bison transport. Our association first coalesced when I was visiting the National Zoo and noticed him looking unusually stressed, quite a change from his normal good nature. I waited until he was alone and asked if he was okay. "My boy's dead. Vietnam," he said. I listened as he shared the painful news and we were close from then on.

I was at Salisbury working when I got a call from Clint. "I'm at the hospital in Centreville about an hour away. Come." No more explanation, just "Come."

I dropped everything and an hour later arrived at the hospital only to be refused to see him because I wasn't a relative and he was in intensive care. I jumped back in the car and returned to Salisbury. I put on a suit, grabbed an old beat-up veterinary doctor's bag that I used for veterinary tools, waited until I was pretty sure the shifts had changed at the hospital and headed back to Centreville. I must say I delivered a convincing line when I got there explaining, "I'm Doctor (mumbled). I've been called in to consult on Dr. Gray's case. I'm in a rush because I have a plane waiting at the Centreville Airport, so if you'd please give me his chart and show me to his room . . ."

The nurse gave me a quick, questioning look, but bought it. "Follow me."

When we got to Clint's room, I turned to her. "Could I have some privacy with my patient?" She checked me out again, but then left. I looked at Clint and shook my head. "What's going on? I could be in a hell of a lot of trouble getting in here this way."

"Heart attack, they say," he answered. "But enough about that. I'm glad you're here, Boy. (He always called me 'Boy.') I need you to get me a *Playboy* magazine and a couple boxes of Russell Stover candy. Some of the nurses here aren't bad." He winked.

He later married Mary Clare, 20 years his junior and the National Zoo librarian. They shared good senses of humor and a love of partying. Folks at the zoo knew Clint was a terrific vet, but that his most productive hours were in the morning, before lunch at The Roma.

I recall one time he and Mary Clare began getting a bit boisterous when they were at an AAZPA Conference. Bob Wagner, executive director of the organization and a close friend, pulled me aside. "Think you could take care of that?" He tipped his head in their direction. "I know they're friends of yours."

I wanted to see the upcoming program, but I couldn't refuse Bob. I went over to Clint and Mary. "Hey there, Clint."

"Hi, Boy," he said. He and Mary Clare both smiled.

I fanned my hand in front of my face hoping the power of suggestion would work. "Phew! It's hot in here, don't you think?"

They looked at each other, nodded and looked back at me.

"What do you say we get out of here and get a drink where it's cooler?" I suggested. They quickly agreed and we continued the 'good times' in their room. We avoided a public scene, but I regretfully missed the program.

The community of Salisbury was extremely supportive of the zoo. They offered not only their money, but also their volunteer services in many capacities. As with most such help, this was always appreciated, if sometimes more frustrating than working with paid personnel. Best intentions don't generally motivate follow-through as effectively as garnered wages or firing. Still, most volunteer efforts are sincere and a plus for the organizations they serve. It was five such young women who were responsible for helping me to compile the excellent first guide book the zoo ever had.

First Salisbury Zoo guide book (Steve Graham)

Salisbury Zoo (1972-1977) – My Career Begins

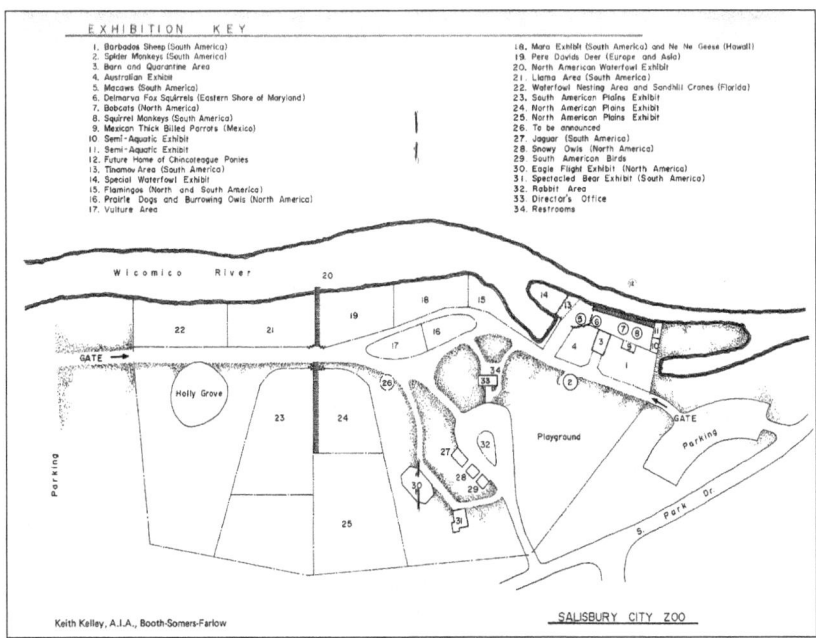

Map of the Salisbury Zoo circa 1975 from Salisbury Zoo guide book

The zoo network is small enough so that even small-zoo directors like me made good contacts with larger zoos. One such acquaintance was Wayne King, the Curator of Reptiles at the Bronx Zoo. He mentioned to me one day that one of their extremely wealthy major contributors to the Bronx Zoo, Nick Griffis, drove to Florida a couple of times a year and was interested in stopping by Salisbury sometime. I said fine, but no formal date was set.

Some weeks later I was making my rounds at the zoo when a stranger stopped me. "Are you Steve Graham?"

"Who wants to know?" I asked with attitude, I'm embarrassed to admit. I was better known than I wanted to be around town and often got tired of the impromptu interviews.

"I'm Nick Griffis," he said. "Wayne King at the Bronx Zoo told me to ask for you."

After my profuse apology, we spent a couple of hours touring the zoo together. Every year after that he contributed $5,000 to the

Salisbury Zoo, a significant amount for our budget, and he often stopped by to visit on his Florida route.

Ward Brothers' Mallard decoys (Steve Graham)

Another of the major supporters of the Salisbury Zoo was the Ward Foundation. The founders, Lem and Steve Ward, were brothers from Crisfield, Maryland. They began their careers as barbers and gained fame, but little fortune, carving spectacular wooden decoy ducks. They are credited with founding this art as one of the seven original Americana art forms. They were befriended by Charlie Bounds who had lived in Salisbury and worked for Dresser Industries, a manufacturer of oil drilling pumps and the main employer before Perdue was established in the Salisbury area. Mr. Bounds went on to become a wealthy stockbroker and staunch pillar of the Ward Foundation. One of his carved geese is the foundation's symbol. Charlie was an outstanding man and great friend.

One of my favorite memories of Charlie involved another member of the Salisbury Zoo Board, Davison Hawthorne, who was not a favorite among the other members. The news of his resignation from the zoo commission was not really a disappointment to them. I discovered that Charlie told the zoo board that *I* was the reason Hawthorne left, but the truth was (and Charlie knew it) I had nothing to do with it. I called Charlie and said, "You son of a bitch, don't ever do that to me again." I said it with a mixture of sarcasm and truth because we did have an unquestioned mutual respect for each other.

"I won't," he said and promptly hung up. We didn't mention it again, though I believe it actually brought us closer together..

His wife Eleanor, a wonderful woman, laughed and told me no one had ever called Charlie that before, but he had deserved it and she loved it.

The Ward Foundation sponsored fabulous annual expositions of wildlife art and carving. I helped set up some of the more elaborate displays, often on a scaffold high above the arena with beads of anxiety on my head adjusting lights and so on.

The cadre of decoy carvers was a strange breed indeed. The Ward brothers had some stiff competition including a really rough little character named Gil Maggioni, a former career oyster shucker. One year he went to great lengths with his display of a Black Duck rising up out of the grass with glistening drops of acrylic water on its feathers. After he finally approved the setup and walked away, another talented carver, Corbin Reed, commented to me, "No damn Black Duck ever looked that good." In the 70s Corbin had made significant money from his art – enough to order a new Cadillac that he refused because the odometer had twelve miles on it when it was delivered. "I ordered a *new* one," was his only comment.

The Ward brothers and I became fast friends, especially Lem. He was like a grandfather to me. They lived together their whole lives, very simply, in a house with no indoor plumbing until 1964. Steve Ward slept nearly his entire life in a small, unheated

Charlie Bounds with Lem and Steve Ward at their Shop

attic with a ceiling so low he couldn't stand up. He used a large saw that nearly filled a large room in the shop to cut the body forms of the decoys and Lem did the artistic detail.

They were very distinct characters. My favorite quotes from each of them exemplify this perfectly. Lem said, "A person don't have to be a college graduate to recognize a friend." While his brother Steve said, "If you think some praise is due him, now's the time to slip it to him."

Lem's early pieces are sometimes called "fat jowls" because Lem exaggerated that part of the ducks' anatomy. They were always favorites of mine, but Lem didn't agree. I was with him in the shop one afternoon and told him how much I liked fat jowls. Lem was a man of few words and thought long and hard before he said anything. After the usual silence that preceded his statements he said, "Yeah, boys (he always used 'boys'), I wish I had every one of those I ever made right now."

"Really?" I said a bit surprised.

"Yeah, boys, I'd throw every one of 'em in that old chunk stove over there and burn em."

The later decoys became more realistic and valuable. The brothers used to ship them in wooden barrels by driving nails from the outside into the bases of the decoys inside the barrels to anchor them and then filling the barrels with sawdust. In 1916 the decoys sold for about $18 a dozen. Years later some of the finished masterpieces brought hundreds of thousands of dollars – even more if they were signed.

Steve, who was three years older, was married only for a few months. Lem's wife Thelma died in the 1960s.

Lem smoked Pall Malls with a vengeance – called them his "vitamins." When I go to visit his grave in Crisfield, I always leave one burning on his grave. He had a partial amputation of both legs due to nicotine foot. I and others had to contact Maryland Senator Mac Mathias to secure Medicare for Lem because he never had a Social Security card, as was fairly common in Crisfield.

It was sad, the people who tried to take advantage of him. One of the major decoy dealers repeatedly had him sign early decoys he had discovered, for no compensation, even though it increased their value considerably. His surgeon took many of his decoys as compensation for the procedures he performed although he had already been paid by Medicare, unbeknownst to Lem.

When Lem really started failing, I often went to the hospital in Baltimore to feed him dinner. He had a tremendous appetite. His favorite was a soft-shell crab "as big as the sole of a gumboot." After consuming a large meal, his response never varied when I asked if he needed anything else. "I could really go for a milkshake," he'd say. I always complied.

He loved to sing and recite long poems – his favorite was "The Shooting of Dan McGrew" and he was always part of a barbershop quartet. He died on August 29, 1984, at age 84. Previously, he had asked me to watch over his daughter Ida after his death. She and I kept in touch until she passed about five years ago.

The Ward Foundation has rebuilt a replica of the brothers' shop. They did a wonderful job taking one small suggestion from me. They added crushed Pall Mall packs to the wood shavings on the floor.

Another member of the Ward Foundation and good friend of Lem's was Dan Brown. He was also an excellent decoy carver, though certainly not as talented a craftsman as Lem. He later replaced Davison Hawthorne on the zoo commission and, in spite of the fact that we were friends, we rarely agreed on zoo issues.

Since my marriage to Susan had fallen as a casualty of my Salisbury job and our irreconcilable differences about 18 months after our arrival there, I was solo during my rare times off work. My favorite getaway was the nearby Chincoteague shore of Virginia, famous for its freely roaming herds of wild horses. I preferred to head for the more isolated area near Nine Milepost, not a popular tourist destination. The horses often hung around and we watched each other at a reasonable distance. I'd mimic their head bobbing to convey my non-confrontational respect for them and their territory.

On hot days when a land breeze as opposed to an ocean breeze heightened the swarms of bugs, the horses would wade in the surf to escape the annoying bites. One day I decided to join them in the water. An old mare close to me had a large open sore that was covered with greenhead flies on her back. I slowly scooped up a handful of wet sand and was pleased that she let me put it on the wound to relieve her misery, if only for a short time. Suddenly the stallion from the herd bit me in the cheek and knocked me down. He stood astride me in the surf to make it clear that I was to keep my distance from his woman. Obviously, he saw me as a threat – one of the herd who had taken unacceptable liberties. I didn't move until he finally gave me leave, but was ultimately more pleased that I had made that connection than I was frightened by the attack. Despite the large cut and broken eyeglasses, it was one of the proudest moments of my life – being accepted as a member of the herd.

All in all, my years at the Salisbury Zoo went quite well. In addition to earning the AAZPA accreditation, the Humane Society of the United States awarded the zoo a number-one rating – the only one awarded in the state of Maryland at the time. Even more impressive, Salisbury was the very first zoo in the United States to complete International Species Information System (ISIS). Again, this proved that no zoo was too small to participate.

Dr. Ulysses "Ulie" Seal, world-renowned expert in physiology, endocrinology, pharmacology, nutrition, genetics and computer modeling, founded ISIS. It is a global, central database that provides computerized animal management information for zoological institutions. Today more than 500 zoological institutions worldwide are cooperating members. The intent is to list every animal in every zoo and its relationship with others of its species in an effort to prevent inbreeding and to keep the species' lines pure. Salisbury Zoo was the first to complete an inventory on ISIS, mostly because we had only 46 mammals. Our presence demonstrated that even small zoos could and should participate in the program.

Ulie Seal had some help developing ISIS from, among others, another local Waynesboro boy, Tom Foose, who worked at the Philadelphia Zoo and had superb expertise with rhinoceroses. We had spent some time together in our youth in our hometown at Carl's Market, though Tom's employment there was very short-lived – about two days, I believe. The practical basics of bagging groceries somehow escaped him, like not piling canned goods on top of a loaf of fresh bread or a dozen eggs.

Years later Tom called me when I was working in Salisbury and invited me to visit the Philadelphia Zoo. Since I already knew most of the staff there, I decided to go. When I arrived, one of the graphics department ladies, an old friend, said that Tom Foose was really happy about my being there. Rumor was that they were more than friends. The zoo community is relatively small and was always ripe with rumors and romping. I felt like it had to be the biggest gossip group in the world. It drove me crazy. This particular one proved to be true as she and Tom eventually married, had a child and moved to Canada and later the Minnesota Zoo. Tom eventually returned to Waynesboro, but he's now deceased.

In keeping with the ISIS efforts, zoos are working together to share the animals for breeding in an attempt to keep various species strong. Some of the most difficult challenges in this area are the expense and trauma involved with transporting animals between facilities. For example, not long after I had taken over at the Detroit Zoo I sent a female orangutan to the Baltimore Zoo. Unfortunately, I didn't directly oversee the shipping, taking it for granted the staff would know what they were doing. I was appalled when I received word from Baltimore that the orang had been severely injured in transport. The shipping container was metal and the screw tips, that faced inside rather than the other way, had cut her numerous times, and no bedding at all had been provided. Granted, this was an extraordinary circumstance but, even under the best conditions, transport is very unpleasant for animals. I asked, not kindly, how any animal could leave the zoo with no bedding and was dumbfounded by their response – "That's the way we've always done it."

Sandy Kempske the Curator of Mammals at Baltimore called to tell me about it. I was sorely embarrassed, but mostly sorry for the orang.

Crating any animal often requires infinite patience. On one occasion at the Detroit Zoo when I was the director, nearly a dozen frustrated keepers were trying unsuccessfully to crate a very valuable and skittish antelope. We finally sent most of the crew away to let her calm down in silence until we could try again knowing it might take hours. Suddenly a foolish keeper burst in on the scene unaware of our plan and slapped the crate thinking she would bolt into it. The antelope panicked and flew against the metal enclosure injuring herself. Such things occurred all too often.

One way the trauma of shipping animals is being addressed is through concentrated research for successfully gathering the necessary sperm intact from the donor and shipping it (a much easier payload) to artificially inseminate the recipient or implanting fertilized embryos in smaller compatible species that can travel more successfully. A leader in this area is Dr. Betsy L. Dresser, a reproductive physiologist who founded the Cincinnati Zoo Center for Reproduction of Endangered Wildlife (CREW). She joined the Audubon Nature Institute in 1995 to lead the new Audubon Center for Research of Endangered Species. Knowledge gained through research at the center has helped scientists and conservationists cope with threats to the most seriously endangered species through the development of new reproductive technologies and reintroduction techniques necessary to ensure their long-term survival. She is an incredibly competent lady and a good friend.

I sometimes forget my audience when I discuss these kinds of issues. When I was Director of the Detroit Zoo, I was meeting with a number of my docents, mostly women, discussing the great apes at the facility. As part of the discussion I mentioned some of the exciting possibilities mentioned above, specifically the possibility of surrogate mothers for implanting fertilized embryos. In staying with the subject of our meeting, the great apes, I unfortunately combined the two topics and remarked that some day in the not-too-distant future a human woman might carry and give live birth to a gorilla. Needless to say, many of them, especially the more mature ladies, were appalled. As I said, sometimes I should just keep my mouth shut, but I still believe what I told them.

Another fascinating and hopefully viable tool being developed and supported by the research and survival centers is the "Frozen Zoo." The reproductive stores of approximately 175 vanishing animal species are maintained there at -320° Fahrenheit via liquid nitrogen, yet another safeguard against the extinction of species.

The AZA also has in place the Species Survival Plan (SSP) to help zoos coordinate and strengthen efforts to preserve species whose natural habitat is vanishing. *The AZA Handbook* lists the five ways SSP can achieve this by:

1. Reinforcing natural populations which may have been so reduced by human activities, natural catastrophe or even epidemic diseases that they are no longer viable genetically or demographically.
2. Providing animals for repopulation of original habitats when that proves practical.
3. Serving as refuges for species destined for extinction in nature.
4. Maintaining repositories of germ plasm in addition to populations of animals.
5. Conducting research and developing more successful techniques of animal husbandry.

I cannot stress too strongly the changing role of today's accredited zoos. They are no longer simply for-profit shows exhibiting exotic species to curious crowds who come to be amazed and entertained. They have become arenas for displaying rare exotic animals in as close to natural settings as possible as a means of educating the public about them. More importantly, perhaps, is the zoos' role as conservationists offering in many cases the last remaining viable means for the survival of many species whose habitat is rapidly disappearing – their *ark*, if you will. This will require global effort and support from everyone.

I count my years at the Salisbury Zoo as very well spent. Little wonder I saved an article written by Herb Clement, staff member of Staten Island Zoo, for the September 6, 1979 edition of *The Staten Island Register* forwarded to me by a friend. It reads in part:

> "...Here [in Salisbury] lies what is unquestionably the finest small zoo in America, a little jewel of a place that can be seen in an hour's time – but can be lingered over and savored for a great deal longer than that. It is, one might say, a gourmet's zoo . . . The Salisbury Zoo comes as close to placing its visitors face to face with the quiet wonder of nature as any zoo that I have ever seen . . . Salisbury has every right to broadcast its exceptional zoological achievement from the rooftops, and its winner of a zoo, not the biggest, but beyond any doubt the best."

The regular zoo visitors were the best evidence that this assessment was true. I enjoyed watching them stroll around, not like the one-time visitors who could then check the visit off of their list of things to do or fulfill a parental field trip duty. The regular visitors didn't just observe the animals and absorb the quick educational references posted by the enclosures. They communed with the animals and the place.

One such visitor was an older lady, very petite and neatly dressed. I often greeted her on early morning rounds before many other people arrived. One morning I saw her before she saw me. She was studying the animal tracks printed on strips of yellow plastic tape that is often used as temporary lane markers on highways. The displays had just been added to coordinate with whatever animals were in the adjacent enclosure. Thinking she was alone, she started following the tracks like an Arthur Murray dance instruction – just hopping around having a ball.

Another day she stopped me as I passed the sea lion exhibit. She was quite distraught at the vigorous interaction between the male and female. "Mr. Graham," she said, "can't you do something about their fighting? I'm so afraid one of them will get hurt."

I thought a minute and replied, "Not to worry. I think she (I nodded at the female sea lion) has a headache."

"Oh." The sweet lady's eyes widened for a second and then she giggled as I walked on.

As the Salisbury Zoo continued to improve and didn't need me as much as it had for the first few years, I became restless for greener pastures. Three times I applied for the director's position at the Arizona Sonora Desert Museum (actually one of the finest zoos in the country) in Tucson, Arizona. The third time prompted a visit from Bazie Tankersly, a gruff character who dressed the part of a larger-than-life cowgirl and had served as head of the zoo board since the 1950s. Her father died when she was 18 years old and she took over many of his responsibilities as editor of *The Chicago Tribune*.

Bazie owned horse ranches in Tucson, Florida and Maryland and preferred to drive between them rather than fly. When I discovered that she planned to stop to interview me on one of her Maryland trips, I arranged for her hotel accommodations and had a fruit basket, my resume and zoo information placed in her room. When she arrived at the zoo she returned the fruit saying, "Here. Give this to some of our animals," and then handed me the paperwork I had left in her room adding "and here's your propaganda."

"It seems pretty clear that you don't want to hire me," I responded. "And, frankly, I don't really want to work for you. But since you're here, would you like a tour of the zoo?" She nodded, we toured, and she left. End of story.

I also made a bid for the directorship of the Buffalo Zoo. The interview process for the final three applicants took an entire weekend. Each candidate stayed at the home of one of the zoo board members. My host was Peach Taylor, a local sculptor of note and long-time member of the board. She was in her 70s, but had the means to make herself look attractive and did so – lots of makeup, fashionable clothes, etc. Her husband Reggie was a tiny, somewhat frail man. They were both big drinkers – cocktails and backgammon every evening. The two nights I spent with them they both got inebriated, but Peach held her liquor better than Reggie.

She took me aside and whispered, "Would you be a dear and carry Reggie up to bed?"

As Peach led me on a tour of the Buffalo Zoo, we passed the llama exhibit and I noticed that most of the animals were moving as an orchestrated group, but one lone llama was pacing back and forth by himself in the front moat. I pointed at the single animal and said, "That llama must have been hand-raised." Peach seemed quite impressed that I had guessed correctly. I explained that when I observed the dynamics of the group, that llama was obviously caught in the no-man's land that happens when an animal loses its sense of identity because of prolonged exposure to humans. "Probably thinks it's a human stuck in there with a herd of furry creatures," I said. I thought that probably gained me some ground in the hiring arena.

As we went on, she paused a few times to order some of the workers to clean something up or move something. I excused myself before I commented, "I really don't think it's a good idea to disturb the workers. That's the director's job. What if they don't have time to take care of the work he's given them because they're doing what you asked?" She seemed to take my advice well at the time, but I didn't get the position.

My later interview for the position at the Baltimore Zoo was much more positive.

I've returned to visit the Salisbury Zoo only two or three times. I once took my step-daughter Hilary who enjoyed it tremendously, much to my delight. Gary Muir was a familiar face from the past. He started as a part-time worker and soon progressed to full time. He would be an excellent director, but has refused the position a number of times.

I've also kept in touch with one of the ladies who created the zoo guide and later served on the zoo commission. Laura McCray is one of the most special persons, inside and out, that I've ever known.

Returning past directors can sometimes appear, though unintentionally, as a challenge to new directors. Comparisons come naturally and aren't always welcomed. In the case of Salisbury, I try to share the following with equal pride and humility. Gary Muir once told me, "The folks of Salisbury have almost canonized you. When you visit it's like the second coming of Christ."

No, I seriously don't presume to have a God complex. Many of my past deeds easily keep me humble, but yes, I'm very proud of the positive differences I made for the Salisbury Zoo, and also happy that the positive changes the zoo made in me have, for the most part, endured.

Chapter 6

Baltimore Zoo (1978-82) – Moving On Up

After six years at Salisbury I needed to move on professionally. One of the places I applied was for associate director at the Baltimore Zoo. Arthur Watson had been the director there for over 20 years. He was a local icon who appeared on *Zoo Parade*, a Bert Claster production on local Baltimore TV stations. Claster also produced *Bowling for Dollars* and *Romper Room*, and was married to Miss Nancy of that show's fame.

The zoo grapevine was well aware that Arthur Watson knew practically nothing about exotic animals or the business of effectively directing a zoo. He was actually afraid of the animals that appeared on *Zoo Parade*. Frank Groves, the zoo's reptile curator, went along to the filming to set the stage for Watson. During one segment a ball python bundled itself as a defense mechanism. Watson took it on himself to begin pitching the snake around like a ball. General opinion held that he was an incompetent alcoholic and the zoo was a terrible mess, but the public (TV watchers) loved him, so the board of the zoo had tolerated him for much longer than they should.

Doug Tawney was Baltimore's Director of Parks and Recreation and a close friend of Mayor William Donald Schaefer, two men I would come to admire a great deal. I arrived at Druid Park, Maryland, for my interview with Mr. Tawney wearing my garish red-plaid sport coat, quite mod for the late 70s. Knowing there was a lot of competition for the job, I felt I needed to stand out in the crowd somehow. I'm not sure if that's what gave me an edge, but I was offered the position. After I was hired, I recall Doug Tawney actually commented favorably on my choice of wardrobe for the day.

Graham's flamboyant interview sports coat in 1978 at Baltimore Zoo (Steve Graham)

Baltimore Zoo (1978-1982) – Moving on up

While I was waiting for my job interview I was invited to walk around the grounds. Two large 1880s buildings stood on the zoo property – the Maryland Building and the Mansion House with a widow's walk on the roof offering a view of the harbor and a wraparound porch that was windowed shut to enclose the Bird House. As I toured the Bird House, I turned the corner to discover two zoo workers in the throes of passion. For obvious reasons, I got out of there as fast as I could. When I mentioned it to one of the three secretaries to the director she said, "Well, they see the animals doing it all the time – gets them hepped up." The scene I had witnessed was obviously more or less accepted practice at the zoo. This gave me an early sense of what to expect in my new job, should I get the chance.

Doug Tawney was a great boss. Our work ethics were very similar in that our day didn't end until there was nothing left on our desks, regardless of the hour. We were both single, so that made this degree of dedication somewhat more reasonable. He was in his 50s, short, with a bald, bullet-shaped head and boundless energy. From day one he made it clear that unless he had cause not to, he would trust me with the zoo. He was good to his word, letting me manage without interference but supporting me when I needed him.

My immediate boss, Zoo Director Arthur Watson, had a palatial office and granted me an office area in the far corner where I began working to rescue the zoo from its current state of physical and financial disarray. Watson was sorely out of touch concerning the pressing needs of the zoo and more concerned with innocuous trivia. He would occasionally call me to his desk to share such important information as, "You know, Steve, it takes 100 years to grow a tree" or "Mary Sue has a butter cream Easter egg that is just fantastic." I usually shook my head and returned to the more pressing tasks at hand.

He once told me, "Steve, you'll never make a good zoo director because you're too much of a naturalist." I'm sure he intended that as an instructive warning that I should change, but I just shrugged and took it as a huge compliment.

The Department of Parks and Recreation hadn't been very vigilant in overseeing the zoo either. During one of my early rounds of the facility I noticed an East Indian family feeding popcorn to a large family of rats believing the rodents to be part of the zoo collection rather than pests. This helped me comprehend the bizarre competition I discovered later. Arthur Watson awarded a weekly prize to the zoo employee who killed the largest rat. They would deliver their entries to the office on a regular basis.

Then I noticed the flamingo population looked very unhealthy. They were molting and the pink had faded to nearly white. Gus Griswold was the curator of birds at the zoo and I had learned from him earlier that he had developed a diet at the Penrose Research Laboratory that enhanced the pink pigment in flamingos, so these sickly birds puzzled me. Gus's flamingo formula of cat food soaked in carrot juice contained a lot of carotene, so I went to the rubber feeding tub in the birds' enclosure to have a look. At first I was shocked to see what appeared to be boiling liquid. On closer inspection I was appalled to see the turbulence was caused by rats that were in a feeding frenzy to eat all of the food. No wonder the flamingos looked sick; they were starving.

Not long after that one of our rare subspecies giraffes died from no apparent reason. The necropsy that followed revealed no disease, only that she was very thin. I started investigating, but before I found the answer, we lost a second giraffe. I had checked what they were being fed and the bags read correctly "omolene." It wasn't until the second death made me more suspicious that I checked the label more closely and discovered the requisition that I had sent to purchase the food had been changed to an omolene with a much lower protein level – and much cheaper. I'm sure the difference in price had lined somebody's pocket. It had also killed two valuable innocent animals.

This event made me truly appreciate the phrase "Hay's a lot cheaper after it's been through the horse." In other words, manure is cheaper than hay.

There was also a dearth of professionalism among the office staff that mirrored Arthur Watson's indifferent demeanor. Not long after I started my duties at the zoo, I was with the inspector of the USDA (United States Department of Agriculture) that regulates zoos. I was very anxious. Considering the condition of the zoo, I knew he would have to grant me many favors to pass the inspections. As we walked in the office past one of the secretaries, she looked at me and said, "You'll never know how much I like you in those tight pants." I was aghast but helpless to correct her obvious faux pas in front of the inspector, who was East Indian and therefore even more offended by her remark. Another day I was giving Bob Wagner from the AAPZA a tour of the zoo. We were riding around the grounds in Arthur Watson's golf cart when we came across some zoo workers who had put a board over the top of an upturned barrel and were playing poker in the middle of the day. They just waved at us as if this was a normal work activity for them. I glanced at Wagner and shook my head. He returned a sympathetic look, knowing I was new to the zoo staff and working for Watson. We were both aware that getting things in order would be a monumental task. We pushed on to the Great Ape House. The design of the building worked well – a U-shaped in/out system with a ramp graded toward the enclosure so the kids could see the animals better. Problem was, the day was gray and dark and we were having trouble inspecting the facility. I asked Mary Wilson, head keeper and a wonderful lady, if she could turn on the lights. She said that she'd love to, but a special key was needed to do that.

"Don't you have one?" I asked.

"No," she said.

"Did you lose it and not get it replaced yet?"

"No, I didn't lose it," she reluctantly confessed. "I never had one."

"How long have you been here?"

She lifted her eyebrows and then lowered her head. "Twelve years. Mr. Watson hasn't been to the Ape House even once since I've been here, and he keeps all the keys."

Ted Roth was the *assistant* director at Baltimore when I arrived. He was the man from whom I had purchased the spectacled bears for the Salisbury Zoo. He spoke with a heavy German accent and had a great deal of experience collecting animals in the wild. He had once been a collector for the National Zoo but had been in a very bad car accident in Africa and spent more than a year recovering. When the Baltimore Zoo hired him after he had regained what he could of his health, Arthur Watson, without proper authorization, had promised him the director's position when he left. Problem was, Ted was never quite right after his accident.

He had a gray Great Dane named Loki that he brought to work with him. They walked around the zoo all the time, often upsetting the animals. Eventually the dog became incontinent and a real detriment to the zoo office environment. When the zoo board told him that he couldn't bring Loki to work with him anymore, he took the dog home and shot it.

For all intents and purposes, I was running the zoo from my first day on the job. Still, outside referrals often made it through to Watson even though the park board had already limited his spending approval to items under $5 and allowed him to open only the fourth-class mail. He spent most days clipping coupons from the paper and giving them to the girls on staff.

I finally went to Doug Tawney about the situation. He was sympathetic, but unsure of how to get rid of Watson without an incident. He was very unpredictable and the general public liked him because of his TV personality. I suggested offering him a

Director Emeritus status. Tawney had never heard of that type of position, but he loved the idea.

Watson jumped at the offer, which solved that dilemma, but then came the announcement that *I* would be taking over *instead* of Ted Roth. It was *not* a popular choice. The staff knew me only as the guy who had been writing policies ever since he'd arrived to make their jobs harder. *No* policies existed at the zoo before I arrived. They joked that I might even make a bathroom policy – I actually should have. Anyway, I anticipated a tough transition, but then the worst thing possible happened. Within weeks of the announcement, Ted Roth ended his own life on the anniversary of the day he had shot Loki.

I knew the staff blamed me, but even tougher, I blamed myself. I felt a terrible, if not rational, guilt about the situation. The next day I stood by the time clock to get a reading on the zoo staff's reaction. Bad – very bad. I called my friend Ted Reed, Director of the National Zoo, and told him I had some upsetting news. Before I could elaborate, he said, "Ted Roth killed himself?"

"How did you know?" I asked.

"Knowing Ted Roth, it's no surprise. I expected it," he explained. "Don't feel guilty, Steve. It's not your fault."

That advice helped me get myself together. Sometimes we just need to have someone we respect tell us what we should already know.

Ted Roth's old office was around the corner from Arthur Watson's and I needed a new office out of Watson's corner. Since I wanted to move into Ted's vacated space, it became my job to clean out his things after his suicide. He always kept lots of cold Pilsner Urquell in his office refrigerator. He cooked there a lot, too.

The filth at the zoo wasn't limited to the animal cages. Roaches and mice were rampant in the offices as well. At night I could see them scurrying across the light panels of the dropped ceilings and hear the mice in the walls. It took me two days at home to clean the filthy pots and pans I found. When I returned them to Roth's widow, she was very gracious, assuring me that Ted's death had nothing to do with me.

I stayed late at the zoo – after hours – to go through his things. Near the top of the pile of folders I found a sizeable collection of memos, some quite sensational and potentially embarrassing.

I called Doug Tawney and said, "I assume you want me to destroy these."

"I'd like you to burn the whole office, but just do the best you can," he advised.

I'll never forget one late night when I was cleaning Roth's office. The zoo was really creepy after dark anyway, but this particular evening the only other person there was the sleeping night watchman some distance away. I was digging through the jammed desk drawers when I suddenly heard Roth's voice – out of nowhere. I have to admit, I was as scared as I've ever been in my life. I was sure in that instant that he had returned to haunt me. Then the initial terror calmed enough for me to realize the voice was coming from the drawer. I had accidentally hit the play button on a recorder that he used to tape his phone calls.

Operating within the political realm is always a challenge and the zoo was no exception. During the sorely needed renovation of the aforementioned large structures on the zoo grounds, the Maryland House and the Mansion House, a faulty bidding system caused numerous problems. A local painting contractor was awarded the job as general contractor by a city inspector and things went south from there.

I was at odds with the decision from the start, but even more so when I discovered that lumber purchased for the zoo project had been delivered to the inspector's residence. Then a newly installed toilet wouldn't flush. When I confronted the contractor about the problem, he claimed someone had flushed a bent Coke can down the toilet and caused the problem. I sent for a case of soda and said,

"I'll pay you $1,000.00 for every bent can you can flush." It took only a few sorry attempts to call his bluff. Still, I'm sure the final bill was substantial for substandard work.

The City of Baltimore owned and operated the zoo, but the Baltimore Zoo Society Board also exerted considerable influence and authority. For example, they paid half the salary for the head veterinarian, Dr. Mike Stoskopf. Johns Hopkins paid the other half. Their funding came from private donations and grants rather than tax dollars which gained them more latitude in some cases, as they weren't so dependent on the public ballot box.

Additionally, the Society Board also had charge of the zoo concessions, a huge business that improved when they finally got rid of the mismanagement of its director. He was a hot mess who had little control over his staff and even less over his temper in dealing with customers.

As an ex-officio member of the Society Board, I attended their meetings. Although I had a great working relationship with Mayor Schaefer and Doug Tawney from the city authority Park Board, I was much more tenuous with the Society Board.

Jim Hunley was the executive director and he, along with many of the other board members, was eager to take over control of zoo operations. Primary to their concern was that they believed that Schaefer would be the last white mayor of Baltimore. Turns out they were correct, but this concern gave them a real sense of urgency to act because Schaefer had just begun his final term of office.

I strongly opposed this move because I felt the timing was wrong. The Society wasn't strong enough yet, and a failed attempt would make subsequent attempts even harder. Better to wait. Luckily I wasn't alone in my opinion and the Society postponed action. A few years later they did take over and have continued to run the zoo well since then.

The zoo encompassed 256 acres, much of it wooded. Ted Roth had blackbuck antelopes, llamas and other animals roaming freely everywhere. They had destroyed the entire understory. No flowers, shrubs, grasses or native plants remained – nothing. Since the Hippo House was giving off heat all night, the antelope and llamas slept on the building's attached outside porch and defecated heavily. I called Karl Mogenson, whose tapir had escaped at Catoctin Mountain Zoo years before, and sold him more than 100 animals. It was one of the very few times I sold to anywhere but another accredited zoo, but I was desperate and I trusted Karl. I wouldn't do it again. I worried about the subsequent soil erosion, but happily that spring, after a heavy rain, hay started taking over from the seeds embedded in all the animal droppings.

The zoo had a number of small, stone-walled enclosures. One housed the yaks, one male and seven females, in a space entirely too small for them. The typical ratio was around three females to each male. When I asked why so many females, they told me that the male yak was named Arthur (like Arthur Watson) and Watson figured the yak liked women as much as he did. He was always regarded as a ladies' man.

In an attempt to improve conditions for animals, I tore down some of the fences that had been added to the original large enclosures to accommodate different species. I eliminated the lesser varieties in order to allow more space for the ones we kept. The revenue from animals I sold to other accredited zoos went toward further improvements to the grounds.

Bobby Johnson became my invaluable assistant director. He had keen insight into what motivated people. I recall complaining to him when a talented employee in the education department, announced she was resigning. "How can we make her stay?" I asked Bobby.

He sighed. "Steve, you know all of us have a switch inside that sometimes just goes 'click' and there's nothing we can do about it. I think her switch just did."

Bobby also developed a unique way to provide more information about the animals to zoo visitors. Our budget for large graphic displays was limited, so the public looked at the animals but learned very little about them. He devised a card that each visitor received when they entered. Specific icons were listed under animals' names on their exhibit signs that referenced the cards with information about diet, habitat, and more. This enabled us to better educate people for a minimum cost within a tight space.

Illustration from The Best of Baltimore magazine in 1978
(Steve Graham)

Diane Nickel was my lifeline in the office to get through most days. She was one of the three secretaries we had, but she was so much more. She was my 'Radar O'Reilly' for you *M.A.S.H.* fans. In fact, I suggested that she replace me as director when I left to go to the Detroit Zoo. Of course, the board rejected it based on her lack of credentials and she was, after all, a *woman*.

Some of my early innovations were less than popular. Visitors missed one of their favorite pastimes, feeding the animals. As in Salisbury, patrons soon accepted the change once they understood the health of the animals was the reason. W.C. Smith wrote an article for *The Best of Baltimore* magazine in July 1978 in support of the move. It read:

> "A woman stood before the camel's pen, popping marshmallows in the animal's open mouth as fast as she could get them out of the bag. When Steve Graham, Assistant Director at the Baltimore Zoo, requested that she stop her feeding, as it was not good for the camel, she stared at him in disbelief. 'Not even marshmallows?' she queried...
>
> [Steve Graham added] Our animals will be a lot healthier now that we can control their diet. Additionally, people will be able to see the animals in their natural state... There is nothing natural about a fat, overgrown bear begging for food."

A bit more challenging was convincing my animal keepers that euthanasia was a sad but necessary aspect of animal management. That option had never been used at the Baltimore Zoo before I came. With the existing policy, aging animals died slow, sometimes painful deaths or were transferred out along with surplus stock, often to unaccredited game parks or roadside zoos under questionable conditions or even shipped to hunting reserves for target practice.

As at Salisbury, I had pledged to be up front about my views on euthanasia. I wasn't about to be accused of covering up what I thought was the preferable policy for the welfare of the animals. It had worked well there so I vowed to continue the policy at Baltimore. As with Salisbury, winning the keepers to my way of thinking was the first big step to ensuring the policy succeeded.

On one of my early inspections of the Baltimore Children's Zoo, a separate facility on the grounds, I noticed three keepers lifting an old British Park cow to her feet. I asked what her problem was and they said, "Nothing really. She's down every morning when we come in. We just pick her up and she's pretty much good for the day."

"That's just not normal," I said. "I doubt she's 'pretty much good.'"

After an exam by the vet determined that her advanced age made treatment for her pain useless, I decided to put her down. She was the first animal I euthanized at Baltimore. The keepers immediately objected despite my explanations.

Soon after that I became aware that Lena, the zoo's only lion, was in deplorable physical condition. She was kept in one of the oldest cages with bars that bent inward at the top and she was obviously miserable. The keepers knew I was considering putting her down and began a good news campaign for her. Every day one of them made a point of telling me how much better she was doing. They definitely were protesting too much as she was clearly deteriorating. When I finally had her euthanized and the necropsy was performed, we discovered that maggots had almost completely eaten the interior of her anus. I made all of the keepers come and witness what condition she had been in – the agony it must have caused her. I had far less opposition from them about euthanasia after this.

Another bone of contention with the keepers arose over my directive that "No keeper is allowed to touch an animal except for administering medication." I explained that I wanted to keep the animals as wild as possible, not as trained circus acts.

Despite my early disagreements with the keepers, I had the utmost respect for them and the difficulty of their jobs. I had been there in my early experience and vowed never to ask a keeper to do something I hadn't done or wouldn't do myself. Vital to making their job easier was educating them about the animals in their care. I made as many opportunities as possible available for them to learn about the animals they worked with every day.

I tried to offer formats for their truthful comments and criticisms about their work. Don't ask if you don't want to know, but I *did* want to know. I had plenty of feedback and complaints. I gave each negative comment my individual attention, if not always the answer the individual wanted to hear. I like to think that if I wasn't well liked, I was respected.

> WILLIAM DONALD SCHAEFER, Mayor
> OFFICE OF THE MAYOR · CITY OF BALTIMORE
> 250 City Hall, Baltimore, Maryland 21202, (301) 396-3100
>
> In reply refer to: MO-63
>
> January 25, 1980
>
> Mr. Steve Graham
> Director, Baltimore Zoo
> Mansion House
> Druid Hill Park
> Baltimore, Maryland 21217
>
> Dear Mr. Graham:
>
> The American Association of Zoo Keepers has cited your keeper-education program as the best in the country and I send you my congratulations! It gives me great pride to know of your achievements, the honor you bring to Baltimore and the excellent care your leadership brings to the Baltimore zoo.
>
> I am grateful for your success and wish you much success in all your endeavors.
>
> Sincerely,
>
> William Donald Schaefer
> Mayor
>
> cc: Douglas S. Tawney
>   Park Board

Letter of Congratulations from Mayor Schaefer – 1980
(Steve Graham)

Two policies I instituted that resonated positively with all of the keepers were increased overtime that they all wanted, as their pay was pitiful, and new required uniforms. I purchased attractive, good-quality winter coats and summer jackets. The workers *looked* far more professional and consequently *felt* more empowered and professional. The cosmetic change was good for the zoo's public image as well.

In 1980 the American Association of Zoo Keepers (AAZK) honored me for my efforts with animal keepers. Below is a letter of congratulations from Mayor Schaefer. This commendation from a man I truly admired meant almost as much as the original honor.

The Reptile House

The Reptile House was located nearly a half mile from the main zoo grounds. It was a popular exhibit, but in many ways problematic. Security was iffy at best for the women working there when they left to get their cars. The building was unattractive and only large enough to display ten percent of the collection. Granted, Frank Groves, the reptile curator had a collector mentality and housed far more animals than necessary, but I liked him. We got along well until I suggested that the Reptile House be closed.

I tried to explain to Frank that closing the inadequate Reptile House was the first step in my plan to get a new and improved Reptile House. Lots of zoogoers enjoy reptiles and the zoo would most certainly have to provide one. He was still upset, unsure of his continued employment, so I suggested that the zoo keep him on as curator during any transition and he could use the time to work on some field research studies he had going. I thought I had won him over until one of the head honchos on the Zoological Board called Mayor Schaefer to protest the closing. Seems his four-year-old son loved reptiles and didn't want to see the facility go away. So it didn't. You win some; you lose some.

Frank's son John Groves was the assistant reptile curator. Despite a significant speech impediment, he was an admirable worker and very knowledgeable. I had known them both since my time at Catoctin Mountain Zoo when John answered my call for help to capture the escaped Egyptian cobra. When Roger Conant, Director of the Philadelphia Zoo, called me asking for some leads on a good number-two man for his reptile collection, I suggested John. Conant had made a poor hire for reptile curator but couldn't get rid of him. John was perfect for the position. Roger was more than pleased to get him, but Frank was upset with me for taking away his son.

The Children's Zoo was in such sad shape that I did my best to undo it. For example, the large wooden rendition of Noah's Ark may have once had some potential, but what I saw were portals that framed dioramas of little toy soldiers painted in psychedelic colors. Besides, a zoo that is well run should provide enough educational opportunities for all ages to preclude the expense of maintaining another one just for kids.

Ted Reed, Director of the National Zoo, agreed with me. He went so far as to jokingly suggest we put electric eels in the Children's Zoo urinals.

I was able to make some good use of the Children's Zoo even if I couldn't close it. There were very few winterized buildings on the zoo grounds, so many of the animals were confined to areas that were much smaller and far less than comfortable. A small concrete structure on the Children's Zoo grounds was vacant and unheated, but by housing one healthy camel in it, its body heat kept the inside warm enough to make the temperature acceptable housing for animals who fell ill over the winter.

The Baltimore Zoo also had a pair of gorillas, but they were always housed in separate, inadequate cages. After I became zoo director, I arranged a permanent loan situation that would allow them to finally be together in a new large primate facility at the National Zoo.

Gorillas are always one of the most popular draws at zoos. Leaving the Baltimore Zoo with none did not go over well. Only the gorillas would benefit. Anticipating a backlash, I made as many prearrangements as possible with Ted Reed, Director at the National Zoo, before I went public.

I had maintained my close friendship with Mitch Bush, head vet of the National Zoo that started when I was at Catoctin Mountain Zoo. He had been the compassionate support I needed at Johns Hopkins when I took our chimp Marlena in for a necropsy. He was often a source of advice and support in the years that followed while I was at Salisbury, too. We were working together to make the gorilla transfer happen as easily as possible. He was already accustomed to covering the Baltimore Zoo when our vet was unavailable.

The day of the move, the male had been anesthetized for transport and was being evaluated by Mitch as protocol dictated. In his late 30s, Mitch was tall, Friar Tuck-balding and wearing his ever-present knit cap as he stood over the huge unconscious ape on the examining table. Suddenly the exam room was full of people. He blew up at the sense of spectacle that had descended on the dignity of the gorilla in his charge. "What the hell are all of these people doing here?"

Such outbursts happen among friends, especially in emotionally charged cases as this when Mitch felt the need to protect the gorilla from gawkers. Our friendship endured and often got me into trouble with the vets at Baltimore. If I disagreed with them on a case, I'd call Mitch for a second opinion. They knew he was considered to be a premier vet by many more people than just me. Still, they resented being second-guessed, especially if Mitch's view fell on my side instead of theirs.

The eventual gorilla transfer was painful for those who were opposed, but ultimately swift enough to avoid a prolonged controversy.

Some years later I was with a large group at an AAZPA conference at the National Zoo, so I stopped by to see if the gorillas might possibly recognize me. They were in a spacious enclosure with a natural setting and a large viewing window. I was glad to see their new situation, but saw no indication that they had any memory of me. I was explaining this to my friend Clayton Freheit, Director of the Denver Zoo, who was also attending the conference.

He smiled at me and asked, "Are you sure they didn't know you?"

"Yes, not even a glance of recognition," I said.

"Are you sure?" he repeated as he pointed to the enclosure behind me.

I turned to see the male poised on the six-inch ledge on the inside of the viewing window in a huge male posture. What a thrill! Again, like the Chincoteague stallion, he had accepted me as a member of the group.

On a lighter note regarding a vet story, I recall the zoo had a substitute vet from Johns Hopkins, Dr. Frank Lowe, who was drawing blood from a very weak lion that had had been dropped on our doorstep and had been raised for entirely too long in a second-story apartment. We were checking its condition before euthanizing it. A new, young female assistant was helping with the procedure and she dropped the first vial on the floor and it shattered. (They were glass back then.) Frank didn't chastise her at all. He simply drew a second vial which she also dropped. Frank winced and said, "You know, there's only so much blood in this lion." The assistant burst into tears and left. I felt sorry for her, but thought Frank handled it very well.

The Baltimore Zoo also had a lone male orangutan that had developed the unconventional habit of staring at me. Contrary to popular belief, primates – actually mammals in general, including your faithful dogs and cats – are threatened with forced direct eye contact. Your pets may enjoy gazing lovingly at you, but if you hold their head and force them to look you in the eye, it frightens them. Anyway, this particular orang made it a point to try to make eye contact with me and hold that stare as if he was trying to tell me something. This directly contradicted my contention that humans should avoid anthropomorphizing wild species – giving them human emotions. I couldn't help but look back at this orang in his solitude and think he was indeed trying to tell me something.

Years later I discovered a lone female orangutan at the Detroit Zoo where I was director. I sent her to the Baltimore Zoo on permanent loan as promptly as possible. This was the transport nightmare I mentioned earlier. Fortunately she made a full recovery. Though I never returned to visit my orang buddy at the Baltimore Zoo, I like to believe this was the request he was making years earlier and he's much happier now.

Another success story involved a partial albino green monkey in the zoo's collection. After several unsuccessful attempts to breed her, she was moved to a separate cage alone. Some time later another green monkey died soon after giving birth. We started bottle feeding the baby, less than happy that it was destined to become yet another primate that would miss her native bonding and think she was a human. Frustrated, I suggested we attempt to put the newborn with the lone partial albino female. Happily she quickly took on the role as surrogate mother. Although we continued the bottle feeding (as she had no milk of her own), the baby clearly preferred the new mother to a warm blanket, and the both monkeys thrived. They were eventually returned to the full colony of green monkeys.

In a wonderful footnote, less than a year later the partial albino bred successfully and gave birth. This brings to mind instances where women unable to conceive prior to adopting a child, then become pregnant. Just a reminder of how much we witness, but really can't explain.

The zoo had basically no funds for improvements. It was – all zoos are – expensive to operate even when well managed. The Baltimore Zoo had lots of room for improvement in the money-management department, so I asked Doug Tawney, Director of Parks and Recreation, if he would give me half of what I saved from current annual cost figures to use for improvements at the facility. He agreed, so I started to take careful note of any hint of waste or fiscal incompetence. They weren't very difficult to find.

I arrived at the large Hippo House early one morning – I always went to work hours before the zoo opened. When I touched the door to the Hippo House, it was so hot that I thought there was a fire inside. I pushed the door open with my shoulder ready to battle the flames, but found only sweltering air. I started asking questions and soon discovered that the heating control had been broken for years. Rather than report the malfunction, the workers figured out that if they cranked up the heat to the maximum before they left for the night, the building would hold enough heat to get the animals through the next day. The hippos had a regular night-long sauna going on in there. We saved considerably on heating bills after the thermostat was fixed.

Stashed behind one of the taller stone barricades was a 40-year accumulation of manure. By regulation, I had to create a paved road leading to a macadam area large enough to manage the daily accumulation of manure once I got rid of the stockpile. The estimates I got from a local contractor were far beyond the zoo's reach. When I explained this to the contractor, he hesitated and then said, "I have an offer for you. I'll swap you my work for the manure. That stuff is gold to the farmers around here." He and I both knew this suggestion made perfect sense, but the proposed exchange would never fly with the authorities. So I didn't ask the *big guys*. I employed the old *don't ask/don't tell* game. I just said "yes," the contractor nodded, and no one ever asked. He hauled away over 40 tractor-trailer loads of manure and the zoo got the road and storage area for no cost. I could have lost my job over that but the solution just made too much sense to ignore.

One story to hit the press not long after my arrival was the escape of a young, newly acquired mountain lion. To explain, a cat can squeeze its body through any opening it can manage to get its head through. The wire fencing at the top of the lion's enclosure had small rectangular openings, but not small enough. Unfortunately, one of the keepers alerted the press of the lion's escape before he reported it to me.

Normally the two locks on the chained zoo gates granted access to either the zoo staff or the fire/police department independently. I wanted to keep the police outside the zoo grounds until I assessed the situation. Luckily it was before opening so I immediately issued an order to add bastard locks that they couldn't open to all the outside perimeter gates. As soon as the report went out, I stood at the top of the rise facing the main entrance at Druid Park and watched 20 or more police cruisers and an armored tactical- unit vehicle, sirens blaring and lights flashing, line up outside the fence.

I went down to meet the chief officer. "I'm ready and willing to work with you on this," I told him. "Outside *you're* in charge, but inside *I'm* in charge." He grudgingly agreed.

The keepers knew the grounds, but the police officers had hand radios for communication. I paired them one-on-one and told them to fan out and "look for crows mobbing." Crows work together like wolves – in a pack – when they sense a predator in their territory, and the new young lion fit the bill. Sure enough, we soon spotted the crows flocking and cawing loudly overhead and tracked down the frightened cat. We anesthetized it, put it in a more secure cage and reported to the crowd that had gathered that all was well.

Doug Tawney had heard the news reports and appeared with the others to see if he could help. I pulled him out of the fray and suggested that we offer free admission to the waiting people as a goodwill gesture. He smiled and said, "Steve, you're a genius."

The police force was very helpful in solving another dilemma at the zoo.

First, I need to remind the readers that in the late 1970s and early 1980s family dogs were allowed to roam much more freely than they do today. Unfortunately, docile house pets become vicious when they join a pack and take on the more aggressive pack mentality.

On more than one occasion a pack of these dogs running amok at night dug their way into some of the zoo's larger outdoor enclosures and killed a number of the free-roaming hoofed stock. One night they mauled four beautiful gazelles. Problem was, the dogs would then return home to their unsuspecting owners. We knew the predators had been dogs, but had no idea where they individually lived.

After a second such raid, I called the police. They decided to set aside certain nights to patrol and shoot the trespassers. Since every official bullet they fired had to be accompanied by a report, the zoo had to provide the cartridges. The results were effective, but slow, so they decided to set a trap. The Mansion House on the zoo grounds had a large storage area under it that the zoo staff salted with rancid, raw meat that would attract a crowd. The first night they corralled and shot more than 20 dogs – even a dachshund in the mix. After three or four such nights, the problem stopped. Guess the word finally got out to the canine community to avoid the zoo, but I'm sure numerous pet owners spent useless hours trying to locate their missing dogs. All in all a very sad story.

Attendance was down at the zoo when I arrived. The location in Druid Hill Park, which was in the center of the black section of the city, was one of the factors keeping people away. Although the park is one of the oldest landscaped public parks in the United States, its location in northwest Baltimore had become economically depressed and potentially volatile. That alone was enough to discourage some folks from visiting, but the weekend drummers intensified the problem. The incessant loud bongo drumming in the neighborhood that accompanied every Saturday and Sunday added a heightened intimidation factor to the atmosphere. There were also many large-breed dogs in the Druid Park area. Unlike the free-roaming ones I mentioned earlier, many were valued household pets and very well-trained, often requiring no leashes as they never left their owner's side and responded immediately on command. Such animals could easily give outside observers reason to pause.

Easter Monday was without a doubt the most problematic. The day is traditionally an unofficial black holiday because many years ago black household staffs were always busy on Easter Sunday serving meals and working. Monday was their day to celebrate. It transitioned into a real Mardi Gras mentality in Baltimore. An urban legend still existed as a part of zoo lore that the police once had snipers stationed on rooftops at the zoo, just in case things got out of hand.

The recent shooting, Easter Monday 2014, at the entrance to National Zoo in Washington, D.C. where two bystanders were injured, brought back memories of Baltimore. I had to wonder if it wasn't somehow part of the same type of celebration though reports didn't indicate so. Still, the association clicked in my mind.

On Sundays the Baltimore Zoo opened at 10 a.m. The attendance from open until 1:00 was 90 percent white, 10 percent black. From 1 p.m. until close, it was reversed, 90 percent black, 10 percent white. Since zoogoing was not generally as much a part of the black tradition as the white, the total afternoon attendance was much lower. Something needed to happen to encourage more white folks to attend more often and longer as they were, to a large degree, the zoo's financial bread and butter.

We pumped up the public relations for the zoo aimed at highlighting new programs and redid the front entrance with some fantastic window dressing. The first thing visitors saw amid the colorful tropical plants just inside the front gate was an immense aviary housing more than 20 vibrant male Golden Pheasants, a real feast for the eyes. They were stunning and affordable. Females weren't an option because their plumage is more subdued and, more importantly, if one female was introduced to 20 males, pretty soon only one male would be left – last man standing for the lady.

Along with the general cleanup and major efforts from the staff, general attendance and conditions at the zoo began to improve.

Zoo Personnel

Not everyone was as big a fan. One of my tougher relationships was with the zoo vet – a short, wiry man about my age with a terrible temper. [Later in this book I'll discuss the difficulties that often arise between zoo directors and vets – usually a battle of egos – and that was true in this case.]

To his credit, our veterinarian was the project manager of the state-of-the-art animal hospital that was built at the zoo at a cost of $4 million (significant funding for 1978) during my tenure. The funding came from the state legislature with lots of lobbying from Johns Hopkins. It was big news in the zoo world with many cutting-edge innovations like positive air flow in the operating room and more.

At an AAZPA conference Clayton Freiheit, Director of the Denver Zoo, asked some details about the hospital. He was a rotund and regal individual who made a habit of having himself paged during group meetings so he could get up and make himself visible and therefore known to everyone. I gladly answered his questions, but our vet was livid that I had done so.

There was little doubt that our veterinarian knew his stuff, but he couldn't control his temper. We were like oil and water – or maybe gasoline and a match. He stormed into my office one day after receiving a memo he didn't like and shouted, "Maybe you don't realize that I'm one of the top three zoo vets in the United States."

"If you really are, you wouldn't have to tell me, would you?" I answered.

He slammed my office door so hard when he left that the glass panel shattered.

I didn't really doubt his expertise. A secretary interrupted an interview in my office one day, aware that only an emergency would allow her to do so. "Ray's in the moat," she said.

"If you'll excuse me?" I explained to my guests. "Ray is one of our giraffes. I've got to go."

When I got to the scene, Ray was lying in the moat looking helpless and pathetic. Our vet had cleverly taken charge of strapping various block and tackles expertly around the giraffe to heave him back onto dry land without injuring him. Not an easy task.

Unfortunately, the doctor's temper continued to be his own worst enemy. I came across him one day fiercely berating a keeper. I waited until the incident died down and then told him, "You just shot yourself in the foot. You've embarrassed that keeper so badly that he'll never call on you after this regardless of how much he needs to."

He detested performing surgery and more than once threw instruments while spewing obscenities during a procedure.

National Zoo Director Ted Reed and I were having dinner weeks later and the topic of our vet's well known explosive disposition arose. "You think he's on drugs?" Ted asked. This wasn't an unusual sentiment when it came to zoo vets. Drug addiction was an occupational hazard for a very tough profession.

Finally, I fired him, raising a storm of protest from some of his more loyal zoo- keeper associates and Dr. Frank Loew, head of Comparative Medicine at Johns Hopkins. The vet I had just terminated was also on staff at Johns Hopkins to boost his salary above the less-than-adequate one the zoo could offer. I defended my actions based on his continued insubordination and unprofessionalism. Dr. John Strandberg, another vet at Johns Hopkins, who shared an apartment with our vet, supported me in opposition to Loew, his boss.

The zoo board ultimately supported my position, but it had been a struggle.

Another one of my personnel issues had a happier ending. I hired a woman as curator of mammals despite the fact that she had less impressive credentials than the other major candidate, Tom Foose, from the Philadelphia Zoo. He was the same Tom Foose I mentioned earlier from Waynesboro who worked with me unsuccessfully for a few days at Carl's Market. I knew our personalities just didn't mesh, so I went with an applicant who previously had a much lower position at the Norfolk Zoo.

She did a great job overall, but went to pieces when an animal died. She had become very attached to an elephant who was suffering from lupus. The medication it required cost nearly $1,000 a week which luckily was donated by the pharmaceutical company, but the pachyderm still died. Now, elephant and rhinoceros deaths present a huge, very unpleasant disposal issue. After the required necropsy, they have to be laboriously dismembered and buried. It's an ugly job, but Sandy's reaction was off the charts.

I called her into my office to console her, but explained that such things happen all the time in the zoo business and I was concerned about her future in the profession if she couldn't learn to cope with it better. She took my advice to heart and controlled her reactions much more successfully in subsequent situations. Still, she eventually left the zoo business. As of five years ago she was working as head of the Humane Society of Baltimore.

The welfare of the animals and pleasing the public are all top concerns of an effective zoo director, but competent staffing supports both of those aims. As with all businesses, this area is an ongoing challenge.

Not long after I took my job as director, Director Emeritus Arthur Watson felt I needed to know the history of the keeper (I'll call him 'Joe') who was responsible for prepping the bird feedings.

Baltimore Zoo (1978-1982) – Moving on up

The administrative offices at the Baltimore Zoo shared space in the enormous Mansion House with the Bird House that was enclosed in the large wraparound porch. I was informed that 'Joe' took a three-hour nap every day in the feed-storage room that was located on the other side of the wall right behind my desk. Sure enough, when I checked at the critical time mentioned, I found 'Joe's' stocky form stretched out asleep on the large aluminum table beside the tall metal trash cans of various feeds. I took one of the heavy lids, dropped it on the large concrete slab right beside the table and ducked out. 'Joe' jumped like a flea in hot grease at the loud clatter as I made good my escape before he saw me. He didn't know who had done it, but he knew he'd been caught.

The problem might have ended there except that 'Joe' had another card to play. A few years earlier a bear at the zoo had bitten his hand. If the old injury got cold it swelled up. The zoo policy provided transport to the medical clinic downtown for any staff with injuries or health concerns. After the feed-room incident, 'Joe' would run cold water over his hand and request the zoo car to drive him to the clinic which would involve at least half a day off for 'Joe' and the driver. This happened on such a regular basis that I had to do something.

I called Doug Tawney and asked if the zoo was required by contract to drive the staff to the clinic. We checked and it stated that the zoo would "send them" to the clinic. If providing transport was implied, it wasn't stated, so the next time 'Joe' came for permission to go to the clinic, I played my card. To my advantage, 'Joe' picked a snowy day for his request. I handed 'Joe' an envelope. "Here's your bus fare to the clinic."

It wasn't a short walk to the bus stop or a short wait. 'Joe' protested. "You can't do that."

"I believe, according to the contract, I can."

"I'm going to my union rep," he threatened.

"Feel free. Until then, here's your transportation." I extended the envelope again.

That ended 'Joe's' visits to the clinic.

Orgie Kimble was a sweet old black woman who worked as a custodian for years at the Baltimore Zoo. I was attending an Ella Fitzgerald concert in the city when I spied Orgie in the audience. That was a little surprising, but I was amazed when Ella Fitzgerald saw her too and came out to see her at intermission. They hugged and Ella explained that Orgie had been quite a singer/performer herself. You can never really know all the people around you, but it was heartwarming to discover that a woman as dear as Orgie had some wonderful past memories before her mundane work at the zoo.

One of Orgie's responsibilities at the zoo was the cleaning of the Mansion House. I remember that before I got rid of the intrusive loudspeaker system at the zoo, one of the first announcements I stopped was paging "Orgie to the Mansion House" when she was needed.

I also eliminated a very loud carillon at the Detroit Zoo that had been donated in memory of Frank McInnis, one of the earliest and best-loved Detroit Zoo Directors. It just didn't fit in and brought some much needed funds to the zoo.

All too often, someone from the zoo board or city council or other position of influence had a recommendation as a zoo hire. One of the more amusing came from Mimi DiPietro, a longtime city councilman. He was short, stout, always flushed, hyperactive and the ultimate Mr. Malaprop. (as in malapropism – the misuse of a sound-alike word. For example, being under the *affluence* of alcohol.) Mimi told me he had an excellent prospect for an animal keeper job who just "loved animals." I obliged, but the interview with his candidate went very badly. I called to let Mimi know and he said, "You found out, didn't you?"

"Found out what?" I asked. "It was just a..."

"He said he wouldn't do that anymore," Mimi interrupted.

"Do what?"

"*Expositioning* himself," Mimi mumbled.

One of my most important hires turned out to be one of my worst decisions. I was in dire need of an assistant director and looking for some advice. I had a good friend Tim who had once worked for Ted Kennedy and had been called in to pull the Boston Zoo out of the same chaos the city of Boston was suffering in the late 1970s. His recommendation, though sincere I'm sure, was a disaster.

The interview with the candidate was less than impressive, but I was so desperate for an assistant that I hired him. The first incident I can recall involved his requesting the maintenance department for some white Krylon paint for his expected baby's crib. They said no when they realized it was for personal reasons, but then reported to me later that some white Krylon paint was missing from inventory.

I called my new assistant director in, telling him that he didn't need to deny what we both knew were the facts, but more importantly I wanted him to realize the message he had just given to staff – that zoo property was free for the taking. It could potentially be a huge cost to the zoo and would require constant and now somewhat hypocritical monitoring.

More such incidents followed until I finally took him for a ride around the zoo lake in the zoo golf cart. That was my way of ensuring that conversations were private. I suggested he look for a new job because he wouldn't be working for me in six months. I also promised to be conveniently out of town when requests for recommendations from prospective job inquiries came in.

A few weeks later I was at the Toronto Zoo as part of an accreditation team. Zoos police each other to ensure they are keeping to standards. I returned to some terrible news in Baltimore. In my absence, my assistant director had accepted a job that I had been offered previously but refused as the assistant to my boss, Doug Tawney. I had explained to Tawney that as assistant to the

Department of Parks and Recreation I would show bias to the zoo over the other facilities which in my opinion was not a good thing.

The man I had privately fired with pre-notice was now my boss and he did everything he could to make my work situation a living hell. He questioned any requisitions, sent critical memos nearly every day, whatever he could do. He was still my boss when I left for my new position in Detroit.

When I announced my leaving, the Park Board invited me to lunch which was a pretty big deal. They asked if I had any recommendations, so I told them my opinion of their new assistant to the Department of Parks and Recreation. I shared a few incidents to illustrate, such as his telling two women in the Park Board office that they wouldn't keep their jobs after he was their boss. Why would he do something that foolish? My comments led to an investigation which led to my adversary being given a *new* position with no supervisory authority. His duty was to write a work manual for the zoo. The first topic assigned was "How to Sweep a Floor." He left soon after that.

Celebrities at the Zoo

Thanks to my position as zoo director, I've met a host of very fine and famous people. Three of the most widely recognized celebrities are closely associated with my tenure at Baltimore.

Oprah Winfrey is undoubtedly the best known of all. She was working for local news station WBAL and sometimes covered interesting stories at the zoo. As with all special visitors, we rode around the grounds in a golf cart discussing the topic at hand. I remember thinking like everyone else who knew her then that she was destined for much bigger things. I never envisioned the heights to which she'd rise, but she was totally delightful and professional.

Baltimore Zoo (1978-1982) – Moving on up

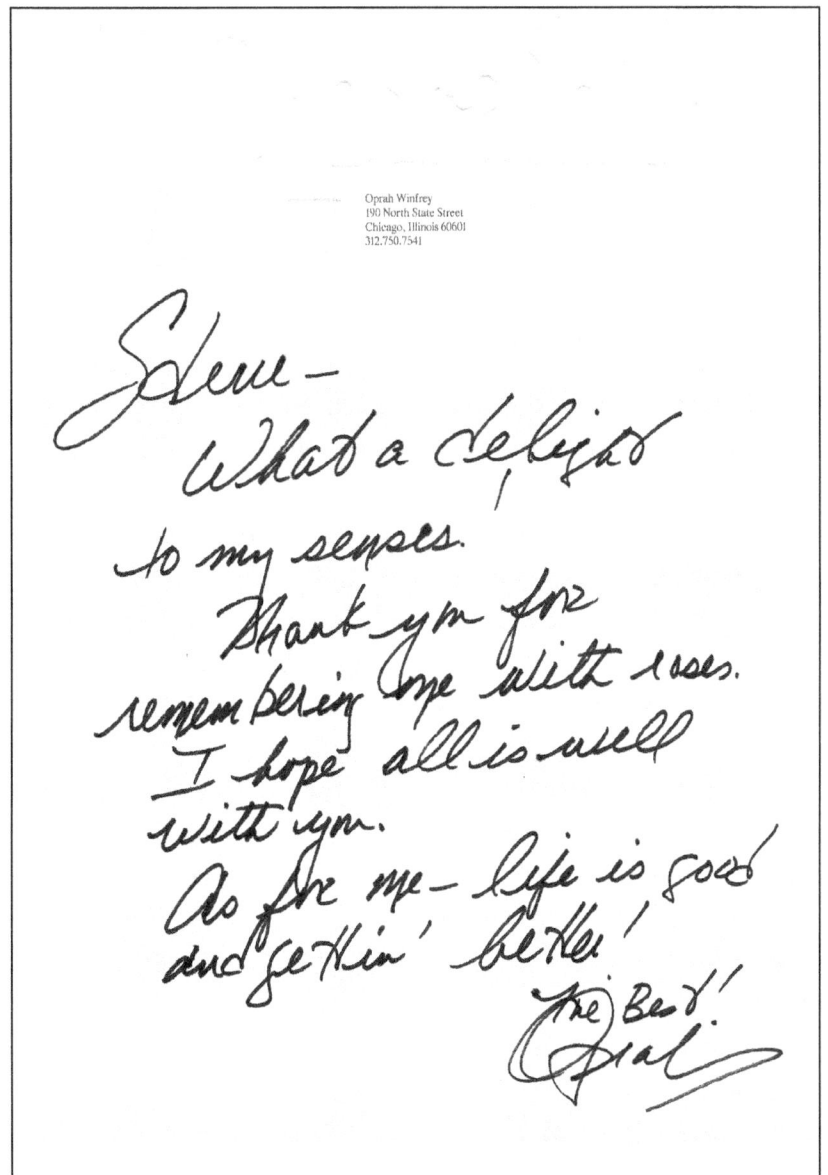

Thank you note from Oprah Winfrey circa 1984 (Steve Graham)

Years later when I was zoo director in Detroit I heard she was in town visiting local station WXYZ. I sent her a dozen roses with the message, "The nicest things happen to the nicest people." I knew it was a really long shot that she'd get them, or if she did, that she'd remember me. To my surprise both happened. I saved her thank you note in return. Who wouldn't?

During my venue at the Baltimore City Zoo Marlin Perkins, Director of the St. Louis Zoo, was a TV personality on the very popular show *Wild Kingdom*. He was a great showman. The public never caught on to the fact that the large snakes he handled on air were actually dead and recently thawed.

His sidekick was Jim Fowler, the real animal handler. He was the *Tonight Show* connection with Johnny Carson. The animals he took to the set were real audience pleasers, but Carson was frightened of all of them. One time Jim showed up with a giant hissing cockroach. It flew right at Carson and plastered itself to his coat. Jim said, "I didn't know they could fly."

Carson replied quickly, "Do you at least know if they're *poisonous*?"

Truth be told, Fowler probably didn't know. He was a good showman but knew almost nothing about the animals he performed with.

I recall seeing Marlin at a conference in Denver. We were standing in the large hotel lobby and I said to him, "Why don't you go and peek around one of those big marble columns and say 'Go get em, Jim'?" This was his pat line from *Wild Kingdom*. He laughed out loud and promptly did just as I had suggested with his usual flair.

My friendship with Amanda "Miss Kitty" Blake that began in Salisbury continued in Baltimore. She was a real zoo groupie along with her friend Jane Brolin, wife of James and mother of Josh Brolin of more recent fame. They attended many national zoo events and were big supporters of animal conservation groups and humane societies.

Amanda also had a friend named Gladys Porter who had singlehandedly financed the Gladys Porter Zoo in Brownsville, Texas. Mrs. Porter had inherited, as the saying goes, 'more money than God' from her father who had been personal assistant to J.C.

Penney of retail fame and fortune. She joined Amanda on a trip to the Salisbury Zoo. The ladies wanted to see nearby Chincoteague, so I offered to be their guide. We stopped for lunch at my favorite Chincoteague haunt, Bill's. When I ordered a hamburger, Gladys's eyes lit up. "I think I'll have one, too. I've always wanted to try one of those." The cultural gap that comment revealed has stuck with me to this day.

Amanda enjoyed her wealth, too – spent money like it was water. I was invited on more than one occasion to her Arizona ranch where she raised cheetahs. She was with her fifth husband, Frank Gilbert, when I knew her. She wore an engagement ring with four diamonds to represent, she said, her first four husbands. If Frank got "out of line," she'd point to her ring and warn him playfully, "Better watch out or you're gonna be just one of the boys." After surgery in 1977 for oral cancer, she died in 1989 at age 60 – far too young.

It was through Amanda Blake that I first met another well-known celebrity, Roger Caras. One of his initial claims to fame was as an assistant director on the iconic film *2001: A Space Odyssey*. He was a wildlife writer and preservationist, the author of more than 70 books, a veteran of television's *Today Show, Nightline, ABC World News Tonight, 20/20* and more. He later became president of the American Society for the Prevention of Cruelty to Animals (ASPCA). I attended one of the many parties for which he and his wife were famous in Queens, New York, as Amanda's guest.

Two very specific details stand out in my memory of that particular evening. First was my all-too-green velvet sport coat that soon became a magnet for the fur of Amanda's white Angora sweater when she hugged me. Second was catching my first glimpse of Roger Caras's daughter, Pamela who was only about 14 years old at the time. I recall thinking, 'Isn't she a bit too young to be up this late?' Little did I know then that years later this very young lady would be my second wife.

At that same party, Roger Caras invited me along on the next safari he organized. I was happily able to take him up on his offer on numerous trips. He and I kept in constant touch after our first meeting through other zoo associations we shared as well. Over that time Pamela had grown up considerably, so much so that she and her boyfriend came along on a later safari to Kenya, too. By then Pamela and I had come to know each other very well– *so well* that while we were all together in Kenya her boyfriend quickly caught on and took the next plane home. Not long after that, despite the nearly 15-year difference in our ages, we were married.

We lived in a very nice 'city' house in Robert E. Lee Park in Baltimore. She brought her horse along with the understanding that her father would pay for the boarding provided by Bobby Johnson, assistant zoo director. Payment was sometimes late and Roger had me call Sid, his money manager, to get a check. Roger Caras made very good money, but he lived very, *very* well. It kept Sid jumping.

One famous and colorful celebrity I met through my association with the Caras family was famed *New Yorker* cartoonist and creator of television's *The Addams Family*, Charles Addams. He was noted for tooling around The Hamptons in his vintage Bugatti and cultivating the poison ivy that covered his home and garden. The gorgeous and vivacious Lauren Bacall was always a fixture at Charles's parties. His birthdays were always memorable, with gifts like a human thigh bone from his girlfriend and a baboon skull with an apple in its mouth from Pamela and me. It was quite a hit.

Charles was once asked to judge a pet show in New York City's Central Park. After choosing a little boy's box turtle, someone advised him against it because the species was endangered in New York state. He thought for a moment and said, "Oh, let's give it to him anyway . . . and then we'll hang him!"

Pamela had graduated from Fairleigh Dickinson University and soon secured an excellent job on her own without using her father's influence working for Williams & Wilkens, publishers of medical texts. Her duties were nearly as demanding as mine and we were spending more time apart than together. The frustration of the situation boiled over when she went to work one morning and was met with a barrage of questions about the infamous mountain lion escape at the zoo that had hit the news the day before. She hadn't read or heard the news but, more importantly, I had never mentioned it to her. I had come home exhausted and fallen into bed. She knew nothing about this huge event that happened where her husband worked. She was understandably embarrassed and furious with me.

The longer Pamela and I were together the farther we grew apart. I began to resent the numerous trips we were mandated to make to her parents' home for gala events and the annual attendance at the Westminster Dog Show where Roger Caras was the preeminent announcer. Although the posh accommodations he arranged for Pamela and me were wonderful, the price tag we had to pay certainly didn't fit our budget. I think he was somewhat aware of our situation which is why he offered me the opportunity to co-author a book with him titled *Amiable Little Beasts*. We wrote the script to accompany more than 100 photos of baby animals that summarized what we knew of their social systems and development from birth to maturity. I appreciated the experience, but it did little to alleviate the distance between Pamela and me.

Before Pamela and I moved to our home in Baltimore, Roger made a request for his daughter's safety. Either we could buy a gun or get a big dog. That was a no-brainer. We got Simba, a golden-coated English mastiff. As her name implies she really looked like a lion. When I came home from work she would put her front paws on my shoulders and lick my face.

Then Pamela decided she wanted a Jack Russell terrier, so her father contacted the breeder who had gotten President Reagan his dog and got Annie for us. When we took her on the required visit to the breeder she introduced us to another puppy, telling us how sorry she was that she was going to have to put her down. "Why?" Pamela asked.

"She's deaf," the breeder explained.

I knew even before I saw the confirming look in Pamela's eyes, that we would be a three-dog family.

Our house sat at the top of a large knoll with a grassy slope reaching down to a walkway bordered on the other side by Roland Park, a very exclusive Baltimore neighborhood. Simba and Annie loved to loll around at the top of the knoll and patrol the small bridge across the walkway and through our gate. For some reason yappy little Annie hated German shepherds and Dobermans. If Annie spotted any she made a beeline for them and then rolled over on her back yelping as if they were killing her. Simba followed at her slow lope and shoved her nose under the uninvited guests and flipped them over her back. They were quite a team.

I used to run five miles every day I could manage with the two dogs. Simba knew how to cut all of the corners and Annie kept running ahead and doubling back so we kept approximately the same pace. When Pamela and I divorced, she got the dogs and I got the Abyssinian cats. One of the first days I was running solo, a very stately gentleman in his tie and tweeds resembling an English squire who often strolled my running path asked me, "Where are your lovely dogs?"

"My wife left and took them with her," I explained with a shrug.

"I'm so sorry," he said. "They were lovely dogs." Not a word about my wife. Guess he sensed I might be missing the dogs more than I did my wife. He was right.

Pamela and I divorced, sadly but amicably, less than two years after we were married.

Baltimore Zoo Politics

No two days were ever the same at the zoo. Demands came from all directions and crises, small and not-so-small, cropped up all the time. Although I've always said the main job of the zoo director is to keep the public happy, that required continually putting out a lot of fires with staff members and in a wide range of situations.

One such busy day I was watching a demonstration of a pretty significant piece of machinery that was under consideration for purchase by the zoo and city parks. A worker rushed up and interrupted us complaining loudly about something. I calmly asked him to wait and he stepped aside, but just a few minutes later he interrupted again and I held up my hand. His response was to publicly crumple his time card and throw it in my face. As deserved, I fired him. Problem was, and I knew this ahead of time, the worker was the union steward.

Anticipating the inevitable backlash, I phoned Doug Tawney to warn him. He said, "Not again, Steve. Sounds like another day with Master Sachs." You see, this wasn't the first time I had locked horns with the union and all the cases went before Master Leon Sachs for arbitration.

Retired judge Master Sachs was a slight man, probably not much over 120 pounds, but he wielded plenty of power in union dispute cases. The hearings were always frustrating. Attorneys for the union members often had little to defend, but did their best, often resulting in monologues of basically crap. In one instance the mindset of the defendant was really off base. He wanted to stop the proceedings claiming racial prejudice because the black female attorney was calling the arbiter "Massa." This was, of course, the lawyer's unfortunate mispronunciation of the judge's title, "Master."

When I told Master Sachs I was leaving for Detroit, but that I honestly wasn't going to miss coming into his room he said, "You really shouldn't have minded so much. You're the only department head in the city who has never lost a case before me."

MEMORANDUM

WILLIAM DONALD SCHAEFER, Mayor
OFFICE OF THE MAYOR · CITY OF BALTIMORE
~~7th Floor, 131 East Redwood Street,~~ Baltimore, Maryland 21202, (301) 396-3100
250 City Hall

TO: Mr. Steve Graham and Mr. Doug Tawney
FROM: Mayor William Donald Schaefer
DATE: February 19, 1980
RE: Zoo Attendance for January 1980

In reply refer to: MO-1

I am very pleased to receive a copy of your attendance memo for January 1980. It is extremely encouraging to note that attendance has tripled even though there has been a slight increase in admission cost.

The zoo continues to be a major attraction in our area, and we are all looking for the continuing improvements being made under the able leadership of Mr. Graham and Mr. Tawney.

I appreciate the report.

Excellent! Happy!!

Letter of commendation from Mayor Schafer – 1980 (Steve Graham)

I smiled. "Master Sachs, you are the fairest arbiter I've ever known and I never brought you a case I wasn't sure I could win."

There's no denying that the position of zoo director is politically charged. City taxes pay the salary and support the facility. I quickly learned that when you had a political job, you had to play the political games – attend the required events and make the meaningful personal contributions. And clearly, if you disagreed with the mayor, you'd better find cover. Luckily, I had very positive relationships with the mayors for whom I worked.

Mayor Schaefer lived for his city. He never married and focused all of his energy on serving Baltimore. Hilda Mae Snoops served as acting first lady to aid in his social commitments, but the mayor was all about the city. Like Doug Tawney, he pledged to trust me to run the zoo unless I gave him a reason to distrust my competence.

He loved to come to the zoo. Whenever he was there, he was smiling. This was especially true as the zoo began to show marked improvement.

We didn't always agree. For example, he really pushed the renovation of the Inner Harbor area. Prior to its new life the harbor was basically a large grassy area for the inner city folks to use as kind of a city beach. I saw the proposed improvements as gentrification that came with a cost to the less privileged who enjoyed it as it was but wouldn't be able to afford it later.

When I saw the plans for the new aquarium I recall saying, "I hope they build a canal from the aquarium to the zoo so some of the money can make its way back to us." That didn't happen, of course. Donors started giving to the aquarium instead of the zoo and the aquarium hired away some of my best staff.

When I was offered an unsolicited job as director at the Detroit Zoo after my interview on November 18, 1981, I decided to take it. They agreed to postpone the announcement of my hiring until I had a chance to tell Mayor Schaefer myself. The next day I called his office to say I was leaving, but he never returned my call. Although my contract with Baltimore required that I have an exit interview with the mayor, it was never scheduled. I finally called two days before I had to leave and his assistant told me, "When your name is mentioned he throws stuff. He's furious with you."

Though the time had come for me to move on, I was proud of what the Baltimore Zoo had become and took the mayor's outrage at my leaving as a true compliment.

My last day on the job, Diane Nickel, my 'Radar O'Reilly', came to me with the final payroll approval I would have to sign. I always detested that job. "Do I have to?" I moaned.

She smiled. "It really shouldn't be so hard, you know. Over 70 percent of the people on the list are your hires."

I smiled back and started my review. 'She's right,' I thought. I really had cleaned house and the zoo was certainly the better for it.

Steve at Baltimore City Zoo – 1980 (Steve Graham)

One of my prized mementos of those years is fabulous life-sized replica of a box turtle modeled after one I had rescued from the highway and kept as a pet for a time. It was crafted by

Tom McFarland, a longtime Waynesboro resident who has been commissioned by various museums and animal care facilities (including the Detroit Zoo) for replicas of turtles of all sizes. They're amazing. The one I have is so lifelike it even fooled my real turtle who postured for it as if it was another male turtle. Tom pointed out the only difference which I never would have noticed without his guidance. He incorporated my initials, a tiny "SG," within the detail of the shell.

I had to admit, the Baltimore Zoo had come a long way since my arrival some four years earlier. I've kept an article by Associated Press writer, Nancy Kercheval, that was clipped from *The Contra Coastal Times* near San Francisco that gave a glowing report of the zoo's progress. Quite a compliment that news had reached as far as the West Coast. It was printed on July 17, 1980. Sections of it read as follows:

> "... Graham is dedicated to making the Baltimore Zoo one of the best inner-city facilities in the country. That is in stark contrast to his first 18 months when, he acknowledged, he didn't encourage visitors to the zoo. 'I was ashamed of it,' he said... [Now] the animals give the children in the city 'an appreciation of life' that they don't find in the streets.' Having added shrubs and greenery to the cages Graham added, 'Bars and dark dingy cages are cruel to the animals ... Children might think the animals have done something criminal. ... I hope this zoo really flourishes.'"

Two months after I started my job in Detroit, I received a large poster of The Baltimore Aquarium opening. It featured Mayor Schaefer in a 1930s swimsuit and was signed "Best Wishes, Don."

CHAPTER 7

Safaris – Another World

Many of the exotic animals popular at zoos make their natural homes in the savannahs, rain forests, waters and mountains of the equatorial regions of Third World countries in Africa, Asia and South America. Much of the natural habitat for these creatures escaped encroachment and human development until recent decades. Many countries with surviving populations of these highly sought-after species are challenged to both protect them and sustain their fragile economic status. Tourism, mainly in the form of safaris is an integral part of their efforts.

One of the perks of being a zoo director was the opportunity I had to go on such trips. Beyond educational enrichment for the zoo professionals who went, the trips were a means of raising funds for the zoos. Many safaris included a mandate that those attending had to be members of a zoo society as financial supporters. One such group included members of the Young Presidents Organization (YPO) who owned businesses that grossed at least one million dollars annually. The experience of the safaris often increased the zoo director's knowledge of the animals and the members' appreciation for the species which would then translate to an increase in future donations to the zoo and conservation efforts. Seeing these magnificent animals in their natural habitat is a truly moving experience.

Steve Graham and wife Pamela (Caras) in back row, fifth and sixth from the left, Kenya Safari trip – 1978 (Steve Graham)

My first of 13 safari adventures was in 1977. I eventually visited Zambia, Zimbabwe, Botswana, Tanzania and Rwanda, but Kenya, home of the very exclusive Mount Kenya Safari Club, was the country I visited most often with the trips I organized at the Baltimore and Detroit Zoos. In the 1950s actor William Holden and some friends purchased 65 acres of land and an inn located in Kenya on the equator 7000 feet above sea level and transformed it into the Mount Kenya Safari Club, a fabulous facility that was and remains *the* destination for the Who's Who of the world.

This all happened after the Mau Mau uprising of the local black anti-colonial forces against the British Commonwealth that began in 1952. Atrocities between blacks and whites occurred on both sides, finally ending with independence being granted in 1963.

Jomo Kenyatta was unjustly tried for his participation with the rebels and imprisoned for nearly nine years. He was elected president of the newly independent Kenya in 1960. The story goes that during the flag-raising ceremony Prince Philip and Kenyatta were on the podium together. The British Union Jack was lowered without a hitch, but as the Kenya flag was being raised it hit a snag. Prince Philip, not known for his sense of humor, reportedly smiled at Kenyatta and said, "Having second thoughts?"

Brochure for safari excursion led by Roger Caras and Steve in 1980 (Steve Graham)

Memberships at the Mount Kenya Safari Club were quite exclusive and costly, but the club welcomed organized tourist groups and individuals as guests. The grounds surrounding the inn looked like putting greens populated by many fascinating animals roaming freely. After a day of game runs, guests could freshen up in their swimming-pool-sized bathtubs before attending the lavish formal dinner in an elegant banquet room, but not the official dining room of the members at the inn. When they returned to their rooms/cabins, their fireplaces were ablaze with local cedar logs. It was amazing, to say the least.

Two thousand acres that surround the club were purchased in 1967 when Don Hunt joined William Holden in forming the Mount Kenya Game Ranch that included pseudocaptive-breeding programs and an animal orphanage. The East African bongo, their rarest species, became the ranch's logo.

In his earlier years Don Hunt, after serving a stint in the army, bought a pet store in Ferndale, Michigan. He brought his younger brothers, Brian and Mickey, into the business and they began dealing with exotic animals from the Detroit Zoo about a mile away. Not one of them had a college degree. Don was the closest with three years at the University of Detroit, while Brian had one year of business college and Mickey a few community college credits. Their acquisition of exotic animals gave rise to *Bwana Don in Jungle-Land*, a locally produced TV show starring Don and Bongo Bailey, a chimpanzee from the zoo. Hunt became a celebrity. He always knew what was good for the media and his pockets.

He formed the International Animal Exchange (IAE) in 1960 and moved to Africa in 1965 to establish an export base. The connections he made after his arrival in Kenya served him very well. He garnered the good offices of President Jomo Kenyatta's wife and then used that influence to facilitate animal exports. The early television series *Daktari* loosely follows his career there.

President Kenyatta was imprisoned for many years during Mau Mau Rebellion– much like Nelson Mandela – and replaced upon his death by a very corrupt Daniel arap Moi. On one occasion before he became president, Moi was at the Safari Club when a member from Texas mistook him for wait staff and called him "boy." The story goes that Moi didn't miss a beat. He took a tea towel, laid it across his arm and served the clueless man.

Don Hunt then endeared himself to William Holden whose good reputation allowed them to purchase the land for the Mount Kenya Game Ranch. Though reputed as an animal expert, Hunt made some very poor hasty decisions. For example, Don suggested that more than half of the population of the rare Grevy's zebra be moved to a more protected area of Kenya. At his suggestion (and to the benefit of his wallet), the animals were captured from the desert area they inhabited and moved to the lush savannah grasses. Within six months, the entire population of the displaced zebras was wiped out by the lions, predators the zebras had no experience with because the desert they came from hadn't equipped them with any instinct to use high grass to hide.

Graham (far left) beside Sydney Pollack, Sidney's companion, and Eleanor Luedtke (far right) at Detroit Zoo fund-raising event circa 1990 (Steve Graham)

Sidney Pollack's motion picture *Out of Africa* starring Meryl Streep and Robert Redford depicts the conflicts and tribulations of earlier colonial farmers of the region like Lord Delamere and Karen Blixen. It is loosely based on the novel by the same name by Karen Blixen herself, written under the pen name Isak Dinesen, the character portrayed by Streep. I had the privilege to meet

Mr. Pollack while I was at the Detroit Zoo through his association with Kurt Luedtke, a supporter of the zoo, who wrote the screenplay for *Out of Africa*. Mr. Pollack (Syd) was a genuinely down-to-earth character and we shared a number of enjoyable lunches and visits to my library together.

The Mount Kenya Safari Club and other such inns were neither the only nor the first famous, or infamous, white settlements in the region. In the 1920s and 1930s the Happy Valley set (largely Anglo-Irish) came together in Kenya and parts of Uganda. The purported hedonistic aristocrats and adventurers numbered nearly 21,000 by 1939. They were renowned for their decadent lifestyle and exploits with drugs and sexual promiscuity. I suppose the exotic setting of Kenya made them more interesting news than similar gatherings of swingers in more mundane locales.

The arrival of troubled socialite Lady Idina Sackville is credited with initiating the notoriety that was to follow in the Happy Valley area.

In recent years, archaeologist Juliet Barnes who has lived in Kenya all her life has investigated the remains of the grand residences that have deteriorated over time. The Happy Valley set has dwindled to a handful of much quieter white Kenyans. They say their homesteads are marauded by itinerant workers driven out of the cities by recent police crackdowns.

Wildlife film maker Joan Root was shot in her bedroom January 13, 2006, just five days before her 70th birthday, one of a number of white settlers killed during robberies. Her 1979 film documentary in collaboration with her husband Alan titled *Mysterious Castles of Clay* was nominated for an Academy Award. She also chaired and funded an anti-poaching task force in the area of her Lake Naivasha farm, causing some controversy with locals. Her last will and testament provided that her land be turned into an admission-free and unfettered wildlife preserve.

Joan was a very exciting woman. She and her ex-husband had many rescued animal pets including a full-grown hippopotamus and an aardvark named Million. 'Aardvark [I'd walk] a *million miles for one of your smiles.*' She and Alan often suffered major injuries to get the spectacular film footage they wanted. Alan has recently released a new book titled *Ivory, Apes & Peacocks: Animals, Adventure and Discovery in the Wild Places of Africa.*

I was also honored to meet and develop a friendship with Cynthia Moss. She had been working as a reporter at *Newsweek* but moved to Africa in 1968 to work with elephant researcher Dr. Iain Douglas-Hamilton. In 1972 she started the Amboseli Elephant Research Project in Kenya where she has studied the same population of elephants for over 40 years. Echo is a herd matriarch who has been the subject of several books and documentaries by Cynthia Moss.

Christmas card from Cynthia Moss, renowned elephant researcher (Steve Graham)

Rarely did I get to Africa that I didn't visit with her. I sent her many volumes of her book that she signed and returned so they would bring top dollar at auctions and fundraising events stateside.

Another exemplary person I had the privilege to know thanks to my safari experiences was Norman Carr. In 1980 he continued his conservation efforts by establishing the Luangwa Valley National Park in Zambia and eventually came to have responsibility for managing all the national park nature reserves in the area. He was about 20 years older than me, about 5'9", his slim frame a bit bent with use, and arms and legs with skin turned to leather by the African sun. I felt an immediate kinship with him when we met and we corresponded regularly. In the States, when I came across copies any of the several books he wrote, I bought them and mailed them to him so he could sign them to sell to tourists to support his work, as I did with Cynthia Moss.

His first love was lions and he raised and released many rescued cubs into the wild even before Joy Adamson, world famous for her work with the lioness Elsa, heroine of *Born Free* which she authored. Norman was one of the few white foreigners to maintain a cooperative relationship with President Kenneth Kaunda and later his successor Robert Mugabe, corrupt firebrand to this day. This was often helpful in achieving good things for the nature preserves under his watchful eye.

According to his obituary in *People* magazine, May 20, 1997, "...he had a small camp deep in the bush for serious walkers. There were huts so flimsy that when you lay in bed you could hear the lions breathing as they padded around exploring human smells..." He worked to keep Luangwa Valley wild and discouraged tourists from tipping guides, suggesting that they donate money to the local native schools instead. On the occasion of being awarded a prestigious conservation award he reportedly suggested that it be given to help preserve the tsetse fly because "in areas from which the fly had been banished, cattle are brought in to graze and people take over. Where the tsetse fly continues to flourish so does wildlife."

Norman Carr died in Johannesburg on April 1, 1997. Donations in his memory were directed to the Kapani School where he once taught the young students the names of the animals in the park where he took them twice a month, so they no longer called them all "inama" which means "meat."

I met Joy Adamson during my safari experiences as well, though less often. She lived in South Kenya in a house that was decorated almost totally with lion skins. Her third husband, George, and his brother Terry maintained a camp in North Kenya. He was equally enthusiastic about lions and actually built his camp inside a cage in the middle of lion territory. He actually shot Elsa's mother in self-defense years earlier which led to their adopting the three cubs left orphaned.

The Adamson's' marriage was rocky, probably in large part because Joy suffered from severe bipolar disorder. One evening at a restaurant gathering with friends (including me), she sobbed the entire time for no obvious reason. She found her connection with nature best in the absence of other humans – the species she most mistrusted. Art was also an expression she often used, leaving nearly 500 paintings and line drawings of animals and plants after her death in 1980.

Joy and her husband, as well as Joan Root whom I mentioned earlier, were killed at various times and circumstances by factions of Shifta (Swahili for thug) tribesmen. The transition from colonization to independence has been rough for most African nations as most of their populations were unprepared for nationhood and still clung to the culture of warring tribes and power struggles. I developed a friendship with Peter Muigai, nephew of Kenyan president Jomo Kenyatta, and hosted him once when he was in Baltimore. Though he enjoyed his association with the ruling power, he was understandably concerned about the African tradition that when a ruler dies, the entire family is killed to insure a totally new transition of power. Luckily he escaped that fate when power transitioned to Daniel arap Moi in 1978 when Jomo Kenyatta died.

I have so many fabulous safari memories of being among such magnificent animals in their native habitats. Probably the best birthday of my life – my 46th – I was within an arm's-length of a family of mountain gorillas. As I watched, the curious primate youngsters mischievously harassed a huge silverback male, the obvious leader of the troop. When I think of that moment, I still marvel at how fortunate I've been in my life.

Augur Buzzard painted for Graham by Norman Arlott circa 1977
(Steve Graham)

On one of my safari trips to Kenya with Roger Caras I was invited to the home of John Williams, the head of the local Coryndon Museum of Natural History, who authored *The First Field Guide to the Birds of East Africa*. He had illustrated his earlier books himself, but hired Norman Arlott from Great Britain for his later editions. Norman's watercolor illustrations are remarkable and highly prized. Arlott was staying with Williams at the time and thus began a lifelong friendship between Norman and myself. He and I actually joined forces with a trusted guide, Omari, to lead groups together in Nairobi. I recall one time John Williams and Norman had captured an Augur Buzzard the day before I was to return to the United States. He stayed up all night to complete a painting of the bird that he then gave to me as a gift.

Several years later I was vacationing in my beloved Chincoteague, Virginia. On returning from the beach to my car, I discovered a note on the windshield. It read, "I'm on the island, Find me!" signed, "John Williams." He had confirmed he had the right car by my license plate that read ZOO-1. Later that day I discovered him in a local restaurant with the inevitable lady friend and we shared a pleasant evening.

Norman Arlott came from humble beginnings in Norfolk, England, and was initially a musician by trade, specifically a drummer, providing for his wife and three children. Steadily his supreme talent for magnificent watercolor illustrations of birds, his first love, began to support him and his family. He has since written, illustrated and published numerous volumes. We've stayed in constant touch to this day.

Norman and I attended the same safaris for years – he as the bird specialist and I as the mammal specialist. I would spend a week with him and his family in Norfolk before going on safari and then take a week after to explore somewhere on my own. One year I headed for Fishing Camp on the coast of the Indian Ocean, very different from the interior. The beach went on forever in one direction and one day I had wandered along the surf far past any sign of human habitation when a group of baboons came out of the adjacent forest toward the water. Now this species can be quite unfriendly and aggressive to humans if they have a mind. I really didn't like the way the large male was staring at me, so I retreated as calmly as I could into the ocean until the water was chin high and waited until they left.

One time when I was visiting with Norman in Norfolk he had a couple of maiden schoolteachers for dinner. They had been on safaris with us previously. Folks affectionately called them Trixie and Dixie after a popular London cartoon. They were quite endearing and at the end of the evening after I had overindulged on the meal I said to Trixie, "I'll never be remembered for my dainty appetite."

She smiled. "Well, I'll always remember you for your unobtrusive kindness." It's hard to forget such a sweet comment from such a sweet lady.

Another of Norman's friends is David Shepherd, a world-famous wildlife artist and outspoken conservationist whose favorites subjects are elephants and steam engines. His artwork today commands as much as $20,000 to $30,000. He is the antithesis of Norman – tall, loud and flamboyant. He was invited to a fundraiser (not zoo related) in Detroit and I was invited to join him. The guest of honor was Prince Michael of Kent, 12th in line to the British throne and a slight, quiet man. Everyone attending had a crash course in etiquette. Royalty cannot shake hands, which is why they are usually seen with hands in their pockets. Men were to bow and women curtsy. My single brush with *royalty* was more than enough. The following day I gave the prince's *man* a tour of the zoo, much to his delight.

Some real characters came with safari territory – usually very wealthy individuals who were often the vast majority of our tour members. One of the guests had photos of her son's Texas ranch who was purported to have had a fence made of new Cadillacs that were lined up end to end and buried to the windshield. Rich *and* pretentious – though they were more the exception than the standard. Most of the folks were a pleasure to be with.

"Fran" was my first experience with an unusually challenging guest on the first safari I ever attended with Roger Caras. She was more than just a little strange – a single, frumpy, middle-aged embarrassment to her well-to-do family who often sent her on trips as far away as possible. Problem was she was a certified kleptomaniac. Items disappeared not only from other guests' rooms, but even the little blue cakes from the public urinals.

Jill Caras, Roger's wife, and I were assigned to search Fran's room for missing articles while she was out. Unfortunately, the front desk gave us the wrong key and room number and Jill and I walked in on a newly married couple consummating the marriage in the bridal suite. Luckily our exit was so quick they never knew we were there.

When our group gathered in the lobby to leave at the end of the week, Fran was wearing every piece of clothing she owned to make room in her luggage for all of her booty. She looked like a tick with her red puffy head ready to burst. Jill had to take her back to the room and straighten things out.

One of the most valued friendships I made among the native Kenyans was with Omari, our driver. We shared a love of birds and he was a font of knowledge about the local sights. We once rented a rickety outboard motorboat at a remote lake where we heard that some extremely rare Pygmy Geese had been spotted. When a pair came into sight, Omari stood up to show me and nearly swamped the boat.

I met Omari's family and spent many evenings at dinner with them – quite a departure from the local custom between blacks and whites at the time. It was normal in Kenya for men to hold hands as a sign of friendship, and Omari and I often did. I was crushed when his daughter told me Omari had been killed in a head-on collision with another bus. Even worse were the false allegations of intoxication brought against him.

One of the most beautiful lakes in Kenya, Lake Turkana, hosts large populations of crocodiles and Nile perch that attract many tourists. It is also home to multiple calderas, the huge cauldron-like remains of early volcanic activity, which dot much of the Kenyan landscape. On one occasion Brian LeFlay, a friend of Norman's, and I were on safari and climbed the impressive outer rim of one of the larger calderas to investigate the wildlife of the lake at the bottom of the gigantic earthen bowl. A soda lake with very high alkaline levels that supported little more than algae had formed at the base. This green slime was ambrosia to two colonies of Greater and Lesser Flamingos that had gathered into two huge but distinct rings around the shore. The Greaters with their deeper pink made up the inner ring in the deeper water while the shorter Lesser species made up the paler pink outer ring. The scene was breathtaking.

On the far opposite wall of the caldera interior was a large patch of white. "I'll bet that's an Egyptian Vulture nest," I told Brian. "All those white droppings." As we watched, one of the massive birds emerged from the small cave and took flight. Brian, an artist himself, painted a picture of it later for me.

On my first safari to Kenya, Norman and John Williams and I were birding in Nairobi National Park, a fabulous wildlife preserve just outside the city limits. The juxtaposition of the exotic animals against the city skyline backdrop was stunning. Suddenly Norman called out to John and me and motioned us to follow him at a run. Now Norman never ran, so we knew something big was up.

Soon we were all standing spellbound watching a pair of extremely rare African Finfoots in the river. John had been in Kenya more than 30 years and had only ever seen one female. As the pair moved along the bank their long tails occasionally popped out of the water and sparkling beads cascaded off their oily feathers. Norman painted this scene later and gave it to me.

One species that I never spotted during my African sojourns despite repeated efforts was the Lammergeier, or Bearded Vulture, the largest of my favorite group of birds. They're most often sighted at Hell's Gate, a drive-thru ravine with high walls so close together you can barely see the sky. Though there were scattered remains from their habit of dropping bones and tortoises from high onto the rocks below to smash them open and get to the marrow, the vultures themselves eluded me. On every visit, I offered any guide who spotted one a $100 bonus, but they were unsuccessful, much to the disappointment of both of us.

Mountain Lodge, a spectacular building in Kenya set on substantial posts 30 feet in the air with a view of a large watering hole, was the site of a memorable elephant moment for me. In addition to the viewing deck, the lodge offered a long underground tunnel leading to a pillbox area closer to the animals. As I spied a group of elephants approaching, I quickly made my way to the end of the tunnel. One of the mothers and her baby were so close that I saw the milk froth on the baby's mouth as she nursed – a magical moment.

Of special note as well is Mzima Springs, a series of four springs fed from filtered rain water that spends nearly 25 years underground before percolating into the crystal- clear, cold water teaming with Nile crocodiles and hippos. Alan and Joan Root filmed their 1969 nature documentary *Mzima: Portrait of a Spring* that featured underwater footage of hippos and crocodiles. Alan was actually bitten in the face by a hippo while filming.

Hippos are responsible for more African deaths than any other mammal. The water is their daytime refuge from the sun that burns their hides, but they graze at night. Anyone who inadvertently gets between a hippo and the water is in danger, especially if the hippo is startled.

In 2009 a catastrophic drought forced additional wildlife to Mzima Springs in search of water as the surrounding grasslands turned to desert. Only five hippos remained of the original population of 70 in 2003.

I love the refreshing African myth about the hippos. As it goes, eons ago the hippos were suffering because the sun was scorching their skin during the day. They asked the gods for permission to go into the water for refuge. However, the gods were afraid that the hippos would eat too many of the fish they had reserved for the other water animals like the crocodiles. The hippos promised that they wouldn't. In fact, they're still herbivores. So the gods determined to give them a chance. However, the gods didn't trust the hippos so they devised a way to check. Knowing that the hippos only defecate on land, the gods made them wag their tail as they defecated to broadcast their manure widely to the ground so the gods could see any fish scales. To this day, it's a good idea to get out of the way when you see a hippo's tail shaking.

The multiple opportunities I had to explore the fabulous lands of the safaris were priceless in so many ways. I only hope they can continue to inspire future generations as they did mine.

More recent 2014 headlines focus on Thomas Cholmondeley, the only son and 38-year-old heir of the 5th Baron Delamere of Happy Valley fame still living in Kenya. He is accused of shooting a black man he claimed was a poacher and faces life imprisonment if convicted. He shot another black Kenyan just a year previously, but murder charges were dropped before the case came to trial. Much hangs in the balance especially regarding the fate of his landholdings. Local Kenyans hope to recoup the lands taken from their tribes generations ago by the British. Delamere has two young sons who might stand to inherit by his estranged wife who is a doctor in Nairobi.

Unsettling reports like these make me cringe when I consider the negative effect they might have on tourism to Kenya. More recently the situation has worsened with attacks on Westfield Mall in Nairobi in September 2013, the slaying of 150 students at Garissa University College by al-Shabab militants in April 2015 and in increasing threats from the terrorist forces of Boko Haram.

I long for a return to the Kenya I remember from my many visits – to a country that was welcoming and relatively crime free. Visitors' dollars helped to fuel the country's economy. In Kenya these monies helped to support wildlife conservation by enabling

Kenyans to preserve land reserves rather than develop them to provide additional income from farming or other financial ventures. With continued violence and loss of tourist revenues I am moved to echo warnings I made when tourism to Kenya was lagging in the late 1980s. As I wrote in *The Detroit News* on August 20, 1989, "African governments will have no choice but to plow their game reserves to create more farmland to offset the loss of foreign-trade dollars brought in by tourism . . ."

CHAPTER 8

Detroit Zoo (1982-91) – Storms of Controversy

When Fred Martin, the deputy mayor of Detroit, called me at the Baltimore Zoo and asked if I would be interested in being Director of the Detroit Zoo, I immediately said "No." When he persisted a bit and invited me to come out for a tour of the zoo at the city's expense, I thought, 'Why not?' However, the trip started out badly with trails of ants parading through my hotel room. Then a quick drive-by of the zoo confirmed it was clearly wanting in many ways.

Gunter Voss had been the last official zoo director. He was involved in multiple varieties of corruption during his tenure, especially those that would line his own pockets. After he was fired, then jailed, some acting directors had barely held down the fort. On one occasion the results had proven especially disastrous. One of the zoo's largest benefactors, James Holden, successful businessman and founder of Holden Fuel Oil Company, had established the Holden Director's Fund to extend assistance to any staff member determined to be in financial need and worthy of the money. Repayment of the loan wasn't required, though many recipients did so. However, one of the acting directors *and* his secretary had purchased new cars using the fund. That prompted the Zoo Commission to change the nature of the trust, but not before the two offenders drove away in their new rides.

The Detroit Zoo desperately needed competent leadership.

After the whirlwind tour, I was seated at one end of a long conference table facing the head of the Detroit Zoo Commission. I'm a little embarrassed to recall how cocky I was, leaning back in my chair with my legs crossed. When the deputy mayor asked why I wasn't interested in his offer I said, "First, this zoo isn't accredited and second, I want no part of this zoo's infamous chimp show."

He just smiled back at me and said, "Those are the first things *we* want to fix and we think *you're* the best man to do that."

I had painted myself into a corner. Here was the chance to correct some large wrongs. I hadn't expected the opportunity to make such a positive difference and felt drawn to the challenge. Besides, the situation was no longer the best for me at the Baltimore Zoo. So I said "Yes."

Apparently they had been pretty confident about my acceptance because when we stepped out of the room reporters were waiting and cameras started flashing. As they began firing questions at me, I asked them for a favor. "Please don't report anything for at least 24 hours. My boss in Baltimore [Mayor Schaefer] knows nothing about my coming here and I want to give him the courtesy of knowing about my leaving before the news goes public."

They complied. That augured well for the positive relationship I would have with the Detroit press in the years to come. I told the reporters I would never lie to them, and I kept that promise. They were, for the most part, supportive. Lots of positive copy came from the desk of reporter Pete Waldmeir of *The Detroit News* and I've saved a tongue-in-cheek feature article by Nancy Ross-Flanigan from the Sept. 18, 1988 edition of the *Detroit Free Press* that discussed my signature wardrobe of choice, safari shorts. I used to order about eight pairs a year from Norm Thompson Outfitters in Oregon.

Graham in fashion photo-op for Detroit Free Press 1988
(Steve Graham)

My arrival at the Detroit Zoo was a newsworthy event. I was about to tackle the status quo and take on some formidable foes on issues that raised emotions on both sides. Within two weeks I had investigated every nook and cranny of the zoo grounds and determined what needed to be done. Neil Shine, publisher and editor of *The Detroit Free Press* once said that he had never seen anyone take the Detroit media by storm quite the way I had. Having the press with me was a real blessing.

Fortunately, I had a good and respectful relationship with Mayor Coleman A. Young. In the 1970s Detroit was struggling mightily with huge economic and racial issues. Mayor Young's actions were controversial and, as in all political arenas, full of tales of questionable deals, favoritism and rampant rumors. One of the major reasons I accepted the position in Detroit was Coleman Young. I had long admired his leadership on civil rights. Given his situation, I respected him for what he was trying to accomplish when I came – and even more so when I left.

This human dynamo was always moving, always on the job. At our first meeting he was watching three televisions and playing solitaire and didn't stop as we talked. He said, "I don't know a whole lot about zoos, so if you report to me once a year that'll be fine."

"No one would like that more than me," I recall saying. "The only thing I ask is that you trust me to have the best interest of the animals at heart and leave any decisions about the life, death or movements of the animals to me."

He agreed.

It was lucky for me that the mayor had a sense of humor – and patience – when a political cartoon parodying my push to have the zoo accredited hit the *Detroit Free Press.*

In order to receive accreditation the zoo needed first to pass the USDA inspection that had been seriously glossed over previously by the inspector who had been a former classmate and close friend of the zoo's vet. Many shortfalls were being ignored that had to be remedied. I couldn't ask for funding to fix the problems until they were confirmed. When I finally got tired of pointing out the violations that the inspector had skipped over, I called the head of the USDA who was a friend of mine – without consulting the mayor. My friend from the agency came personally, writing up the violations that Mayor Young then agreed to correct. What followed cost the city a lot of money in order to gain accreditation. I was the hungry lion that had duped the mayor – "had had him for lunch." Since the positive rating for the zoo was unquestionably a good thing, the mayor couldn't really say much, though I'm sure he was tempted.

Mayor Young was also frustrated with my effect on his publicity another time, although, unlike the accreditation issue, I did nothing knowingly in this instance. The occasion was Devil's Night, October 31, 1986. Detroit has a history of burning buildings on this night before Halloween. Most were arson of structures for insurance payment or other financial advantage with as many as 100 buildings being torched. In response to this unofficial local *custom* the mayor enlisted all of the city appointees (department heads and assistants) to patrol in their cars all over the city on Devil's Night.

Being aware of the situation, I was driving around the city when I saw a house on fire and stopped. After I called it in on the radio, I noticed the fire jump to the roof of the adjacent house. When I hopped out of the car, I spied a water hose in front of the house and started spraying the second roof to prevent the fire from spreading. As fate would have it, Channel 7 news crews were in the vicinity and saw me. Reporter Steve Kay brought in the camera crew and I made the evening TV news – the very spot that the mayor was hoping would be his. This was to be the mayor's big PR coup, but I had unintentionally upstaged him.

Conditions at Detroit Zoo gradually improved but the long hours and continual conflicts played havoc with my chronic depressive disorder. Having left my marriage to Pamela behind along with my tenure in Baltimore, I felt the loss of a personal companion for comfort and support as well. Having maintained my sobriety, I had neither time nor interest in the bar scene which somewhat limited my options for meeting women.

Editorial cartoon about Detroit Zoo policy circa 1983 (Steve Graham)

Sensing my dilemma, a few of the docents at the zoo with whom I'd become friends determined to rescue me. They arranged a meeting with Karen Krabbenhoff, a registered head nurse and the daughter of a well-known local radiologist. The attraction between us was immediate and mutual. I realized how much I had missed such close companionship and didn't want to risk losing this new found love. I began an intense courtship despite my concerns that she had two young sons from her previous marriage. I had determined never to have children and risk being a failure as a father.

As it turned out my positive relationship with these two wonderful boys lasted longer than my whirlwind marriage to their mother. She and I both worked long hours and shared the parenting. The boys totally enjoyed accompanying me on daily rounds of the zoo and we became very close. Meanwhile, Karen and I got caught up in our own frenetic schedules and as other passions cooled we came to realize we were very different people who had wed too quickly and needed to part. This was far more apparent to us than to the boys. After our separation and divorce, I continued to spend time with them, but eventually we grew apart. My biggest regret about those short years was that the boys had been hurt in the process.

The zoo docents were probably disappointed by my divorce but approved of my prompt redecorating of the long hall leading to my office. The walls had been lined with multiple stuffed animals' heads, often prompting questions from children about when and where each had been killed. There were also exhibits of props from the infamous chimp shows that I intended to eliminate. The heads and props were sold at a high-end yard sale for substantial funds after I was assured all the profits would go solely to the zoo instead of the city. Then the hall was tastefully repainted.

Though my three previous marriages had stumbled, I wasn't content with a solitary life. Caught up again with the demanding business of zoo I again began to feel the absence of a life partner.

Years earlier, not long after moving to Detroit – before I began dating Karen – I was part of the accreditation team that went to the Binder Park Zoo in Battle Creek, Michigan. While inspecting the grounds, I met Lori Canterbury, one of the animal keepers, and was immediately smitten by her intelligence and good looks. However, her boss told me she was married, albeit not happily, so I didn't pursue my first inclinations.

I never really forgot that first meeting with Lori, so when the position of education curator came open at the Detroit Zoo, her name immediately came to mind. I discovered that she had left the Battle Creek Zoo after her divorce and moved to Cincinnati where she had a good paying job in a chemical plant. I knew we couldn't match her salary, but I also remembered from our earlier conversations that she loved zoos. Using that as leverage, I persuaded her to come for an interview and began professionally courting her until she accepted and moved to Detroit with her daughter Hilary.

Within less than a year of their arrival, Lori and I were married.

As I mentioned earlier, Pete Waldmeir, featured reporter for *The Detroit Free Press* was typically very supportive of my efforts, but he was also one of the mayor's harshest critics. For my part, I was a fan of Mayor Young. Though I didn't agree with everything he did, he was most certainly a visionary with positive intentions and boundless energy.

I recall the first time I met Pete. One weekday in the zoo's early winter off-season I was making one of my many solo walking tours of the grounds. Other than the month of May, my vacation time, I made a complete walking tour inspection every day. This particular day I noticed a man with two young children around five to six years old stopping at various exhibits. The man was taking time to share lots of information with the kids. When I walked over to them he turned to me and said. "You're Steve Graham, the zoo director, aren't you?"

I acknowledged that and we went on to spend two or three hours strolling together discussing the zoo. I finally extended my hand to him and said, "You know, we've been talking for hours and I don't even know your name."

"I'm Pete Waldmeir," he said with a knowing grin as my jaw dropped. Here I was having such a positive exchange with the infamous critic of the mayor I so admired. It was the beginning of a positive relationship between Pete and me that would endure for my nearly ten-year sojourn at Detroit – much to the chagrin of the mayor.

The Fred Silber Company held the concession contract for the zoo. Fred's son Dennis took over for him and was a very close friend of Mayor Young. He was a little younger than me and quite dapper head to toe with monogrammed shirts and manicured nails. He and the mayor shared bagels every Sunday morning at the Manoogian Mansion, the mayor's official residence.

Although I had a shaky relationship with Dennis because of some of his less-than-acceptable practices with the zoo concessions and cleaning services, he was my best conduit to the mayor's ear. I would tell him "Please don't tell the mayor" and be pretty sure he *would* tell the mayor within the hour. I used to joke that he was the highest-priced errand boy in Detroit.

It was better to stay on Dennis's good side. So when he was less than happy about my don't-feed-the-animals policy that compromised his big moneymaker of peanuts and popcorn, I conceded to allow beer to be sold as long as it was a very small amount of beverage for a very high price. It never caused a problem

As much as I admired the mayors with whom I worked in Baltimore and Detroit, they had little affection for each other. This did work to my advantage at one point when Detroit was beginning to consider its grand aquarium complex. When I was at Baltimore during the aquarium's construction, the head builder/designer and I had butted heads quite often. He had built his first one in Boston and gone on to be the go-to person for any large city considering building an aquarium. I suggested to Mayor Young that he could simply contact Mayor Schaefer and borrow the plans from him since the aquariums would probably look alike anyway. That pretty much derailed the idea.

Coleman Young's funeral in 1997 was a huge event in Detroit that he had orchestrated long before his passing. People lined the street three and four deep for miles as the hearse passed through the city. During the services a young local girl rocked the church with her rendition of *The Wind Beneath My Wings*, a favorite of Coleman Young's. The mayor had dedicated the song to his appointees before his death. In his own words, Young once said, "I suppose I'd like to be remembered as the mayor who served in a period of ongoing crisis and took some important steps to keep the city together, but left office with his work incomplete." I truly admired him.

One of the mayors who came after Young was the former pro basketball star for the Detroit Pistons, Dave Bing. He also owned Bing Steel, a successful Detroit company, and was a member of the Zoo Society Board during my tenure. He was a real asset for the zoo, being both a good person and an effective link to additional sources of revenue.

Coleman Young's name resurfaced many years later on one of my visits back to Waynesboro. While lunching at The Parlor House, one of my favorite neighborhood haunts, I met Steve Waltz, an older black man who ate there regularly too. As we reminisced, he shared that he once served with the Tuskegee Airmen, a famous United States Air Force flying unit from World War II. I told him that Coleman Young, the mayor I had worked with in Detroit, was also a Tuskegee Airman. Steve's face lit up. "You mean Reds?" he said. "We were good friends. I didn't know he was the mayor of Detroit. I never kept up with him after the service."

"Yes," I said. "I didn't know he got that nickname so early. When we were working together in Detroit, people thought the nickname alluded to Communist tendencies because he pushed the civil rights movement so hard." Steve just grinned. Coleman had passed by then, but I would have loved to get those two wonderful gentlemen together.

The Detroit Zoo

The Detroit Zoo had three separate venues. The largest section is located in suburban Royal Oak. The much smaller Belle Isle Zoo and the Belle Isle Aquarium were on an island in the Detroit River approximately 15 miles away. Mayor Young spent many of his younger years at Belle Isle and remembered it as I did Hershey Bars – that they were ten times their actual size. His family often escaped the summer heat of the city by camping on Belle Isle. He always favored it over the other sections of the zoo because it was far more familiar to him.

Fallow deer, a species from Eursia, had nearly taken over Belle Isle. Someone had donated a pair of them years earlier that had propagated profusely and were eating most of the vegetation on the island. The animals were so crowded that males often swam across the river to Windsor, Canada, and we would get the call to come remove them. Also over-populating Belle Isle were the resident Canada Geese. Unlike the migrating variety, these birds stayed on the island year-round and created an awful mess with their profuse droppings.

I developed a proposal to round up the geese and deer and send them away, but the mayor balked at the idea. He finally agreed to the geese removal when the Michigan Department of Natural Resources agreed to take them. We used a cannon trap that shot a huge net from its barrel and trapped the birds on the ground where we had spread some corn. They were shipped to one of the western states.

As for the fallow deer, the mayor agreed to my plan as long as I didn't take all of them. We euthanized many of them and sent the venison to the city soup kitchens. In that time of economic hardship and hunger, this was a popular move. What the mayor didn't know was that the remaining small herd were all males. Hence, the *problem* of the deer soon nearly disappeared.

The Belle Isle Aquarium and Zoo was finally accredited on June 25, 1985, some time after the main zoo complex. It closed several years after I left due to the city's financial woes. It has since reopened under the Michigan Department of Natural Resources as Belle Island Nature Zoo.

Prior to my arrival at the zoo, the major exhibits were equipped with a series of talking boxes. Keys shaped like elephants purchased at a concession stand fit the boxes and triggered an explanation of the animals in the exhibit. Over the years the boxes had fallen into disrepair but hadn't been removed.

One snowy night after closing on my usual end-of-day walking inspection of the 125 acres, I had the zoo in the eerie late hours all to myself. I knew the sole night watchman was nowhere close. Suddenly, I heard a strange voice behind me. To say I was spooked is an understatement. I finally discovered the source was a malfunctioning talking box. Needless to say, the first order of business the next day was to make sure the power to all of them was turned off. They were all removed not long after that.

As at the Baltimore Zoo, among my first initiatives to improve conditions for animals at the Detroit Zoo was to tear down some fences that had been added to the original large enclosures to accommodate different species in smaller areas. I incorporated the lesser varieties in order to have mixed exhibits in more space. The revenue from animals we sold to other accredited zoos went toward further improvements to the grounds.

I respect all animals, but primates have always been special to me. Two of the most troubling exhibits involved the crab-eating macaques and baboons. The moated-island enclosures for both species were too small and the climate was too cold. Many of them had frostbitten tails and toes. They were put outside on exhibit too soon in the spring and brought in too late in the fall because the inside accommodations were sadly inadequate

– cramped and filthy with poor ventilation. We simply couldn't care for them adequately, but I had few options as to where they could go.

My best, though not pleasing, option was to sell them for research. With the macaque species, I didn't have much choice. The best home I could find for them was with Giselle Epple who was working at Washington University in St. Louis in research to treat arteriosclerosis, a crippling disease that hardened arteries. She wanted *all* the crab-eating macaques and agreed to use them for one research only. Many times research animals are used endless times for ongoing testing over many years. I didn't want this for my monkeys and she signed an agreement that they would all be euthanized within 30 days to check them for signs of the disease.

When word got to the press that a "research" facility was involved, it created quite a kerfuffle – but nothing compared to what would come later.

Snow monkeys replaced the crab-eating macaques, but the island was too small even for them. Periodically the hierarchy of the dominant females resulted in severely abused young males who had to be removed and euthanized. Still, these casualties were a definite improvement over an entire group of maimed animals.

The baboons also were transferred to a research facility with the same one-procedure-only contract, but I missed a serious loophole. Their offspring could be used for testing multiple times. I've never really forgiven myself for that mistake. The only happy note here was the healthy population of ring-tailed lemurs that took their place so happily in an exhibit that suited them perfectly. We had adopted them from a facility that I discovered was in search of another facility large enough to house all of them and not disturb the group. Such happy endings are heartening to recall.

The Chimp Controversy

One of the most popular attractions for many years at the zoo had been the chimpanzee shows starring, among countless others, Jo Mendi, their first headliner. The shows started in 1934 and continued for nearly 50 years. Arthur Forsythe was one of the early trainers and his daughter recently released a personal account, *The Chimp Trainer's Daughter*, remembering his abuses both at home and with the zoo chimps. She shares much of her research about the history of the animals that her father and other zoo trainers worked with to bring in substantial income for the zoo at a tragic price to the chimps. Jo Mendi earned more than $30,000 in 1930s dollars as a performer during his 31-month career at the Detroit Zoo.

The Detroit Zoo used Jo Mendi to encourage public donations to the Community Fund during the Great Depression
(Steve Graham collection)

Most of the chimpanzees came to the zoo from Africa. The only method of wild capture involved killing the young chimps' mothers who refused to give up their young and the males who tried to protect them. On average, an estimated ten chimps died for every baby taken in the wild.

The chimps usefulness for the zoo shows lasted only two to five years because older chimps no longer submitted to the trainers in order to be dressed like little people and forced to perform such foreign acts as riding bicycles and smoking cigars. Few people know that a chimpanzee's smile is actually a sign of abject fear.

The average lifespan for chimpanzees is 40 to 50 years – at least one lived to be 80. The zoo would retire many of the rebellious teenagers to research or breeding facilities with notoriously inhumane conditions for the remainder of their lives.

Dawn Forsythe remembers the 'Jo Mendi days':

"It all makes sense now," says Dawn. "At home, dad was a brutal man, often punching my mother and my little brother… He thought it was okay to use violence to 'teach' his kids and 'discipline' his wife …in a way, the chimps were an extension of a dysfunctional human family… Dad was fired sometime in the late 1950s after someone saw him throw a young chimp against the wall. I'm betting it wasn't the first time."

Though widely popular with the public, the chimp shows continued to be blatantly degrading and destructive to the chimps. I made it my business to eliminate the shows and construct a new world-class chimpanzee exhibit that would allow them their natural dignity. They had earned it for bringing so much revenue to the zoo for so many years. The zoo had been built on the back of the chimpanzee.

I had to go in search of the massive funds the chimpanzee facility project required and so encountered David Lawrence, Jr. He was publisher of the *Detroit Free Press* and, at the time, orchestrating the impending joint operating agreement with *The Detroit News*.

I recall pitching my case to him the first time and being pleased that he didn't say "no" immediately. Before he could, I requested that if his answer was leaning toward the negative, he had to tell me "no" *twice*, at a later date. At our *second* meeting over a stack of buckwheat pancakes at the exclusive Detroit Club, he actually said yes and we began planning how to raise the money. With his widespread respect and influence he was able to tap into the resources we needed. Our original estimate of $3 million quickly ballooned to $8 million, but the exhibit named Chimps of Harambee (Harambee is Swahili meaning "let's all pull together") was eventually a sight to behold.

Near the completion of the fundraising campaign David Lawrence and I led a trip to the Arnhem Zoo in the Netherlands, home of the premiere chimp exhibit in the world. We left invigorated enough to complete the funding sufficiently to begin construction. David, who doesn't understand "can't," carted a card table-sized architectural model all over Detroit in search of support. In large part, his efforts put us over the top.

I didn't hesitate to contact the best people in the field. Dr. Richard Wrangham (then at the University of Michigan, now at Harvard University) is among the world's most highly regarded primatologists. He was in Africa at the time, but I still managed more than one very expensive phone conversation with him. Frans de Waal, who has authored more than 20 books on primates while on staff at Emory University, advised me in his strong Swedish accent how to make the facility the best possible.

The new chimp facility was a monumental task with many people offering their support. Alan Schwartz, head of the city power company and a highly revered philanthropist, offered the services of his head engineer, Harry Tauber, as construction manager – easily a $400,000 to $500,000 savings. This was good news for the budget, but not for me as we went head-to-head on nearly every issue. His take-no-prisoners attitude prevented him from considering any other options. Once he had his mind set he would not change.

Nearly 20 years older than I, he was quite tall, gaunt and severe. He rarely smiled, actually *never* softened his expression when we were together that I can recall. He didn't know how to compromise and we were always at odds with each other. The tension was so bad I developed back spasms and was forced to wear a back brace. Not surprisingly, as soon as I got on the plane for a scheduled safari to Kenya, I didn't need it any more. The pain went away.

Every meeting between us was bad. Finally, I heard he had let it be known he was determined to have a showdown with me. We had always met on neutral ground at the Detroit Zoological Society's office, so I called and asked him to come to *my* office, knowing it would rile him. I didn't feel like being nice. When he arrived, irritated as I had anticipated, I never offered him a seat. About halfway thorough our scheduled topic I finally said simply, "Harry, if it has to be you or me working with the Commission, I'm going to win." He stormed out of the office.

At a meeting at the prestigious Detroit Club, the Zoo Commission confirmed my prediction and chose me over Harry. I was relieved, but no one was smiling when it was over.

One of the first requests I made after I took my post in Detroit was to see the records of all the chimps. The abuse was obvious, but the medical X-rays of multiple broken bones added even more proof. The chimp handlers were initially furious about my intention to close the shows. When they found out it would not involve losing their jobs, they relented, somewhat.

One of my early meetings with the handlers cemented their respect for me. The chimps were housed in individual cages that lined the perimeter of a large stage in the Great Ape House. Each animal had a handler. One way they maintained control without revealing any cruelty to the audience was by a large chain that was sewn into the collars of the shirts that all the chimps wore for the performances. The handlers could easily gain a controlling choke hold if necessary.

Publicity spoof with David Lawrence circa 1988

Great apes intuitively know who's in charge. They act differently around the handlers' boss – namely the zoo director. They probably sense the handlers' attitudes toward the boss and alter their behavior. As I faced the gathering of chimps and handlers on my initial visit to the facility and was talking to them, the largest male, Joe Joe, broke loose and charged at me. Before the handlers could react, he jumped on me and put his open mouth over my face. It was startling, but I could sense he was just testing me. Still not completely sure of what Joe Joe or the handlers might try to do, I stayed calm. I told them to stand still while I had a quiet conversation with the chimp. Slowly he closed his mouth. I lowered him to the ground, took his hand and walked him back to his handler. That made a huge impression on everyone there.

On one occasion Neal Shine, the executive managing editor of the *Detroit Free Press* working for David Lawrence, requested that I bring one of the zoo's chimpanzees to a talk David was giving to a local high school. My reply was, "You know better than to ask me that." Then I quickly counter offered to dress up like a gorilla instead and play the crowd for him. It was a huge hit, especially for David who was the featured speaker and unaware of my plan. Award-winning photographer Tony Spina captured the moment.

The Great Ape House had a large amphitheatre attached and was among the largest buildings at the zoo. It was horrible. The fronts of the cages were glass and all the gorillas, orangutans and chimpanzees were kept in separate cages with no socialization. In their isolation and boredom, they soon discovered that the audience found it amusing when they threw things against the glass. What they had in most abundance was their feces that consequently plastered the viewing glass most of the time. I couldn't wait to tear it down. Still, I expected opposition when the wrecking crew arrived, so I sat right out front in a lawn chair and watched until the Great Ape House was demolished enough so that it couldn't be saved. The new facility I envisioned would have nothing in common with this disgraceful ruin.

During the construction phase of the exhibit, some of the chimps had to be relocated. My choice of placement raised a storm of protest. I have never in my career sent any animal under my charge to any unaccredited facility. My first choice for the chimps was the Primate Foundation of Arizona run by a dear friend, Jo Fritz. I had quite successfully placed Charlotte Levine's chimp Mia and two other chimpanzees there in 1979 during my tenure at the Baltimore Zoo. Still, some individuals in the public heard the word 'research' used in association with the foundation and went on the

Detroit Zoological Parks

Detroit Zoo • Belle Isle Zoo • Belle Isle Aquarium

8450 W. Ten Mile Road • P.O Box 39 • Royal Oak, Michigan 48068-0039 • (313) 398-0903

Coleman A. Young, Mayor
City of Detroit

10 December 1990

Ms. Connie von Hundertmark
79-08 147th Street
Kew Gardens Hills, NY 11367

Dear Ms. von Hundertmark:

In reply to your letter of 3 December regarding four chimpanzees owned by the Detroit Zoo, I can tell you that you have been given some misleading information about them.

We sent those four animals to a facility in Arizona operated by people who are as knowledgeable about chimpanzee care as anyone in the world. The animals were 2-3 years old at the time. Three of them had been taken from their zoo mothers when only a few months old so that they could be sent to the Detroit Zoo to be trained for the chimp shows that used to be held here.

This happened long before I arrived in Detroit. By the time I got here, the three show chimps were extremely maladjusted and I sent them to the Arizona facility because the people there had more experience than anyone else in successfully rehabilitating chimps that were socially inept. The fourth chimp had been born at the Detroit Zoo and was in an unacceptably crowded situation. Fortunately we were able to leave him with his mother until he was a little more than two years old, so his social adjustment was considerably more advanced than the other three.

The year I arrived in Detroit I stopped the exploitive chimp show. Last year we opened a much better chimpanzee facility than we had in the early 1980s when the four chimps were sent out. We would like very much to bring them back to our zoo, but the one female has never advanced to the point where she can fit in with adult chimpanzees (we have two adult males and five adult females at present); she self-mutilates whenever she is with animals that she considers threatening, so she has always had to be kept with younger chimps. The three males have made tremendous progress, and if we did not have two adult males at the present time, we would bring those three young males back. However, they are now 10 and 11 years old. At that age, the adult males would perceive them as a serious threat and would bully them unmercifully. We do not want to take a chance of having those young males injured, so we will not bring them back, at least until they are fully adult.

ACCREDITED BY THE AMERICAN ASSOCIATION OF ZOOLOGICAL PARKS AND AQUARIUMS

attack. One such reaction was in a letter I saved dated Dec. 3, 1990 that read in part:

Dear Mr. Graham,

It is horrifying to hear that you abandoned your four chimpanzees to a research facility instead of taking them back.

Everyone feels you were bribed quite well for this. There is no other logical explanation for it.

How can an animal abuser like yourself keep your job? People should hear about you.

Sincerely,
Connie von Hundertmark

Responding to letters like this always required a little breathing time to stay professional, but I did my best – most times. I was more successful with written comebacks than I was with my usual shoot-from-the-hip direct conversations. In the case of Ms. Hundertmark's comments, I was especially eager to defend the Primate Foundation of Arizona as much, if not more, than myself. Jo Fritz had more than earned my respect for her outstanding devotion to the chimpanzees fortunate enough to come under the care of her and her husband, Paul.

```
Ms. Connie von Hundertmark
10 December 1990
Page 2


I must say that your conception of "research" seems to be that you
think these animals are in some kind of situation where they are
used for painful biomedical experiments.  They are not.  They have
been cared for with skill and compassion ever since they were sent
to Arizona, and I have great admiration for the people at that
facility.  Because we cannot take the males back at this time we
are looking for suitable zoo locations for them, but as long as
they are in the Arizona facility I am confident that they will
continue to be properly cared for.

Best regards,
ZOOLOGICAL PARKS DEPARTMENT

Steve G——

Steve Graham
Director of Zoological Parks

SG/dja
```

Graham's response to negative correspondence (Steve Graham)

Briefly, the Primate Foundation of Arizona was founded in 1973 whose Mission Statement reads in part:

> *"The first and foremost aim of the Foundation is to solve at least a portion of the problem presented by captive Chimpanzees and their future. Up until this time, there was no place for the captive chimp once it outgrew his home, became too difficult to handle or completed his duty as a laboratory animal. Many have been destroyed as a result. The Foundation provides a home for these chimpanzees, giving them a semi-natural environment and the special care necessary for good mental and physical health."*

Two of the six "Policies of the Foundation" included (#3) "The Foundation will never allow any scientific investigation that would involve harm in any manner to the chimpanzee" and (#6) "the health and welfare of the chimpanzees will always be the foremost consideration of the Foundation."

My personal connection with Jo Fritz and her facility involved my friendship with Charlotte Hunt Levine, owner of the Hunt Brother's Circus mentioned earlier, and her need to find a place for her *child* Mia, a female chimp that had been part of her circus act – and her family – for years. The Hunt Brothers' Zoo had finally folded around 1970 and she had come to Rick Hahn at Catoctin Mountain Zoo about placement for all of their animals, but some years later she needed to find special placement for Mia, the one female chimp they had kept. So I contacted Jo Fritz at the Primate Foundation of Arizona.

Mia's move to Arizona was very difficult for Charlotte and Mia. Their separation anxiety was immense. Jo was very sympathetic to the situation. This letter to Charlotte Levine from Jo and Paul Fritz illustrates their exceptional devotion to Mia and all their chimpanzees.

PRIMATE FOUNDATION of ARIZONA

April 27, 1976

P.O. Box 86
Tempe, Arizona 85281

Mrs. Charlotte LeVine
9313 Overlea Drive
Rockville, Maryland 20850

Dear Charlotte:

You have been on our minds constantly these last three weeks. We hope the really rough days are now behind you. I have a delightful story to tell you.

Remember, in my last letter I told you about Willy Lenz and his 12 year old male chimp? Willy brought Pedro here on April 6th and it was the saddest parting of man and animal that we have ever seen. Willy carried Pedro out in his arms crying and put him into a small portable cage so we could roll it into the room and release him. Pedro held out his arms to Willy and cried, I cried, Mrs. Lenz cried and you know the feeling, don't you?

We kept Pedro by himself for a while although he was used to being with other chimps. We wanted to watch him and get to know him ourselves. He is big and exceptionally pretty. Across the next days we spent a great deal of time with him because he was so depressed and would only eat hand-fed tidbits. He is soft and gentle and talks all of the time. I have absolutely no fear of him, so you should know how good he is.

He did not rally around and really begin eating and we were becoming very concerned about him. Paul decided he must have a cage-mate, but the big question was who. We could not house him with another male and take a chance on him being hurt and most of our females are also very aggressive. Paul made his decision and on April 19th Pedro was given his cage mate.

Paul first shifted Pedro to the next cage so his cage was empty and then opened the door to the empty cage. The female Paul had chosen was in another room. Paul felt certain he could handle her and did not anesthetize her to be placed in a transfer cage. He separated her from her companion, opened her door and said, "Come on." She would not let him hold her hand and I was having nervous tremors. This was an adult female that he purposely had let out. She yelled at him and he yelled back and told her to go in that room and get in that cage and she did! He shut the door, locked it and let her explore and look at the new people around her. So far so good.

LeVine   2   April 27, 1976

Then he opened the door to Pedro's cage and let him in with her.
There was not a sound. The female then went down from the bench to
Pedro, held out her hand and said "Uhhhhhhhhhhhh". Pedro sniffed
her hand and turned his back to be groomed. They then moved together
up to the bench and put their faces together. She stood up and turned
her back to him and he stood up and bred her. Then the grooming started
again. All of this was in silence and left us with our mouths hanging
open. These two chimps acted as if they had known each other all of
their lives, there was no male dominence, it was a mutual act of
breeding and that just isn't normal chimp procedure. Paul was beaming
like and proud father saying, "I knew they were perfect for each other!"

The female will not be pregnant because it was not the right time in
her cycle, but we feel certain they will eventually hit the right time
and present us with a baby. It may sound corny and like I've lost what
little good sense I had, but I think when they do it will be a love
child.

The day they have that baby will be one of the happiest days of my
life. I will be able to pick up a telephone and call you to tell
you that MIA and Pedro are parents!

You need not worry about her any longer. She is truly happy now and
spends hours each day hovering over her man.

Please let us know how you are feeling.

                                Sincerely,

                                PRIMATE FOUNDATION OF ARIZONA

                                Jo Fritz
                                Secretary

JF:jo

Letter from Jo Fritz of Primate Foundation of Arizona
(Steve Graham)

PRIMATE FOUNDATION of ARIZONA

24 July 1979

P.O. Box 86
Tempe, Arizona 85281

To: Members of the Board of Directors and Advisory Board

From: Paul and Jo Fritz

Due to three very tiny, but very large problems, we will be unable to leave Malacandra in the evening for the next eight or nine months. This will necessitate some discussion regarding Board of Director's meetings, which are held quarterly (October, January, March & May).

The three problems are:

<u>Jayme</u>: (named after James Garland, M.D.; James Ebert, V.M.D., & James Mahoney, D.V.M., Ph.D.) female, born 2 months prematurely on 22 May 1979. Weight at birth: 2 lb. 7 oz, respiratory and neurological problems, blind in one eye (cataract?) and possible limited vision in the other. We hope the cataract will respond to surgery. Time will tell with the other problems. Jayme required feedings every 2 hours 'round the clock and is now on a 3 hour schedule.

<u>Babad</u>: (Frog - Papago) male, born on 1 June 1979, one week after Jayme. Weight at birth: 3 lb. 14 oz. His mother literally tried to stuff him back where he came from following birth and when that wouldn't work, she walked away from him. He has now developed a hernia, which will require surgery in the very near future. His feedings are also every three hours.

<u>Hahshani</u>: (Saguaro Cactus - Pima) female, born 10 April 1979. Her mother thought the whole thing was a big joke, played too rough and would only nurse the infant when Paul demanded she do so. Paul supplement fed the infant for 9 weeks. Then the mother started sticking pieces of straw and sticks in every orifice. Hahshani was taken from her on 10 June 1979 and added to the already over-flowing "nursery". A stick had punctured her ear drum and we are still battling infection. She too eats every three hours.

Besides the additional day and night hours (that were not there to begin with!), the initial cash outlay for nursery supplies (bottles, nipples, diapers, blankets, baby shirts, humidifier, baby beds, etc.) has been tremendous. Monthly costs for just formula and diapers is averaging $70.00 and this will increase as the size of the babies increases. If anyone has suggestions on the solution of both the time and the $ problem, we would be grateful for them.

Milly Chambers (with help from Jeff Rogers) cared for Jayme while Jo was gone. The James Ebert family cared for Babad for a week and then he too went to Milly's. Hahshani was taken from her mother three days after Jo's return. Paul held the remainder of Malacandra together. Needless to say, we are very tired, but we are also very grateful to those special few who assisted with the babies and with Jo's trip and during her absence.

The Washington, D.C. - New York trip was very successful. Another meeting in Washington is scheduled for next year preparatory to a national open meeting on chimpanzee breeding. Jo has again been invited to serve as a consultant and was requested to prepare and submit the Foundation's behavioral recommendations to be included in a national report. Preliminary discussions took place in New York regarding possible affiliation with New York University.

We are going insane, but the babies are dear. Hope all is well with you.

Jo

Letter indicating conditions at Primate Foundation of Arizona (Steve Graham)

As with all zoos and most caring animal institutions, time and money are always in short supply. It's a 24/7 proposition as the letter below illustrates:

The situation finally became more than the Fritzes could manage. An online source from *National Geographic*, July 2013, reported, "In 2006, Jo Fritz announced that PFA would close its doors and all the chimps would be transferred to the MD Anderson Cancer Center's Keeling Center for Comparative Medicine and Research in Bastrop, Texas." They will join more than 100 other chimps at the NIH-funded colony where they have improved housing with larger social groups for play and interaction.

Not everyone was a fan of Jo Fritz due principally to her connection with research placement for some of her chimps. I understand others' reservations with this, but realized it was the only way she could afford to maintain her facility to save as many animals as she could.

Dennis Merritt, Curator at the Lincoln Park Zoo in Chicago, had little respect for Jo's choices. I was friends with both of them and got letters from both of them within days of each other that said practically the same thing. In an effort to bring them closer together, I mailed them each other's letters. Jo thought it was enlightening, but Dennis was furious and didn't speak to me after that.

Three of the smaller chimps from the Detroit Zoo that were sent to the Primate Foundation during the chimp exhibit construction were so mentally damaged that they could never be integrated with other chimps. The zoo had housed them in a cage entirely too small in the Great Ape House in Detroit and they were psychological messes before being sent to Arizona. In Arizona they suffered severe stress if they were kept together, so they sat in solitary cages holding themselves and rocking behind vacant dead eyes. Their fate had been sealed before they ever left Detroit.

Four or five of the larger chimps that the Primate Foundation couldn't house were sent temporarily to a Texas facility run by the International Animal Exchange – definitely not my first choice, but the only one available at the time. Within a very short time we received word that two had died. I immediately went to investigate and found deplorable conditions. The chimps were in small cages in a dark, damp building and the roar from the primates was incredible when I opened the door. They were not happy creatures.

The Detroit chimps weren't hard to find. They sensed my presence and cut loose with a cacophony of noise that was incredible. I sat with them for hours grooming them through the bars of their cages while I berated myself for ever allowing them to be sent here. Why hadn't I checked it out before I sent them? The least I could do was to get them out of there as quickly as possible. I had them shipped back to Detroit and housed them at the animal hospital that could barely spare the room, but we managed until the new facility was complete.

In addition to chimps, three gorillas and an orangutan also lost their home when the Great Ape House disappeared. One male gorilla, Jim-Jim, died before he could be transported from his temporary enclosure at Detroit. The other, Sheldon, had been sent to San Antonio, Texas. It wasn't a successful transition because the environment was so foreign to him. He had no idea how to cope with the outside, grassy area, as Detroit only offered a suffocating interior space. Sheldon never came out of the interior section of his San Antonio home and died there.

On Sept. 2 the zoo vet and I accompanied Mesou, the female gorilla, to the Brookfield Zoo. It was a harrowing trip. The crate holding the sleeping ape was too large for the plane, so we moved her to the floor of the craft and covered her with a cargo net in case she woke up. During takeoff the plane skidded sideways with the uneven weight, but we made it.

What was even more problematic about Mesou's departure was the deal I made regarding the move. Instead of selling her to Brookfield for the going price of $30,000 – $40,000, I donated her to the SSP (Species Survival Plan) because it would be better able than the Brookfield Zoo to control the direction of her future placement and breeding. Not only did Detroit lose the money, I had set a precedent – this being the first time an animal was *given* to the SSP – that would pressure other zoo directors to follow suit. It wasn't popular, but I knew it was the best thing to do.

Years later the headlines recounted a story about a child falling into the moat of the gorilla exhibit at the Brookfield Zoo. One of the female gorillas picked up the child and carried it unharmed to one of the animal handlers. When we read about it in Detroit we all wondered if Mesou was the heroine, but we never knew for sure.

As for the lone orangutan, I sent her to the Baltimore Zoo to be with the lone male orangutan I had left there. It was a happy ending for both of them, despite the unfortunate injuries she suffered in transit due to inadequate shipping practices that I missed personally supervising in Detroit. I always felt terrible that I hadn't checked out what was going on since the staff was new to me, but to my knowledge it didn't happen again on my watch.

Happily, the positive changes for the Detroit chimps that began with the Harambee time have continued. As of 2009, the Detroit Zoo had 11 chimps, four males and seven females, living in a Garden of Eden compared to the conditions endured by their forerunners. Of the current chimps, four were born at the Detroit Zoo.

Unfortunately, Dawn Forsythe reports from her research that although the Detroit Zoo's chimp shows are no more, the practice continues in different parts of the world. Orangutans appear in boxing matches in Thailand, and as late as 2004 Universal Studios Hollywood theme park featured them as performers.

There's still much to be done.

My early introduction to Jane Goodall grew with my vision for the Detroit chimps. She was there when we broke ground for the Harambee exhibit...

Chimps of Harambee groundbreaking – Larry Buhl, Coleman Young, Jane Goodall, Graham, and David Lawrence (Steve Graham)

...And again for the jubilant opening

Chimps of Harambee grand opening with Jane Goodall (Steve Graham)

As proud and happy as we were with the new chimp facility, fate threw us a curve with the first birth much later, just months before I left Detroit. I was present for the event which went well until the vet said, "There's another one." I stormed out of the chimp house in frustration. This twin was *not* good news.

Chimpanzee twins are very rare – and tragic. A chimp mother won't raise both babies; one will be rejected. The only alternative is to hand-raise the unlucky one that the mother doesn't want. This feels like positive nurturing at the beginning, but never has a good ending for the chimp that gets trapped between being a chimp and being human. I left it to the deputy director to decide to save the abandoned baby because I was so conflicted about the situation.

I never heard the eventual outcome of the adopted chimp, but I hope it had a happier life than the majority of other human-nurtured animals that never really 'belong' anywhere.

Statue of Carl Hagenbeck, designer of the Detroit Zoo (Steve Graham)

The Detroit Zoo already had a number of Hagenbeck moated exhibits named after Carl Hagenbeck of Hamburg, Germany who was among the most famous European importers of exotic animals during the 19th and early 20th centuries when capture and transport involved primitive methods with high animal casualty rates. He later made partial retribution for his earlier practices by advocating for and constructing more humane, natural settings for zoo animals, most notably the moated exhibits that removed the bars and cages of the past. He designed the original plan for the Detroit Zoo.

The new chimp exhibit was also moated. Before we opened it I issued a challenge to members of a local mountain-climbing club to attempt to escape. They jumped at the offer, but were surprised at their inability to get out of the enclosure. We had a winner, it seemed.

On Oct. 18, 1989, the first chimps were given access to the new exhibit. Two had been with us before the new facility, two were purchased from the Cleveland Zoo and four females came from Germany through animal broker Fred Zeehandelaar. One of the German females motioned empathically to a keeper who was passing the transport cage with a bucket and rag. When he gave her the rag, she calmed and cleaned the inside of the cage top to bottom that day and every day after.

We chose a Wednesday to introduce them to their new home when the zoo was closed and prepared ourselves with rifles and cap-chur guns (air rifles that shot hypodermic darts) just in case. When the sliding steel door was opened for them it took a while before the dominant male ventured forth. He kept pressing the grass with his hand because it was all new to him. Eventually he came out followed by a bold female and the remaining group of six. The first female soon made her way to the top of a mound of dead trees in the center of the exhibit and did a slow 360-degree assessment. "That's the one that'll get out," I recall saying.

Within a year she confirmed my prediction. She managed to scale one of the specially designed inclined walls to escape to the top of a building just outside the enclosure. The public was at the zoo at the time so when the alarm was sounded they were quickly escorted to zoo buildings until we could capture the chimp.

The chimp leaped off the roof into the rear trash area and encountered the zoo vet Dr. Robyn Barbiers who reacted perfectly by not attempting to wrestle with a much larger and stronger opponent. Robyn stooped into a submissive pose and the chimp hit her on the back soundly as she passed. Then the chimp met head-on with a head keeper, a short but powerful body builder. She grabbed him by the ankles and flipped him over her back before making her way to the top of a tall maple tree beside the eight-foot-tall chain link fence of the zoo grounds. Part of the tree extended over the fence into the adjacent upscale neighborhood of Huntington Woods.

As we watched and hoped she wouldn't move, maintenance personnel brought in a cherry picker, a cap-chur gun and a crate. Head veterinarian Dr. Nadine Richter and I agreed that we needed to hit the chimp in the thigh where it could penetrate enough to inject the sedative. I told Nadine that as head vet the shot was hers but that I'd take it if she wanted. She handed me the gun and got in front of me so I could rest it on her shoulder. We waited maybe ten minutes to get a clear shot at the half-dollar-sized target. When the dart hit the mark we were both a little shocked.

The chimp pulled out the projectile and threw it right at me, as expected, before the sedative kicked in. I climbed into the cherry picker that took much longer than I liked to tack between the branches to the top of the tree. I lifted her lethargic arms around me and pulled her into the basket. As the workers slowly tacked us back to the ground, the chimp began to groom my chest hair. It hurt like hell but I let her continue until we were down, but by then she had recovered enough so that she hopped out and loped to a downed tree nearby.

Finally, I shot another dart from the cap-chur pistol that fully sedated her and she dropped two feet to the ground unharmed. She was crated and taken back to the facility where prongs were immediately added to the faulty wall.

Detroit Zoological Parks

Detroit Zoo • Belle Isle Zoo • Belle Isle Aquarium

8450 W. Ten Mile Road • P.O Box 39 • Royal Oak, Michigan 48068-0039 • (313) 398-0903

Coleman A. Young, Mayor
City of Detroit

4 October 1990

Mr. Rick Swope
11390 Culver Road
Cement City, Michigan   49233

Dear Rick:

I want to thank you and Cynthia for the lovely flowers. You are the most gracious people on Earth. Here we were trying to thank you, and you thank us! Your gesture was most appreciated. Please tell Matthew, Nichole, and Brandie hello also, and remember that you have a standing invitation to visit the Detroit Zoo, including tour and meal.

The Society is still working on the photo of "Joe-Joe" which I promised you, and you'll be interested to know that Swope Grove is half planted as of today and should be completed tomorrow. We'll send you a picture of that also.

We can never thank you enough.

Best personal regards,

ZOOLOGICAL PARKS DEPARTMENT

Steve

Steve Graham
Director of Zoological Parks

SG/dja

All Hope to see you soon.

ACCREDITED BY THE AMERICAN ASSOCIATION OF ZOOLOGICAL PARKS AND AQUARIUMS

Thank you note to Rick Swope who rescued chimp from moat 1990 (Steve Graham)

Despite extensive research as to what would provide a safe and adequate barrier, in April 1990 a chimp drowned in the moat. In the wild a very small stream will divide whole colonies of chimpanzees, but this day, according to on-the-scene reports, the female that had cleaned her crate earlier simply walked toward the crowd into the moat. Her huge body mass, three times that of humans, sank easily and as she got chin deep she opened her mouth and swallowed, almost purposefully. It was almost as if she recognized someone in the crowd and was going to them. As soon as we pulled the chimp from the water, Dr. Barbiers did mouth to mouth resuscitation on her and tried to clear the water from her lungs ... but she was gone.

After this incident, experts assured us that it wouldn't happen again and that the facility was safe for the remaining chimps. Nonetheless, a few months later on July 29, 1990, Joe Joe, a dominant male, deliberately threw another male into the moat. A zoo visitor, Rick Swope, jumped into the moat and dragged the chimp to safety. Strangely, Joe Joe backed off his original aggressive behavior and didn't attack either Mr. Swope or the rescued chimp. The headlines were huge.

This courageous act could have ended badly for both parties, but fortunately didn't. Neither Mr. Swope nor the chimps were injured. The exhibit lost no more chimps to the infamous moat.

I honor and respect all animals, but I readily admit my preference for the primates. Unfortunately they are very susceptible to tuberculosis (TB). At the Baltimore Zoo they were kept behind glass to help prevent their exposure to those and other harmful germs from human carriers. The City of Baltimore had a high incidence of TB.

Detroit didn't have the same precautions, so I added the protocol that anyone working with the primates had to be TB tested every six months. This was not very popular with the staff, so I volunteered to be the first. The Wednesday before Thanksgiving I got word from the lab that I had tested positive. I was a carrier.

I was horrified. This branded me a Typhoid Mary for TB. This would severely limit my contact with the primates and, nearly as bad, my dating career. I quickly called my friend Jo Fritz hoping for some sort of alternative. She said it's not unusual to get a false negative reading for TB, but very hard to get a false positive. The CDC (Centers for Disease Control) confirmed her opinion. I was calling anyone, desperate for a solution.

It was an awful and eternal weekend, among the worst I can recall. On Monday when the lab reopened I called to check results for the rest of the zoo workers who were tested and told the technician how upsetting the positive reading was for me. He seemed puzzled and checked. "Mr. Graham, sorry for any inconvenience, but I'm afraid we made a mistake. You didn't test positive. I'm looking at your results right now, and they're negative."

All's well that ends well, but that was one of the longest weekends of my life.

Years later after I sent my resignation from the Detroit Zoo to Mayor Young, I never went back to the chimp house that I had normally visited two or three times a day. I'm not good at goodbyes and this one would have been exceptionally painful. One female in particular used to recognize my voice or my gait or something about my presence because the keepers knew as soon as she started shaking her hand that I was somewhere near by.

Most recently in the news related to chimpanzees is the controversial case being heard in the New York state courts. The Nonhuman Rights Project (NhRP), headed by founder and President Steven Wise, filed suit to grant captive chimpanzees in that state the same rights as a "legal person." If successful, captive chimpanzees would be moved to a sanctuary "where they can live out their days with others of their kind in an environment as close to the wild as is possible in North America." Three New York courts have rejected the group's efforts, but an appeal is planned. In fact, they plan to file more lawsuits on behalf of captive animals "who are scientifically proven to be aware and autonomous," not someone's property. This would eventually include "elephants, dolphins and whales."

I admit to some bias in considering my reaction to this legislation. Of all the species I've worked with, chimps are my favorite – ever since Jackie made his introduction with me at Catoctin Mountain Zoo. To my mind, Jane Goodall, the ultimate chimp-person and close friend of mine, would have been on the side of the NhRP. In principle, I am as well, but I'm pretty confident the declaration of chimpanzees as "persons" isn't going to happen.

In all practicality, consider the consequences if the group won its suit. What would happen to the freed chimps? The placement called for in the suit that would offer them the most natural settings possible in North America is impractical at best as such areas are sorely limited. The chimps would most probably end up in Bastrop, Texas, a facility that once used chimps for testing serums – most notably for the treatment of HIV – until they discovered the chimps' reactions are not the same as humans' despite our close DNA correlation. Many chimps suffered before this was determined. Since the NIH's (National Institutes of Health's) more recent move away from using chimps for research, this facility has remained a very acceptable sanctuary for chimps, but it would soon be overtaxed if this suit succeeded.

On a more positive note, Bryan Walsh reported in *Time*, 2013:

> *"Chimpanzees and their advocates have had a good year so far, with the National Institutes of Health deciding to retire most of the lab chimps owned by the government, and the U.S. Fish and Wildlife Service proposing to add captive chimpanzees to the endangered species list, which would severely curtail research on the primates..."*

Since that time this proposal has been approved.

As far as the long-term plan of the NhRP to include elephants, dolphins and whales is concerned, the same problems exist. Although the oceans have more natural habitat remaining, recent news about the plight of captive orcas and their attacks on trainers are disturbing and if dolphins are such friends to man, why are we keeping them captive? Valid questions, but up against the vast influence of the 'Sea World' attractions worldwide, animal rights lose ground quickly.

The Tiger Controversy

The second and perhaps larger issue that arose early in my tenure was my decision to euthanize four of the zoo's old and ailing Siberian tigers. One was so crippled she had to lean against the wall of her cage to stand up. Another had a severe behavior issues causing her to attack any other tiger she got near. She had to be kept in a separate cage and was unpredictable with keepers as well. My choice to have them put down really struck a nerve, especially with longtime zoo visitor, Krescentia B. Doppleberger who said my decision deprived her "of the enjoyment of visiting the tigers."

Eventually Doppleberger and a group of animal rights organizations headed by Cleveland Amory, well-known author/reporter and prominent animal rights advocate, sued the zoo and me for $1 million each. The case opened on Sept. 24, 1982, and was heard by a blind judge, Paul Teranes, whose area of jurisdiction was critical as the city line was at 8 Mile Road, but the zoo was located at 10 Mile Road. At one point in the trial, I asked to move the site to the zoo. The question of the judge's authority was resolved, but the judge wasn't happy with the move because he wasn't able to take his Seeing Eye dog to the zoo venue with him. Zoo policy dictated any animal brought on the zoo grounds must undergo permanent post entry quarantine (PPEQ) to avoid possible spread of disease to the collection. That might have worked against our case, but ironically the judge's experience with Seeing Eye dogs worked to our favor. Seeing eye service dogs are often humanely euthanized when they outlive their service. The judge had been through this enough times to sympathize with the situation of putting animals down.

Mrs. Doppleberger eventually lost her suit regarding the four tigers. I'll never forget Cleveland Amory's very bright lawyer pulling me aside after the decision. "Never repeat what I'm about to tell you," he whispered. I nodded as he continued, "You know what they feed the tigers at the zoo? Dopplebergers."

Amory then revived the controversy in 1990 when we euthanized four scimitar-horned oryxes following the same protocol as we used for the tigers and other surplus animals. He reported to Andrew Cassel in the May 13, 1990, edition of the *Detroit Free Press*, "He's [Steve Graham] a kind of efficiency expert; there's a coldness to him. A zoo should be a warm place. Animals should be happy. I don't think he buys happiness the way we do."

Jack Hanna, then Director of the Columbus Zoo, took it a significant step further when he told Cassel, "Steve Graham is a very intelligent person. Hitler was also an intelligent person."

However, the general tone of Cassel's article was positive about some of my actions stating, "Since he arrived from Baltimore in 1982, Graham, 45, has revolutionized Detroit's municipal animal park, reviving an institution that had been close to collapse. Budgets are up. Attendance is soaring. Membership in the Detroit Zoo has increased tenfold."

Despite the tiger ruling protests continued for years whenever I made decisions to euthanize any zoo animals. I retired more than 20 years ago, and the problem *still* persists for other zoo officials who take similar stands. I shake my head in frustration and sympathy for the Copenhagen Zoo officials dealing with the 2014 outrage about their, to my mind, legitimately euthanized young giraffe, Marius. As Bob Dylan sang, "When will they ever learn?"

My views on the necessity of euthanizing animals as often the best alternative to the ongoing dilemma of dealing with surplus animals within the zoo's limited space were never a secret. Indeed, euthanasia is often the ultimate kindness.

At my previous positions in Salisbury and Baltimore, I was always very candid about preferring this more humane end if transfer of a healthy animal to another accredited zoo or acceptable research facility was unavailable. Many of my fellow zoo directors agreed with me in theory but either didn't follow this philosophy in practice or did so, but not openly, to avoid the anticipated negative public reaction. My approach was to be honest and instructive in sharing my views – in other words, educating the public as to why the emotional subject of killing animals was not something I took lightly, but something that best served the animals and helped preserve the species.

When the tiger controversy broke out in Detroit, the ensuing outcry often drowned out my attempts to explain. It seemed never ending.

One day I was in my office at the zoo meeting with Ruth Glancy, head of the Detroit Zoological Society and a wonderful woman. I had received reports that PETA was conducting a significant demonstration protesting the tiger euthanasia at the zoo entrance a good distance away and I wanted to personally investigate. Ruth didn't think it was a wise idea, but I finally convinced her to lend me her luxury car so I could investigate at the scene undercover. No one would expect *me* to be driving a car with that kind of price tag.

The ruse was short-lived with the protesters. One young woman recognized me through the car window and yelled, "You're not only a killer, you're a rapist." The illogic of that accusation says something about her less than rational take on the situation.

The phenomenal amount of correspondence I received that was generated by the situation was intense. Much of it was in response to the widespread publication of an article that was almost criminally biased and misleading, as it suggested that my reasons for euthanizing the tigers were to "ease overcrowding" and "weed out breeding problems." Not that these weren't valid points, but the article neglected to mention the tigers' severe disabilities that were causing them pain and suffering – dental, hip dysplasia and more. The news article included a photo of Czarina titled "Death sentence." One letter from Hudson, Ohio on Oct. 6, 1982, referred to this photo and read, "May this face haunt you."

Death sentence
Czarina, 17, is one of three Siberian tigers that will be put to death next Tuesday as part of the Detroit Zoo's policy to ease overcrowding and weed out weak breeding specimens.

The multitude of letters from as far away as Texas and Colorado covered the full gamut of suggestions and downright threats.

Letters from kindergarten classes to retirement communities covered a vast range of suggestions and emotional appeals – sharing everything from the recent death of a pet to wishes for my eternal damnation.

A 12-year-old girl from Cleveland wrote:

". . . P.S. I am not writing this letter to be mean. I am just asking you to save their [the tigers] lives. P.P.S. My dog just died. I had him for 11 years and he died Thursday, Sept. 16, 1982 at 3:30 a.m. That article made me think of him and made me cry. Thank you."

A lady from Chesterland, Ohio, wrote of saving my soul:

"I am a Christian person so I will pray for you and hope that you find another way to rid your overcrowded zoo of these unwanted animals."

Another suggested that my choices carried the responsibility of the nation:

"The United States must set an example to the world of wildlife conservation and this practice must begin in our zoos and parks. Please change your mind and let these tigers live. There is already enough killing in this world; don't add to it."

One gentleman thought I was deranged:

"I really do believe Steve Graham, zoo director, should have his head examined"

One lady wanted my death:

"Why not do the world a favor and switch places with Czarina?"

Finally, a letter dated January 18, 1983, ironically signed "A Friend to Animals" called me a "sorry son-of-a bitch" and continued:

"... I wish I could put you in a small, slippery-floored cage... then I would torture you each day... until you died. Then your sorry bones would be thrown aside so your spirit could burn in Hell for eternity... My only consolation is that you will pay for your deeds in this life and the hereafter."

```
                      O.C.
                                          September 19, 1982
Dear Sirs:
          I happened to glance at my newspaper to see a
picture of a very beautiful Siberian Tiger, only to be
heartsick and full of terrible thoughts of the zoo's
administrator.
          How can you broaden your policy of weeding out
the week? Or did you just find yourself a little over
crowded?
          It sounds like you just don't give a damn.
Why not kill off a few animals because they are WEEK?
          Well let me tell you one thing, if society, I am
talking about the human race now,killed off its week
people only the strong would survive; and some of those
so called "less than adequate" people could be you.
What are you a son of Hitler? Sure go ahead and kill off
the week.
          Sure go ahead and kill off those tigers and any
other animal that just doesn't fit your standards of
livng. Or do you have any? But don't you dare ask for
donations fore fund to buy animals with, or do you
use that money so you can go an a safari? Animals have
rights too, thank god for that.
          After all you bring the animals over to the U.S.,
removing them from their natural habitat,force them into
a cage and then put them on dxibit. After a while you
get tired of having them around so you take upon yourself
to "kill them off". Realy do you think that a small child
nows the difference between those tigers?
          I thought it would be a treat to go to the zoo,
but after this little incident I think I would rather
go find a rock and crall under it.
          I will saythis about killing off the week,
nature has it's own method it doesn't need help from man.
          I am beging to think that your zoo is being run
by our own Mr.James Watt.
          When ever I read a story about a zoo getting a new
animal I thought it was like having a baby, but oh was I
ever wrong. You just take it all upon yourself to destroy
animals so you can have the best ones only. I have one
thing to tell you life is not perfect and neither are
people so the same thing goes for animals.
          Zoos are always talking about endangered species,
and how man's plot for conquest is taking it's toll on
our animals. But what zoo's don't say is that they are t
the ones who reely take the lives of the animals.
          What makes me sick is the fact that you have enough
guts to say that the animals is less than adequate. Did
you try to sell those tigers to another zoo? Or possibly
take them back and try to fit them into their animal kingdom?
          I want a responce to this letter.
                                   Thank-you
                                   Jennifer L. Coppage
                                   1113-34th. Street
                                   Ft. Madison, Iowa
                                                   52627
```

One of many letters to Graham from irate citizens in response to tiger euthanasia (Steve Graham)

Some notes, like the one below, have to be seen to appreciate the emotion of the writer.

> To DETROIT MICH. ZOO DIRECTOR: DEAR SIR;
> MANY ANIMAL LOVERS READ IN CLEVELAND
> PLAIN DEALER THAT YOU ARE ABOUT TO PUT
> TO DEATH CZARINA 17, + OTHER SIBERIAN TIGERS
> TUESDAY! PLEASE LET THEM LIVE AND
> IMMEDIATELY CONTACT ALL HOMANE SOCITIES
> AND OTHER ZOOS — THEY MIGHT TAKE THEM—
> TRY! HURRY PLEASE! WHY SHOULD EVIL
> CRIMINALS LIVE AND BE FREE, WHILE BEAUTIFUL
> ANIMALS DIE? HAVE A HEART!! WHEN EVER
> CHILDREN HEARD ABOUT THIS, THEY CRIED!
> " CLEVELAND + ALL OHIO ANIMAL LOVERS!"

Emotional note about tiger euthanasia (Steve Graham)

Equally distressing for me were the letters from people who genuinely cared for animals and were supportive of conservation organizations that I generally admired. It was difficult to feel their hate.

> Friday, September 17, 1982
>
> Detroit Zoo
> 8450 W. Ten Mile
> Royal Oak, Michigan 48068
>
> Attn: Steve Graham
>   Zoo Director
>
> Mr. Graham:
>
> I saw a photo of Czarina, the Siberian Tiger in my local paper "The Gazette Telegraph" with only a photo and the caption under the photo reading "No more: Czarina, 17, is one of three or four Siberian Tigers that will be put to death Tuesday as part of the Detroit Zoo's policy to ease overcrowding and weed out weak breeding specimens."
>
> I would like to know what your "policy" is that says you have the right to put an end to these wonderful animals lives. Also I would like to know why there is an overcrowding in your zoo. Don't you realize what you are doing? How do you come to the conclusion of a weak breeding species?
>
> I am a member of the World Wildlife Fund, National Wildlife Federation, International Wildlife Federation, Greenpeace and the Audubon Society. I do not see why in the first place these animals are subjected to being drugged, snared and put in cages for people to come and stare at them. Then when YOU decide they are no longer useful you put them to a very painful death. I am truly OUTRAGED at this being done to our animals friends. Do you know that without animals in the world that people would die. I expect an answer from you regarding this, or you will hear from me and many other people again, and this time it won't be a friendly letter.
>
> Regards, *Marianne Fuhr*
> C/O Colo. Outward Bound School
> Marianne Fuhr
> 431 N. Cascade Avenue #1
> Colorado Springs, CO 80903

Negative response from an advocate of conservation groups (Steve Graham)

Some of the letters had petitions attached with a long list of names. Again, they came from a wide variety of sources. Many were from grade schools.

> **Class Letter**
> September 17,
>
> Dear Zoo Director,
>
> We were really sad when we saw this picture in the paper. We think that it's disgusting that anything should be taken from his or her friendly family, and home. Try to sell it to another zoo. We really think the tiger should live. Tears came to our eyes when we heard about that terrible deed.
>
> Sincerely
> Katie Diehl
> Michael Shulman
> Cameron Goodyear
> Julie Lorber
> Jamie Luce
> Lawrence Dempsey
> Joey Staruch
> Andrew Simms
> Amanda Ballew
> Edward Salanga
>
> Sincerely
> Katie Diehl
> Hannah Thomson
> Eric Klein
> Scott Prekins
> Liza Studen
> Laurel Sahley
> Oliver Gratry
> Kate Hawley
> Mike Harvey
> Jessica Zellner

Grade school petition against tiger euthanasia (Steve Graham)

I tried to be reasonable and calm in my response letters and I *never* failed to answer *any* inquiry, but sometimes my patience grew thin. The letter and attached petition from a group of retirees in Saint Simons, Georgia, on Dec. 14, 1982, challenged the limits of my professionalism.

> 533 Bartow Street
> Saint Simons Island
> Georgia, 31522
> December 2, 1982
>
> Mr. Steve Graham, Director
> The Detroit Zoo
> Detroit, Michigan 48226
>
> Dear Mr. Graham,
>
> Enclosed is a petition signed by over one hundred of our fellow animal lovers in Georgia. The time set for the hearing on December 10th prohibites us from getting more signatures.
>
> We entreat you to find a more humane solution for your problems with "Anna", the Siberian Tiger, than the one you presently are planning. The Schulers, of Waldo, Florida, who are quite famous in our part of the country, have offered to take the cat and we are at a loss to understand why this is not a possible solution.
>
> We have contacted "60 Minutes" and "P.M. Magazine" both CBS news magazine shows, about the situation. You will be hearing from them soon. "P.M. Magazine" has already done a feature article on the Schuler's Wild Animal Retirement Village. This reel was viewed nationally.
>
> We realize that you are a professional administrator in animal care and we are sure that you have what you consider adequate reasons for your plans. However, the publicity is not doing you or the Detroit Zoo any good.
>
> We are writing in hope that you will find a more humane solution than lobotomy or death.
>
> The residents of Florida and Georgia, where the circus tradition is strong, have a strong attachment to the big cats and, frankly, we are outraged.
>
> Yours Sincerely,
>
> Enclosures: Petition with over 100 signatures.
> Letter from the Schulers.

Plea from Georgia retirees in response to planned euthanasia of Detroit Zoo tigers. (Steve Graham)

> 14 December 1982
>
>
> Mrs. Mary C. Hanley
> 533 Bartow Street
> Saint Simons Island, Georgia 31522
>
> Mrs. Hanley:
>
> Thank you very much for your letter of 2 December and the attached signatures.
>
> Let me give you some information that you may not currently be aware of. First, the injunction against euthanatizing Anna, the fourth tiger, was lifted in court on 10 December, as the judge agreed that the zoo had acted in a professional manner in making the decision. The other point that I would like to make is on the record in the local press and elsewhere, and that is that the decision to keep Anna alive was made prior to the injunction obtained by Mrs. Doppelberger and the Fund for Animals.
>
> We would stand by the professional commitment of our early decision to euthanatize Anna, but we have 3,000 other animals to care for in the zoo and we did not want to expend an inordinate amount of time and energy defending our actions with one animal who has become a "cause." We are instead looking into ways to provide Anna with outdoor access and to strengthen the exhibit so that there is no possibility that she may come in contact with other tigers, as in the past she has attempted to kill several other tigers. We would hope that you would be equally as concerned about the tigers she would potentially attack as you are about Anna.
>
> In regard to the Schulers, I have never met these individuals and have only talked with them on the phone, but I must tell you that people who make statements like the fact that we would do a lobotomy on a tiger have no credibility with me or my professional staff. This is so far from the truth as to be totally ludicrous, and if these individuals are so desperate as to make such fantastic statements, can they be credible to the signers of your petition?

My response was sincere, if not righteous, indignation to their insinuations and not so lightly veiled threats to alert the national media.

```
Mrs. Mary C. Hanley
Page 2
14 December 1982


The Detroit Zoo currently has a professional staff with 50 years
of experience in maintaining tigers, plus two full-time veterinar-
ians. The area where we keep our tigers is much larger than Mr.
Schuler indicated his facilities are in Florida. Additionally,
the Detroit Zoo is backed by a $6 million budget from the City of
Detroit. Would you suggest we send a tiger to the Schulers knowing
the following:
1. That their exhibit would be smaller than the one Anna currently
   has.
2. That there are no veterinarians on the staff of the Schulers.
3. That we know of no professional training that the Schulers have
   for caring for wild animals.
4. That their facility does not even contain a telephone to call
   a veterinarian if one were needed.
5. That the Schulers have indicated to us that they have funding
   problems, and what would happen if we sent Anna down there and
   suddenly they ran out of money? Who would then care for Anna?

I think we have made the best judgment, both professional and
humane, and I just wanted to make you aware of our concern and the
reasons behind our decision.

Best regards,

ZOOLOGICAL PARKS DEPARTMENT



Steve Graham
Director of Zoological Parks

SG/dja
```

Graham's response to retirement community criticism (Steve Graham)

After I started receiving numerous death threats, Mayor Coleman Young assigned me round-the-clock bodyguards. My position provided a house on the zoo grounds, but I had an armed escort every time I left the premises. The most memorable guard was the guy who always had a gym bag hanging from his shoulder. It held an Uzi.

One evening I was at home alone talking on the phone. In the middle of my conversation, two cops burst through the door at high post and low post, weapons drawn. They had received reports that I had been killed and they thought the killer was still in my house.

For all the nasty moments, there were also voices in the wilderness that supported me. They were very uplifting and helped me in my resolve to stand my ground. Letters like the one exerted below confirmed that my arguments were valid and my intentions were clear to those who chose to listen to them. The Sept. 25, 1982 note read in part:

". . . My first visit to the zoo was . . . when I was 6 years old . . . I remember one gorilla, Jim-Jim, who just sat there & stared. The next time I visited was in 1977 [34 years later] . . . Jim-Jim was still there, only now he was silver. How sad that he spent all those years in that cage.

It is never an easy decision to euthanize and animal. . .

I support your decision to destroy animals for which a home can't be found or those that are overly populated. . .

I would think that the goal of a zookeeper would be to create as natural an environment as possible for the animals and that this would be the goal of any responsible animal lover. . .

Please keep up the good work. My family appreciates it as I'm sure all the animals in your care do."

Such examples of support were encouraging validation of the many hours I spent both hands-on and at my desk to ensure that the Detroit Zoo was worthy of its lofty, well-earned reputation. One of my self-imposed duties was to respond as thoughtfully as possible to every piece of correspondence and phone call I received. I often staying at work until 9 p.m. or later.

The negative ones were distressful and more of a challenge as the one dated Sept. 10, 1990 that read in part:

"Dear Mr. Graham,

Yesterday I visited the zoo . . . with great anticipation of viewing all the million-dollar renovations I have heard of. . .

Detroit Zoo (1982-1991) – Storms of Controversy 241

Understandably, many of the animals were not out to be viewed which I assume may have been attributed to the heat of the day. However, I did not expect to see this throughout the zoo...

... at the refreshment stand... I found the food, specifically the hamburgers, to be horrible.. garbage cans overflowed throughout the park and bees swarmed everywhere near them... the restroom were filthy...

... I wonder how the animals are treated and cared for after seeing the deplorable conditions of the visitors' area..."

As difficult as it was to get reports like this, determining how to remedy such problems was a matter of training and dealing with zoo staff and vendors – much less convoluted than the philosophical questions of animal management.

Some letters were hard to take seriously, but I did. Each one was important. Regardless of the author or the content, they deserved a proper, reasonable response. Below is an example.

A somewhat bizarre letter about zoo conditions (Steve Graham)

My response to Mr. Cushman read:

Detroit Zoological Parks

Detroit Zoo • Belle Isle Zoo • Belle Isle Aquarium

8450 W. Ten Mile Road • P.O Box 39 • Royal Oak, Michigan 48068-0039 • (313) 398-0903

Coleman A. Young, Mayor
City of Detroit

3 October 1990

Mr. Mark Cushman
3154 Willet
Rochester Hills, Michigan 48309

Dear Mr. Cushman:

The comment form that you completed on 1 September has been brought to my attention.

Using life preservers for chimps sounds like a good idea except that, unlike humans, they would have no idea how to use them or what they were for.

In regard to Councilman Hill, I guess it goes to show that we all make intemperate remarks which we later regret.

Thanks for sharing your thoughts with us.

Best regards,

ZOOLOGICAL PARKS DEPARTMENT

Steve G.

Steve Graham
Director of Zoological Parks

SG/dja

ACCREDITED BY THE AMERICAN ASSOCIATION OF ZOOLOGICAL PARKS AND AQUARIUMS

Graham's response to Cushman letter (Steve Graham)

Detroit Zoo (1982-1991) – Storms of Controversy   243

I had to remind myself on many occasions that the public was not familiar with all the ramifications of working with exotic animals, and individuals were sincere in their suggestions, no matter how bizarre. For example, after the zoo and I won the euthanasia case, one local entrepreneur offered to have the tigers stuffed and load them in a van for a statewide, money-raising tour. We respectfully declined his offer.

I'll never forget one letter I received from Isabella Fiesselmann in the spring of 1982. She was a sweet lady who wrote from her nursing home in the Detroit area about her love of the zoo and how much she missed visiting it. This prompted me to call the facility where she was staying and arrange a visit for her to tour the zoo with me in a golf cart.

The day with her was such a delight that the zoo decided to establish Isabella Fiesselmann Day every year to invite and honor area nursing home residents. As many as can make it are granted free admission and given whatever assistance they need to enjoy a visit to the zoo. This kind of innovation helped to balance the scale of frustration and fulfillment that characterized the management of a zoo.

Still the protests persisted. In September 1990, much to the chagrin of Detroit City Council President Maryann Mahaffey, I ordered the euthanizing of a young elk at the zoo. Pete Waldmeir, columnist for *The Detroit News*, came to my aid writing in his September 10 column, "Graham has been besieged for years by 'animal rights' sharpshooters who'd like to hang his carcass in their trophy room. His main hang-up is that he insists on running the zoo in a humane, realistic manner . . ." He went on to support my honesty in the case as opposed to the more deceptive route often taken by other city officials who reported to the Council what would be easily received rather than the truth. He wrote that it would have been tempting for me to take an easier course and give the Council the "Dr. Doolittle" version, ". . . the one where all the animals in the forest live to be 105 and die in bed." You had to love the guy who came up with this quote – and I did.

A less controversial if equally necessary improvement I quickly made in Detroit was to the zoo entrance, although the estimated $1 million project finally came in at $12 million. I'll claim much of the responsibility for that. The prospectus called for *replacement* of existing features at the entrance. Having received well-founded complaints about the lack of adequate restroom facilities, I upgraded the new entrance to include them. Problem was the "existing" facilities consisted of a tiny closet toilet for the gate attendant. Though this significant upgrade could have been challenged as not technically above board, no one could challenge the need for the bathrooms.

The zoo benefitted from a new highway project that brought Interstate 696 right beside the zoo. The zoological park was compensated nicely in exchange for the property the zoo lost to the project. The original figure was $1.2 million, but by the time the dust settled, we had received more than $12 million for improvements.

Sorely needed front-entrance parking and a three-story parking deck were added, although that still didn't put an end to my Sunday parking duties riding around in a golf cart jockeying places for zoogoers to park their cars without getting hopelessly trapped. I was pretty good at it and it was actually a nice change of pace from my other weekly duties.

I also pushed to construct an eight-foot grassy mound and privacy fence that my two strongest keepers couldn't get over, as a buffer between the zoo and Woodward Avenue, in addition to a new brick wall the entire length of the zoo.

Just opposite the zoo entrance was an iconic huge water tower with "Detroit Zoo" emblazoned on it. The mayor had taken a lead from Baltimore's Mayor Schaefer and started putting his name, Coleman A. Young, on everything, including the water tower. At the dedication ceremony I was standing in front of the gathered dignitaries and crowd with my younger stepson Chris who was just learning to read. He looked at the edited water tower sign and misread aloud, "Coleman, 'a' young mayor." I couldn't help but use that line when I introduced the mayor to the audience. He laughed so hard his shoulders shook.

More humorous was the case of the lumpy-jawed eland.

Directly adjacent to the Detroit Zoo was the Rackham Golf Course. Errant golf balls often landed on zoo property where groundskeepers gathered them as a minor addition to their incomes.

Elans are the largest species of the antelope family. Their enclosure was only 50 feet from the golf course. One day an animal keeper noticed a large lump on the lower jaw of a male eland. After a few days of observation, we anesthetized the animal and found a golf ball wedged between his cheek and jawbone. We removed the obstruction with no damage to the eland. However, several months later another lump appeared – another golf ball. For some reason, he must have developed a taste for them.

In my earlier days at Detroit, even minor shortcomings at the zoo bothered me. For example, there was a large bin at the commissary marked "Day-Old Bread." I discovered the stale bread was being fed to the zoo animals. This was certainly not nutritionally sound, so I ordered a stop it. A few days later the bin was still there, but only about half full. When I asked, the explanation was that I shouldn't be concerned because it was only being given to the mixed bears, those who had mistakenly crossbred. I nearly lost it, but explained that *all* zoo animals were important. *None* of them should get a less than the appropriate diet. The bin never reappeared.

When I first came to the zoo, I noticed an adult eagle flying in a large, domed cage. She had been rescued by the Fish and Wildlife Service. I ordered the unpopular release of the recovered bird, replacing it with one having a bad foot. We fitted her pretty successfully with prosthesis and she eventually aged to the point where we mercifully euthanized her.

I also noticed hundreds of mice in the aviary. This is no exaggeration, as we trapped more than 400. After that I ordered the keepers to cut back the bird feed by 20 percent. This was soon followed by their concerns that the birds were starving. "Are they dying?" I asked. "Do they look lean or unhealthy?" When they said "no" I reminded them of the absent mice. The vermin had been eating the additional 20 percent of the feed previously. That ended the keepers' concerns.

I waged an uphill battle soon after I arrived with some of the horticulturists on staff. Tied into the zoo's huge central forced-air heating system were three separate greenhouses – two used solely to start flower seedlings for annual plantings. I suggested switching to perennials and claimed these two greenhouses for the flamingo population as winter housing to replace a dingy basement chamber enclosure. The gardeners weren't happy, but the flamingos were. They even bred later – something that is very unusual in zoos and had *never* before been accomplished at a latitude as far north as Detroit.

To ensure the quality of the fabulous gardens wouldn't suffer, we started the "Adopt-a-Garden" program. Various civic and gardening groups from the city were granted entrance two hours before opening to work on whatever section of the zoo grounds they had volunteered to take responsibility for. The results were stunning and cost effective, a perfect public-private partnership.

I also ran into some opposition when I removed a group of large pine trees surrounding a beautiful fountain. The trees had become so overgrown that the fountain was almost completely hidden. The final result was a bit painful for the most nostalgic of our patrons, but the end result was aesthetically pleasing and opened up more usable ground that was always in short supply at the zoo.

Although I sympathize with how difficult and often unpleasant the job of animal keeper can be, I also envy the close relationship they share with their animal charges because of the day-to-day nature of their job. I hope they sensed my respect for them despite some of the disagreements between us.

The chimp handlers and I had found common ground despite the chimp show cancellations, and the same kind of initial friction I had with the elephant handlers eventually resolved itself. Elephants suffer from chronic foot ailments, many due to prolonged standing on hard surfaces. I suggested that the keepers who were working with our elephants, Ruth and Kita, take them out of their cramped quarters and walk them the length of the 126-acre zoo before the public arrived, two days a week.

That request was, to say the least a bit risky, but I taught the staff a few tricks I learned from Mahout natives about a subtler, kinder use of the ankh, the traditional long stick with a hook on the end used to control elephants. Soon the keepers looked forward to *walking day* as much as the elephants who often trumpeted their delight making everyone smile.

Likewise, the keepers at the sea lion exhibit were not pleased when I cancelled their balancing ball performances. I told them, "A zoo isn't a circus. The sea lions' stunts should be more attuned to their natural behavior." Again it was a learning curve for both the staff and the public that ended up pleasing to all, making the struggle worthwhile.

One noble experiment the zoo attempted had a tragic end. We had hoped we were situated far enough north to successfully house a moose. The massive animals are a rarity at zoos in the United States because they require consistent cool temperatures. We should have recognized the signs early on when the young bull escaped and I had to herd it back to the enclosure, but sadly we didn't. At one point it was necessary to house him temporarily indoors and a radiator cracked, shooting the temperature so high that the poor animal basically parboiled to death. What a horrific way to die! It still haunts me.

Specific protocols were in place regarding potential animal escapes. For example, depending on which species got loose, a cap-chur gun would be used to stun the animal, but a polar bear or leopard necessitated a rifle. A general code red radio alert warned of any dangerous escape while the Reptile House had a red button that signaled the escape of any hot (venomous) snake. The alert was sent to staff throughout the zoo grounds to the appropriate areas as needed rather than disrupt the animals and visitors.

Twice I pushed some red buttons as practice drills. They went very well, but the staff was not happy with me. They were really madder than hell when I called a code red at the polar bear exhibit over the two-way radio while a group of vet students from Michigan State University was making rounds with the staff. It was just a drill and the response was excellent, but the staff didn't share my positive take that they had demonstrated to the students how well prepared they were for such possible emergencies. I won no popularity awards.

From July 13 until August 3, 1986 the keepers union went on strike. There were seven unions represented at the zoo, so we were fortunate not to have more work stoppages. The keepers' main dispute was their wage scale. I sympathized with them, but the animals had to be cared for. Everyone on staff, including me, put in long hours until the keepers resolved their issues and returned to work. Some keepers came to work through the backdoor out of sympathy for the animals. I appreciated their efforts and was grateful that their compassion and willingness to cross the picket line never became an issue with the other union workers who honored the strike vote.

The Penguinarium

In 1984 I undertook the renovation of the zoo's Penguinarium that had been built in 1968. The original facility was intended to combat the low breeding success and extremely high mortality of the penguin population in zoos. At that time the improvements resulted in a much healthier environment for the birds by providing more protection from contamination by human contact, better lighting and temperature control, improved safety features and better viewing areas. However, by 1984 an additional upgrade was sorely needed. Among other maintenance issues, the birds were eating the deteriorating fiberglass of the faux ice and the glass panels looked dirty because they were severely damaged by the high metallic content of the water.

The improvements took six months. We reduced the original five penguin species to three – all Subantarctic so we could better accommodate them. Three separate habitats were established according to their species– the King Penguins' simulated a granite coast, the Macaroni/Rockhoppers' depicted small stones and decomposed sandstone, and the one for the Blue Penguins consisted of softer sand embankments.

A large pool was available to all three areas that allowed the penguins to swim in a circle continuously with no barriers, yet the species were segregated by natural barriers when they were out of the water. Visitors could watch the birds feeding though the pool viewing windows when live minnows were released. Although the penguins torturously played with their prey like cats do mice, the crowd made no complaints. They relished watching meal time.

Lighting and graphics were upgraded in the public areas and colorful educational/interactional displays, murals and signs were added. A favorite feature depicted the various stances of the penguins and encouraged the children to imitate them.

The proposed cost was $600,000 and the final cost was $630,000, 25 percent of which went to fund educational graphics. The grand opening was in June 1985.

Illustration from article discussing controversial panda loans
(Steve Graham)

Then Came the Pandas – or Not

April and May brought the panda conundrum to the zoo.

The Chinese government had initiated numerous short-term loan agreements of panda pairs. The contracts carried high price tags that were beneficial in two ways. The first benefit was that the Chinese would supposedly use the revenues to enhance the wild habitat and improve captive breeding of the dwindling endangered giant panda. The second benefit was increased patronage at the zoos where the pandas were on loan. The $1 million per panda per year would not only cover the loan agreement cost but also provide additional income through increased attendance for other pressing

Detroit Zoo (1982-1991) –Storms of Controversy 251

zoo needs. Many zoos were lining up to participate. Why hadn't I requested such a loan for the Detroit Zoo? The public asked this question many times and not everyone agreed with the reasons I gave.

Although it wasn't completely legal to import endangered species in commercial transactions, the United States government had been persuaded to designate these loans as non-commercial. That cancelled one of my arguments, but my other reasons were more important anyway.

Transport was traumatic for the pandas and the short-term nature of the stays made such moves more frequent. The relocation discouraged the animals from acclimating enough to breed or interrupted breeding cycles. *Long-term* panda loans became more unlikely, as they were less lucrative for the Chinese. Popular demand for the panda pairs threatened to necessitate actually removing more pandas from the wild to meet the need. This was totally counter to the species' survival.

A front-page article in the Sept. 7, 1988 issue of *The Detroit News* read as follows:

> CINCINNATI – *Zoo officials are giving panda Chia Chia five days to see if he can overcome homesickness.*
>
> *Chia Chia went on display Friday at the Cincinnati Zoo, at the start of a three-month stopover on his move from the London Zoo to Mexico City. But administrators closed the exhibit because the 290-pound panda stayed in his den.*
>
> *. . . When keepers tried to keep him in view, the panda began pacing rapidly and bumping the walls.*

Not surprising, to my mind, was the dubious reason The Cincinnati Zoo gave for the closing in an attempt to avoid controversy. They had been the architect for the three-way trade in the first place, calling Chia Chia's visit to Cincinnati "a model for the way panda loans ought to be handled." They also reported to *The Cincinnati Enquirer* that the exhibit had closed temporarily because "the plan to control traffic in the rare bear's exhibit was too complicated for consumers." Additionally, no refunds were being given for those who had paid extra but missed their scheduled viewing time due to the zoo's closing of the exhibit.

UPDATE ON GIANT PANDA

AAZPA BOARD OF DIRECTORS' ACTION REGARDING IMPORTATION OF GIANT PANDAS

As reported in the April 1991 edition of COMMUNIQUE, the AAZPA Board of Directors voted unanimously during its meeting in March in Greensboro, North Carolina, to continue the temporary moratorium on the acquisition of giant pandas by AAZPA members. The original moratorium was imposed by the Board during its meeting in August 1990 in St. Louis, Missouri.

Shortly after the Greensboro Board meeting, the U.S. Fish and Wildlife Service (FWS) published in the FEDERAL REGISTER its Policy on Giant Panda Import Permits, thus lifting its moratorium on the importation of the species. The AAZPA Board of Directors has formally addressed its concerns to the Secretary of the U.S. Department of the Interior, noting the policy falls far short of the expectations and recommendations of the world conservation community and will likely cause a flurry of activity by those seeking to import giant pandas. In the publication of its policy, FWS notes no world registry of captive pandas yet exists and that they will accept applications from those desiring to import giant pandas only for public display.

As a result of the action by FWS, the Columbus Zoological Gardens has informed AAZPA of its plans to pursue a permit to import giant pandas as a part of the activities in Columbus during 1992 in celebration of the 500th anniversary of Christopher Columbus' discovery of America. Because the Columbus Zoo's efforts to import giant pandas preceded AAZPA's action regarding the species and based upon our knowledge that the City of Columbus and the Columbus Zoological Gardens had received formal authorization from the government of China in 1986 and 1987 to receive giant pandas on loan and even though our moratorium remains in effect, AAZPA will take no formal action against the Columbus Zoological Gardens; but we have informed the Director of the Zoo and the Chairman of the Zoo's Giant Panda Committee of our concerns and that we cannot support the importation of giant pandas until the concerns of AAZPA and others in the world conservation community have been adequately addressed.

(R. Wagner)

Opinion of AAZPA about Panda loan situation (Steve Graham)

The AAZPA eventually discouraged the panda loans for many of the above reasons and in May of 1988 they took the U.S. Department of Interior to court. But the public still clamored for a view of these endearing animals.

My newspaper response to the Detroit zoogoers about my nonparticipation in the panda bear program was, in part, as follows:

> "I'm sure that Detroiters love pandas, but I'd like to think that we also respect pandas – respect their right not to be trundled around like a circus act and not to be manipulated by people with dollar signs in their eyes.

"A short-term exhibit of giant pandas at the Detroit Zoo? No. At least not as long as I'm the director of this zoo. And I hope that after reading this article you will agree with Robert Roselle, president of the Detroit Zoological Commission, that, as far as the giant pandas are concerned, 'We're on the side of the angels.'"

The good news is we finally did prevail in being angels for the pandas. The short-term loan agreements finally ended.

from the desk of
STEVE GRAHAM

15 September 1988

TO: Panda Conspirators

It would appear that the recent decision by the Chinese government to stop short-term panda exhibits in the United States indicates that victory is ours--at least temporarily. I suspect that "victory" may not really be the proper word, but I think that what has happened has obviously been of great benefit for pandas.

As a memento of all the information that you have received from me over the past few months, please accept the enclosed copy of <u>Michigan Out-of-Doors</u> proclaiming "Pandas Coming to Michigan." This may not have the historical significance of "Dewey Beats Truman" but it will at least be an interesting footnote to all our memoirs.

SG/dja SG

Distributed to: R. Wagner, P. Krantz, W. Iliff, G. Schaller, J. Luoma, K. Cook

Final resolution of the panda dilemma (Steve Graham)

Elephant House Renovation

Like most of the buildings at the zoo, the Elephant House was constructed of gunite, a concrete substance that was blown onto mesh rebar. It was very versatile as it could take a variety of shapes. However, the floor of the Elephant House was rather like large-sectioned hardwood parquet. It was impossible to clean properly and held bacteria contributed to foot infections among the stock. Replacing the floor, along with a general facelift, amounted to a nearly $2 million project, though I would like to have done more. The new floor was concrete topped by a rubberized compound mixed with crushed black walnut shells. It was extremely durable, easy to sanitize and offered good cushioning and traction for the animals.

As part of the process I called on my old friend Lyn de Alwis, the head of zoos in Ceylon. I first made his acquaintance through my many consultations with the National Zoo while I was at the Salisbury Zoo years earlier. He was a short, slim man with impeccable manners and a real penchant for sampling such unusual foods as pig fallopian tubes, a Chinese delicacy. I went to visit him at a meeting of the Asian elephant specialists group of which I was a member in Chiang Mai, Thailand, to learn as much more as I could about elephants. The forest elephants there are valuable work animals – each one assigned a master or "mahout" for an entire life. The animals' size limits their endurance to four to five hours of hard labor a day after which the mahout spends hours every day in the water scrubbing their hides with halved coconut shells. It was there I learned that elephants in the United States are gray because they aren't properly bathed. Their natural skin is really black.

Lyn was the world authority on Asian elephants and served as a specialist in that area for the International Union for the Conservation of Nature (IUCN), the world's first global conservation organization. Formed in 1948, the more than 1,200 member organizations in some 160 countries work to find practical solutions to conservation and development challenges. Tom Foose, who as I mentioned earlier was from my same small hometown, was the IUCN Specialist on Rhinoceroses.

Also in connection with IUCN, I was privileged to meet Harold Coolidge, the organization's founder, during my years at the Baltimore Zoo. He additionally founded the World Wildlife Fund (WWF). He was wealthy, highly educated, lived in Massachusetts and had hired my girlfriend at the time to catalogue his prodigious book collection. One day we were both invited to tea at his home. His charming young wife occupied much of my girlfriend's time, so Hal (as he requested I call him) and I had a marvelous afternoon visiting and sharing our philosophical views on many things, but chiefly our concerns about conservation and our love of the primates. I was deeply touched when at the end of the day this man who I so admired told me, "Today I have truly met a kindred spirit." The IUCN established the Harold Jefferson Coolidge Memorial Medal in 2006 to honor those who have made internationally significant contributions to effective conservation.

Detroit Vets

When I took over the directorship at Detroit, Dr. William Appelhof had been the head veterinarian for nearly 25 years. He wasn't pleased with the way I did things from the get-go. In fact, he went to the press when I decided to euthanize the tigers and stirred up the whole uproar initially. This was a complete hypocrisy on his part because his unwritten, unmentioned, but well-known practice when animals didn't respond to medication was to shoot them.

Nadine Richter was another vet at the zoo who had been hired right out of Michigan State a year before I arrived. She was younger and less experienced, but very competent.

Dr. Appelhof finally resigned before the tiger issue went to trial. During the proceedings of the tiger trials I was asked why I had taken Dr. Richter's advice over the more experienced Dr. Appelhofff. I said I had chosen to believe her because her one year of experience was better than Dr. Appelhoff's one year of experience 40 times. His last day at the zoo was Dec. 22, 1982.

In need of a vet, I heard that the veterinarian daughter of a friend of the mayor would soon be looking for the job. Wanting to have more of a say in who I hired, I needed to move quickly. I offered the opening to Dr. Robyn Barbiers who became a valued member of our staff.

I also hired Dr. Cynthia Kispert (through the mayor's connections) who also worked out very well. She stood her ground when she needed to. One time the zoo received a tractor-trailer load of butterfish from Maine for the sea lions. It was clear from the stench that the fish were spoiled. She told a very large truck driver to take them back to Maine. I was really impressed. She eventually earned the new position as animal nutritionist at the zoo when the need for three vets was raised.

The Holden Museum of Living Reptiles

The reptile house at Detroit was in relatively good shape when I arrived. The individual display cages needed a bit of sprucing up and I eliminated a huge revolving circular display in the middle of the building that was divided into pie-like wedges holding different species. I asked the acting curator, "How natural do you think that is for the reptiles, going round and round continuously all day?"

The reptile house used to be closed on Wednesdays to allow the staff to feed the animals other live animals, their usual diet. I determined to go ahead and open on feeding days with a posted warning to the public that live feeding would be going on and suggested that if parents didn't want their children to view this, to come back another day. Within a relatively short time, attendance was actually higher on Wednesdays than other days.

Unfortunately, many reptile curators follow the sausage school method of feeding their collection. The animals become grossly obese because they are overfed and expend no energy pursuing their prey as they would in the wild. At Detroit, I encouraged the natural school of healthier portions and sleeker creatures.

We did not overfeed our animals, but we fed them well. For example, many zoos and animal parks keep their supply of mice and rats for feeding in barrels with a little sawdust and some raw potatoes. This keeps them from starving and provides enough water to eliminate the need to provide additional water. What it *doesn't* provide is a healthy population of animals. At Detroit, the mice and rats were fed high quality feed and clean water. The healthier the rats, the better the nutrition for the animals that ate them. Besides, who decided which animals are *better* than others, deserving of *better* treatment. At the Detroit Zoo we fed *all* the animals as if they were endangered species.

One of the three small lakes at the zoo was Pierson Lake, named after longtime generous zoo supporter during my tenure and long before, Lynn Pierson. Pierson became a dear friend who I highly respected. Zoogoers could watch the teeming population of bullheads, a type of catfish that flourished there.

The fish were also a favorite of the over-150-pound alligator snapping turtle at the zoo reptile house. This curious creature had an appendage extending from its tongue that it used to lure prey near its mouth. Our early attempts to provide the crowd with the opportunity to watch this fascinating scenario had failed. The surplus fish from the Belle Isle Aquarium we offered as food were in no way attracted to the turtle's unusual lure. It wasn't an evolutionary tool the fish were familiar with, so they weren't fooled. Neither the turtle nor the crowd was happy. Then we decided to try some of the surplus bullheads from Pierson Lake. Worked like a charm – a lesson from evolution.

My personal slice of Eden at the zoo was an idyllic little strip of land near the Pleasant Ridge Fence. A small artificial stream fed by city water had developed over many years into a natural stream bed spanned by a unique concrete bridge resembling branches crafted by Mexican artist Dominico Rodrigues in the 1970s. I added a bronze replica of a snapping turtle – all in all a rarely visited vignette nestled on the edge of the zoo.

On one of my many solitary visits to this quiet spot I was shocked to see an American Woodcock, colloquially known as the timberdoodle, a short stubby bird with a thin bill ending in a highly sensitive tip used to probe for earthworms. I had seen some males previously during their courtship flights going high in the sky and then plummeting to earth, but never one so close. Despite its highly secretive nature, it returned for several months year after year. We cherished the tranquility together.

When I arrived at Detroit, I was immediately in need of a new curator of reptiles. Kathy Latinen's name came up as formerly holding the position. She had done an outstanding job, but during the investigation into accusations against former zoo director Gunther Voss that eventually led to his dismissal, she felt betrayed by her fellow curators. Evidence that she discovered and passed on appropriately was thrown back into her lap leaving her as least senior curator to field the questions from the FBI and others – so she left. Years later after I arrived as director, Kathy's husband was still working as an animal keeper at the zoo. When I offered to return her to her position as curator of reptiles, she was so happy she cried. "I loved that job," she said. "It's the best thing I've ever done."

She is one the most amazing people I've ever known – sweet-natured, intelligent – the single best employee who ever worked for me. She advanced at Detroit Zoo to curator of mammals and finally general curator. However, when her marriage failed and she fell in love again, her new love interest took her to the Minnesota Zoo where he worked and they later married. I was devastated for the zoo to lose her. I tried my best to persuade her to stay, but, as they say, "You can't beat love." While she was still at Detroit, she became Species Survival Plan (SSP) coordinator for chimpanzees, a very important position. Currently she works for the Minnesota Department of Natural Resources.

The Detroit Zoo had a pair of green anacondas, the largest snakes in the world, that bred prodigiously. We had covered the demand for anacondas at other accredited zoos many times over and still had more than we could handle. At the same time, we were feeding our ophiofagous snake population (snakes that eat other snakes) with snakes taken from the wild. After confirming with Kathy that this could easily put a strain on a small wild population, we decided to feed them the surplus anacondas instead – a great argument to support supply/demand theory.

We determined that the most humane way to euthanize the surplus snakes was to first cool them in bags on the reptile house floor, then move them to a refrigerator to slow their metabolism further and finally into the freezer. As always, this prompted a negative headline in the *Royal Oak Tribune* – "Snakesicles at the zoo." However, we stayed with the policy because it had the added bonus of cutting down on surplus snakes disappearing out the back door to the likes of a nearby pet dealer for resale as pets or worse.

The debate that ensued prompted Jim Langhammer, my occasional opposition among the zoo staff, to call his longtime friend and world-renowned herpetologist Hobart Smith for support. His effort totally backfired. Dr. Smith called me to hear my side of the issue and I soon received an inscribed copy of Smith's fourth edition of *Snakes as Pets*. It read, "For Steve Graham with the best wishes and support of Hobart M. Smith." It gave me a real boost.

When I got to Detroit, many of the surplus animals were available to the highest bidder – a commodity for convenient, if questionable, funds. This was a common practice at many zoos at that time and probably still is. The Curator of Aquariums, Jim Langhammer, was often involved with such dealings. Although the zoo was always in need of extra funds, the animals suffering, in my opinion, outweighed any monetary gain.

When I discovered that some of our beautiful freshwater stingrays were part of this backdoor trade, I called Jim in. I reminded him, "Apart from it being illegal, don't you realize those rays are venomous?"

"That doesn't matter so much," he claimed. "They won't live that long anyway."

He simply didn't buy my argument that *situational* ethics means *no* ethics. There are no modifiers for ethics. In my mind they don't change at a whim; they're consistent. Such differences of opinion between us were more the norm than the exception with many zoo issues.

To Langhammer's credit, the money from these dealings *all* went to the zoo – none to him. He was scrupulously honest with zoo funds. Additionally, he successfully expedited the firing of former zoo director Gunter Voss by going public with evidence of the director's misconduct.

The Aquarium where Langhammer worked was on Belle Isle, and I didn't come into contact with him as often as I might had he worked at the main facility at Royal Oak. The distance made it easier for us to work together. Firing him could have been an unpopular messy situation. Instead, I admit that, when I could, I made his job as miserable as possible until he finally resigned. I had a sense that others at the zoo and in the mayor's office shared my sigh of relief when he left.

Previous directors and Detroit train

Frank McInnis was a longtime, well-liked director of the Detroit Zoo. He served for more than 30 years. After his passing came Jim Savoy who stayed briefly before going to Phoenix. Next in line was Doc Willson, a vet not overly-effective in his role but pretty well-liked, who remained on the Society Board. Finally came my immediate predecessor, Gunter Voss.

Larry Buhl had been head of the Zoo Board for years. Both father and son were very wealthy and loved to play pinochle. He was a constant thorn in my side.

At one of the first board meetings the topic of the zoo train came up. One rather mundane tractor train that ran on wheeled tires and transported zoogoers short distances was currently in operation. However, a much more impressive 2/3-sized replica of an actual train that ran on tracks and carried passengers the entire length of the zoo had been a popular attraction but was sidelined in 1980 after a crash that resulted in multiple injuries. Still in mothballs, the engine required extensive repairs to be done in Canada, among other things, and would require significant money to restore.

Audrey Rose, another board member whose husband was big in the savings and loan industry, agreed to head the campaign to bring the train back, on condition that everyone on the society board supported the idea with more than their voice. She started the ball rolling by pledging $10,000 and then proceeded around the table for additional contributions as is customary in the Jewish community. She looked at Lloyd Semple, a lawyer with the good old boys network on the board. He stuttered around a bit and then said, "I'll pledge $400 over three years." Now that doesn't even make good mathematical sense. Then there was silence as no one else made a move to offer any money at all.

Audrey Rose just shook her head and left. The door no more than closed when one of the board members made a scathing sexist prejudicial slur against this gracious lady and another member laughed and nodded. I was appalled but kept my mouth shut, being new to the scene. I thought to myself, *What the hell have I gotten myself into. How can I ever work around outrageous attitudes like this?* I was sorely tempted to leave the room with her.

Happily, someone else picked up the reins and raised the funds to get the old train rolling again.

Maryann Mahaffey was the second most powerful person in Detroit after Mayor Young. A fiery, grandmotherly-type former civil rights demonstrator, she was head of the Detroit City Council and constantly at odds with the mayor and me.

During one of our more heated disagreements I suggested that she "buy a seventh-grade civics book to learn the roles of the legislative and executive branches of government." This comment quickly hit the papers in the form of a political cartoon by Bill Day.

Editorial cartoon about Graham's conflicts with Detroit City Council

Not long after moving into the directorship at Detroit, I noticed someone moving into the former assistant director's office across from mine. As I came to the door to investigate, the tall, aristocratic-looking black woman in her early 50s turned to me. "Hello. I'm Khadejah Shelby, your new deputy director."

I soon discovered she was also one of the mayor's girlfriends and she knew nothing about running a zoo. Well, she did have a pet cat. Her appointment was part of the mayor's affirmative action campaign to hire black assistants as deputy directors for every white director position in the city government. Ours was not destined to be a good match.

Some weeks later, I was asked to speak before the Detroit Press Club. I noticed her standing in the back of the room, but she had disappeared by the time I had finished. At the end of the day she came into my office weeping. "I can't believe you didn't introduce me to the press people today."

I looked at her and shook my head. "That's not really a part of my job here. I didn't even know you were going to be there."

Not long after that my business manager, Beverly Davis, came to me and said that all the requisitions I sent to the treasurer's office were being refused. She warned me that the rumor was that the mayor was planning to fire me but just hadn't gotten around to it yet. I'll admit I wasn't always in agreement with my superiors in Detroit, but I had no clue what would warrant his wanting to get rid of me.

A few days later I got a call that the mayor was coming to my office within the hour, so I put on my three-piece suit, went to the main entrance facing the wide-open parking area and waited, with Khadejah standing behind me on the front step. Soon three cars came barreling in full of the mayor's official escorts, including the guy with the Uzi in his gym bag and his entourage.

The first indication of trouble was that Bob Berg, the mayor's press secretary, and Carol Campbell, the zoo's representative to the mayor's office, stepped out and didn't make eye contact with me though they were usually my staunch allies. Then the next revelation hit when the mayor stepped out of his car and Khadejah ran around from behind me and gave him a huge hug that he returned in kind. This was not good.

We proceeded to my office and sat at the large conference table, the mayor opposite me and Khadejah beside me. I was working up a pretty good sweat and as I stood to take off my suit jacket the mayor said, "So Steve, I understand you don't like black people."

I immediately slammed my fist on the table less than six inches from the mayor's face. "Mr. Mayor! I have a public record just like you. Either prove what you just said or I never want to hear it again."

A tense silence followed. No one even drew a breath both out of shock at my response and in anticipation of the mayor's reaction. He finally said calmly, "I also understand you don't get along with your deputy director."

"That's an understatement," I said.

He looked me in the eye. "Do you think you can work together anyway?"

I returned his stare. "We have to."

He looked at Khadejah across from him. "From now on I talk to the director, not the deputy director." Then he pushed back his chair and smiled. "Steve, how about we go look at some animals."

I had been director for nearly a year and this was the first time he had toured the zoo with me. Joyce Cohn, a Zoo Commission member I deeply respected who had been at the meeting, rode along in the golf cart with the mayor and me. At one point Joyce pointed to the side and said, "Oh, look at the ostriches."

"They're not ostriches, Joyce," the mayor said. "They're emus."

"E-what?" she asked. "How do you spell that?"

"E-M-U-S," he said. "It's in half the crossword puzzles I do."

The mayor's many talents included knowing his audience. He spoke like a Harvard graduate to captains of industry, but used the dialect of his people when meeting with them. When I accompanied him on several meetings with African American groups, I could barely understand him, much like President Obama at Reverend Pinckney's funeral following the tragic church shooting in Charlestown, South Carolina on June 26, 2015.

I spoke with Carol Campbell a few days later. She was a wonderful friend and served as liaison in the mayor's office for the zoo and a few other city departments. All of my official communications to the mayor went through her and she often advocated for me. We kept in touch for quite a while after I left. After the scene at my office about Khadejah I said to Carol, "Guess I dodged that bullet."

She laughed, "Well, don't unpack any boxes just yet."

One valued friendship I made at Detroit that still continues was with Chuck Hammond. He was as outstanding in personality and stature as he was unassuming in appearance. He was five or ten years younger than me when he was hired as the executive director of the Zoo Society; I was actually part of the hiring process. We had a wonderful working relationship and I came to totally admire him. He missed the recognition he truly deserved as the spotlight was usually on me. I truly thought of him as my co-director.

Depression

When I was working at the Detroit Zoo I briefly dated a woman who was dealing with depression, having lost to suicide a husband who had convinced her to have a child she really hadn't wanted. She recognized some of the same symptoms in me and referred me to her psychiatrist. The diagnosis of manic depression explained many earlier behaviors and reactions in my life – the very highs and very lows and constant obsessions.

Some are very early memories. When I was just a small child I had a favorite little rocking chair stuffed and upholstered in red vinyl. I often had bouts of indigestion after eating, but didn't tell anyone while thinking to myself that I might die. I would sit in my chair and grip the arms and rock obsessively until the pain passed.

During my college career I worked for a few months at Victor Cullen Center, a large, somber complex of stone buildings in Cascade, Maryland, that provided court-ordered housing for indigent, adjudicated juveniles – primarily blacks from Baltimore. I worked eight-hour shifts with one of the units, handling around 18 black teenaged boys. Lorenzo Meeks was one of the shorter inmates and a target for many of the other tougher boys. I signed him out a few times to get a break and took him to lunch and some free time at my apartment in Emmitsburg. When he hesitated to go into the back yard, I discovered he was terrified of the squirrels. He could only relate to them as 'flying rats,' recalling the marauding pigeons of his inner-city background. He was afraid the squirrels would attack him.

The cases of young men I worked with were so sad. After a few weeks there, extreme lethargy hit that left me feeling so shaky I became unable to safely drive my car. I had to hitchhike the 20 or so miles to work and back. Though I was perplexed by my condition back then, I recognize it now as a classic sign of depression. The day I came to work and found Lorenzo pacing like a caged polar bear in the solitary confinement room, was my last day working there. The room was about 6x8 with one small window too high to see out of and a slot peephole in the door. As punishment, inmates were isolated, had meals delivered, and got a thin mattress and blanket for eight hours every 24. Lorenzo wasn't really crying as I watched him through the peephole, but tears were tracking down his face. I went to the office, dropped my keys on the supervisor's desk and walked out.

In Salisbury, after Susan and I split, whenever I had time and the weather allowed, I rode my bike. Many of the days there were over 50 degrees even throughout the winter. I usually pushed for 15 miles or more – not so much a pleasure ride but a therapeutic escape.

Maybe my manic depression also accounted for my drinking and drug abuse all those years as well – a kind of self-medicating before I even knew what ailed me.

It was such a relief to finally have a diagnosis and begin treatment. I'm still on the medications these many years into my retirement and still wondering how I ever managed without them.

All in all, by early 1990 my experience at Detroit was going well. My plan to work another 20 or so years toward a comfortable retirement was right on track, but the situation began to derail later that year.

CHAPTER 9

Leaving the Zoo Behind
(1991 – present)
Retirement

In August 1990 I ran head-on into a controversy at the Detroit Zoo that was extremely painful for me personally. As I shared earlier in this book, the black family I had on The Hill in Waynesboro was as loving and important to me, if not more so, than my biological white family. I spent many hours and took multiple risks supporting black civil rights in my youth and thereafter. I hadn't hesitated to become involved in the most radical of groups including SNCC (Student Nonviolent Coordinating Committee) and SDS (Students for a Democratic Society). It's therefore understandable that being called on the carpet publicly for making racial slurs struck me to the core.

In the summer of 1990 the Detroit Zoo was assigned a number of black teenagers as part of a government youth employment program. I stopped to see the head of maintenance who was in charge of them and said, "I need a couple of monkeys for a job."

One of the youths overheard me and took the term 'monkey' as a racial slur and reported me to the press. Had he been a regular zoo employee, he would have known better, but such was not the case. The accusation hit the already racially charged media. I was stunned to say the least.

My regular zoo employees would never have questioned my opinion on race. They *knew* that I sometimes called both black *and* white zoo employees 'monkeys.' The habit came from my Grandmother Steck who had used the term 'monkey' generically referring to ornery kids. It wasn't always a compliment, but it most certainly wasn't racial.

The story was front-page headline news for a week or two. Many people, including one of my white Zoo Commission members, came to my defense saying they, too, used the same appellation for their children. However, Mayor Young couldn't very well ignore the accusation as he had spent so much of his administration embroiled in the issues of prejudice against "his people."

I gathered my courage and called the mayor's office to offer my resignation. His secretary, Pat, could tell how distraught I was and broke standing protocol and put me thorough to the mayor immediately. A significant silence followed my formal offer to Mayor Young who finally said, "Steve, I guess you think I don't know you. Let me think about this awhile and call you back." Within a very short time I got my answer. He calmly told me, "I'm going to dock you two weeks pay, but you'll work those weeks anyway."

"Absolutely," I agreed. "Thank you, Mr. Mayor."

I've often reflected how this man who had endured so much racial injustice in his life could have supported me. My already high respect for him increased tenfold after this.

Within the hour I got a second call, this one from Walt Stecher, Budget Director of the City of Detroit. He was my long-time supporter getting the zoo money when we needed it most. He offered to cut me a check for those two weeks anyway, but I refused.

One of my sources of comfort during the 'monkey' controversy in Detroit was Dr. Lionel Swann. He was a very tall, square-shouldered, distinguished black medical doctor who had been a long-term appointment of the mayor to the Zoo Commission. In his younger years he had been a 'black soldier' in the civil rights movement that was a cause close to my heart. At 93, he had grown old quite gracefully but often said, "I don't fool myself. I don't buy green bananas."

One of the most ridiculous statements made about the 'monkey' incident was that if I "wasn't white" I would have been fired. I felt I owed Dr. Swann, especially, a personal explanation of what had happened. He listened thoughtfully and replied, "Well, boy, (ironically, he always called me "boy.") you're so much like us that you think like us. We call each other N*#/* all the time. Even if you meant 'monkey' the way they're suggesting, it wouldn't have been a racial slur."

Dr. Swann's comments helped me regain some perspective, as did Blanche Washington's remarks when I called her in Waynesboro for counsel. This wonderful black woman who had been such a significant part of my growing up said exactly what I need to hear. I would never deliberately say anything racist. How I loved that woman!

Not long after that, I was on my way to an appointees' meeting of nearly 50 fellow appointees of the city headed by Deputy Mayor Fred Martin who had originally hired me. En route I noticed some racial graffiti on one of the overpass bridges. It struck me especially hard as I thought, 'They think that's *me*.'

When I got to the meeting Fred agreed to my request to speak, though he cautioned me not to. I apologized to everyone, not for what I had said, but for the way it was interpreted. I choked up a bit. As I turned and headed for the door, I was stunned and blessed with a standing ovation from the group.

I couldn't have received a better sendoff, but I never really got over the 'monkey' incident. Dennis Silber, one of the mayor's closest friends, told me, "The mayor said you were never the same after that, Steve." The cloud over my reputation changed me. As long as I stayed in Detroit, it was a taint I could not escape.

The Final Straw

I was still, most probably, wrestling with this accusation of racism on December 23 when I got the call and went to check in on Kita, a 30-year-old Asian elephant who was suffering from crippling foot infections. What followed was the sad tale of my shoulder injury and Kita's demise that opened this book.

With Kita was gone, the pain of the "monkey" incident still fresh, and my shoulder injuries confounding doctors, I tendered my resignation to Mayor Young in January 1992 to be effective May 1. He accepted it confirming that I was "resigning for personal reasons related to his [my] health." The news was leaked by a former disgruntled employee who had transferred to the mayor's office.

Columnist Pete Waldmeir laid some of the blame for my retirement on Mayor Young, as he wrote:

> *Personally, I'm tired of writing Young's political obituary, tired of describing him as a wounded, aging lion heroically fighting off the hyenas.*
>
> *The guy's no heroic lion. He's dead meat. And the only thing that's powerful about dead meat is the aroma...*
>
> *Mainly because of his [Young's] lack of hands-on control, nepotism and cronyism have riddled the upper echelon of Young's*

administration. Competent appointees like Zoo Director Steve Graham and Budget Director Walter Stecher grow tired of long hours and impossible tasks and quit.

The Associated Press picked up the story and my resignation was carried by numerous national newspapers – actually above the masthead in *USA Today*. As always, reviews were mixed, but nearly all made positive mention of both the undisputed improvements at the zoo during my tenure and the controversy surrounding my stand on euthanasia and the charges of making racial slurs. I was constantly barraged with questions about why I was leaving and I tried to keep them honest and as uncomplicated as possible.

My controversial stand on euthanasia was well known and required little comment on my part, the issue of my shoulder injuries was more than reasonable, and of the racial accusations, I told Michael Betzold of the *Detroit Free Press*, "The incident was and is the lowest point of my life. There is no doubt that it took something out of me, but it basically didn't have anything to do with this decision to leave. They're two separate issues." Plus, I wanted to leave at the top of my game.

Twenty years of pain later, technology had finally advanced enough so that I finally had both shoulders replaced.

I repeated many times that I planned to move to Virginia to retire. I told Pete Waldmeir, my long-time supporter in the press corps that I had originally planned on retiring from Detroit after 20 years when I was 56, but the shoulder injury had changed my lifestyle and plans. That I was "not exactly handicapped, but [I'm] limited now. And the time to live my own life has come just a little sooner than I expected." His reply was, "To tell you the truth, I believe 90 percent of it." Yet another article in the *Detroit Free Press* recalled that "One thing you can usually count on about Steve Graham is that he won't put any varnish on the truth."

The many personal notes of thanks meant a lot to me. Some were high-ranking officials for the city or at the zoo, like the one from Paul Garceau, assistant district engineer that read in part:

> "Steve:
> I'm one of the vast number of people who are sorry to see you leaving . . . I don't think the city realizes how much they're losing with your departure . . . Should you need a personal reference please feel free to use my name . . . Lots of luck in the future!"

Other equally touching well wishes came from members of my zoo staff, like the one dated May 23, 1991 from Leslie Keys, an animal keeper stating in part:

> "Dear Mr. Graham,
> Now that there is no chance of raising suspicions of my intent, I can send you this note.
> . . . I can say that working under you has been no burden to me. You have been able to bring this zoo back from the edge of collapse. I doubt that anyone else could have done that in the space of just a few years as thoroughly as you.
> . . . you have made me proud to say I am an animal keeper at the Detroit Zoo. Thank you and good luck wherever you go."

My last day was May 21, 1991, following two months notice. My preference was to depart quietly, but my friends at the Detroit Zoo had other ideas.

Lori, Hilary and I moved back to the Eastern Shore, but the festivities that had been put in place for my farewell made our refusal to attend impossible. We had dutifully returned to Detroit, but the afternoon of the event I was struck by horrific pain in my abdomen. Unable to stand, I crawled into the Harper Hospital emergency room on my hands and knees.

RESOLUTION HONORING DIRECTOR STEVE GRAHAM

Steve Graham was appointed Director of the Detroit Zoological Parks on 1 February 1982.

He swept through the Zoo like the proverbial new broom, bringing fresh ideas and a new philosophy to the Department.

First, he "winterized" our animal collection in order that visitors could be charmed by snow monkeys, Bactrian camels, and other winter-hardy species. Then he eliminated the explotive chimp shows and closed the inhumane Great Ape House.

Annually he managed to raise our City budget in order to renovate and enhance existing exhibits and build new ones. Perhaps his greatest accomplishment, in conjunction with The Detroit Zoological Society, was the Chimps of Harambee.

Seeing the dire need for educational and directional graphics, he set about improving that situation.

From Memorial Day through Labor Day, it was his practice to work seven days a week, often starting with a VIP tour at 8:00 a.m. and ending with another VIP tour at 6:00 p.m.

Steve upgraded the requirements for Zookeepers and Curators and left us with what is probably the zoo world's first affirmative action reorganization plan. A perfectionist in the best sense of the term, he urged the staff always to put forth its maximum and most professional efforts.

Through Steve Graham's diligent efforts the Detroit Zoo, the Belle Isle Zoo, and the Belle Isle Aquarium were first accredited by the American Association of Zoological Parks and Aquariums in 1985 and reaccredited in 1990.

> An avid natural history collector, he recently reintroduced "art in the park" and we have added life-size sculptures of: a baby Asian elephant, Galápagos tortoise, eastern box turtles, Kemp's ridley sea turtle, snapping turtle, and, soon, a chimp troop.
>
> He gave unstintingly of his time, personally answering hundreds of phone calls and letters when controversial matters were reported in the media, thereby informing the public of the true facts and usually making converts to his policies.
>
> Everyone who has known Steve has enjoyed being enlightened, rejuvenated, invigorated, and stimulated; no one will forget his charismatic personality.
>
> Although Steve Graham's last day worked was 21 May 1991, he has left us with a better understanding of animal husbandry, and has educated us in his philosophy of managing Zoo animals in accord with the principles found in the world of nature.

Resolution honoring Graham's retirement (Steve Graham)

The diagnosis was a kidney stone that required surgery. That might have resolved the issue, but in the days to follow my condition worsened. Seems the surgeon had nicked my ureter during the procedure and waste was leaking into my abdominal cavity. After another emergency procedure, I ended up in a very posh suite at Harper Hospital at the insistence of Ruth Glancy, a quite well-to-do supporter of both the zoo and me whose husband was chairman of the hospital board. The retirement tribute had to go on without me. The resolution adopted by the Zoological Parks Commission on May 29, 1991 honoring my service was very gratifying. My hospital stay eventually extended to five months.

The following month, June 18, 1991, I served as honorary chairman of the annual fundraiser auction and raffle event at the zoo, although I was still hospitalized and unable to attend. The proceeds were designated to benefit the newly created

Steve Graham Conservation Fund to support the Conservation Endowment Fund of the American Association of Zoological Parks and Aquariums (AAZPA) and the 21 Species Survival Plan programs at the Detroit Zoo.

Yet another awesome tribute that I truly treasure is the sculpture designed by Marshall Fredericks in my name on display at the Detroit Zoo. It features a marble plinth that supports flying Canada Geese that rotate with the changing wind currents. It was to symbolize Lori and me flying from the zoo to the Eastern Shore of Virginia.

Mayor Young asked me to remain for a short time as part of the hiring process for the new director. I agreed, hoping to improve the chances that the policies I had begun would continue. When asked my opinion of the zoo's future after I left, I tried to be positive. In February 1991 I told Constance Prater, City-County Bureau Chief, "I don't think there's anything to slow this train down . . . I feel that with all the regrets of leaving anything, what I feel best about is that the mission is going to continue, the programs are going to continue and the philosophy is going to continue." I said this despite the not unexpected reports that some folks weren't unhappy to see me leave and more than eager to derail the train. Most notable were Doris Dixon, Michigan director of The Fund for Animals who told the press, "It doesn't come as bad news to us." and activist Cleveland Amory. I told Pete Waldmeir that I could just picture Amory "rubbing his hands together and gleefully saying, 'We did it! We did it!'"

My first recommendation for director as my replacement was Kathy Latinen. In reply to my letter of inquiry she wrote, "Steve, you were the most inspiring, challenging and rewarding person that I ever worked for and with. What I learned working with you changed the way I address many problems and altered my expectations within the profession . . . I really don't see myself as 'director-material' but it means a lot to me that you think I may have the potential . . ."

The Zoo Commission finally decided on Ron Kagan who has been director of the Detroit Zoo since I left. Friends of mine like Ruth Glancy of the Zoo Society, which eventually took over management of the zoo, have told me that the zoo is thriving – attendance and quality are both high, but the philosophies that I had worked so hard to put in place have disappeared. In fact, Ruth Glancy continues her support, having just partially financed a new animal hospital at the zoo. So the zoo is continuing to flourish.

However, Ron Kagan is in many ways everything I wasn't. He's a good public relations guy with an animal background who garners lots of favorablel publicity for the zoo, but his animal policies are totally unlike mine. New policy at the zoo accepts any exotic pets from private owners who no longer want them. I hadn't allowed this because it enabled the owners to purchase more cute exotic babies and continue the cycle that needed to be stopped. Also many of the adopted pets that came to the zoo had previously been with multiple owners and developed major behavior issues that were a vexing challenge for our own stock and zoo staff.

The most notable philosophical difference between the two of us has been Ron Kagan's public denouncement of euthanasia, though I suspect he employs what I consider far less favorable solutions for his surplus animals, as do many of his zoo cohorts. He also discourages captive breeding, even to the detriment of compromising the health of the species. For example, he opted to spay a rare anteater rather than continue to produce surplus for the zoo when he may have found other suitable accredited zoos for the offspring.

Nighttime at the Zoo

For nearly 20 years of my life I had the privilege and challenge to be a zoo director. Aside from the triumphs and regrets, I will forever cherish my nightly rounds of the zoo grounds. In these dark, silent hours I had the zoo and the animals all to myself.

In Salisbury, my first charge, I discovered during the nightly rounds (that I very rarely missed) a peace and connection that soothed my insecurities and counterbalanced pressures of the arduous days.

I'd start at the barn, as quietly as possible so as not to disturb the sleeping inhabitants. When Ollie, our sweet baby elephant, was there she would be sound asleep on her side snoring loudly. The monkeys outside were huddled in a tight ball to keep warm and the birds had their beaks tucked securely under their wings. The macaws, perched close to their windbreak and heat lamp, would occasionally give me a one-eyed peek. The sleek sea lions spooned or slept in the shadows with the moonlight, on clear nights, sparking the water.

The adult Burrowing Owls had been rendered flightless, but their young had free range outside the confines of their open-topped enclosure. In the summer I watched them darting around the streetlights catching insects drawn to the halos. What fun they had. When I got within 20 feet of the Bald Eagle, she greeted me, day or night, with her shrill call. As a special treat, some nights one or two wild Bald Eagles came to roost in the pine trees surrounding her aviary and kept her company.

The lone jaguar was always asleep in her den close to the drowsing bison and guanacos (a wild species of llama). I usually spotted at least one of them awake on the lookout for predators, a throwback to their wild lives.

I'll always remember the rattle of the key in the lock when I went in and the comfort I felt when locking it to go home.

In Baltimore I had to forego the nightly rounds because my residence was miles away from the zoo. But my Detroit home had easy access to the zoo grounds so my ritual walks began anew.

Step one was calling from my kitchen window to the nearby tapir. She always returned the call. Either my imitation was convincing enough that she thought another tapir was close by, or she was simply humoring me. Whatever the case, it was fun.

Detroit was much larger than Salisbury, so I often varied my route with the exception of a few spots that I never missed. At the elephant house, Kita was generally lying down asleep, but Ruth, as a rule, lumbered over to greet me through the bars with her trunk and grumble her contentment. Likewise, the rhinos that were awake smelled my hands though their bars. The wolverines usually paced at night, probably to compensate for the many miles they would have traveled in the wild during the day.

Summer nights often grew hot and steamy. The tapirs and boars that were housed together thoroughly enjoyed the cool spray of a high pressure hose coupled with back scratches with a garden rake. Regardless of how long I indulged them, they gave up this Nirvana grudgingly.

The one resident I avoided was the uninvited wild skunk that hunched behind the granite rock camouflages in the various exhibits. That fat character preferred to stay away from me, too – a good mutual avoidance agreement.

Much like the legendary postal carrier – neither sleet nor snow nor rain nor dark of night would stay me from my self-appointed rounds. Alone in my mission, the zoo was all mine. In the softer dim of night, the barriers that denied the animals their freedom and confirmed the distance between us faded into the shadows. A peace and gentleness, an intimacy of mutual respect in the imagined absence of walls and confines allowed me a connection with the animals few others will ever know. I will treasure those times as long as I live.

Life after the Zoo

I stayed nearly a month in the posh Merrill Suite of the Harper Hospital in Detroit. Though my condition persisted, I was discharged to free up the magnificent accommodation for a more distinguished patient and was referred to a kidney specialist and an additional four months in a hospital in Cincinnati, my wife's hometown. They finally diagnosed the nick in my bladder from the original surgery and repaired it and removed my dead kidney. Throughout this long process I became addicted to Lortabs, a powerful pain medication. The withdrawal was worse than any alcoholic recovery I experienced. I would pace incessantly around our small house in Chincoteague, Virginia all hours of the night, unable to be still. Rock bottom was when the shells I got for the gun I managed to acquire were the wrong size – otherwise I would have probably shot myself.

Not long after my health finally returned, Lori developed increasingly alarming symptoms of severe chronic fatigue eventually diagnosed as Lyme disease. Her long recovery threw me into whole new and totally unfamiliar position as fulltime parent for my step-daughter, Hilary, compete with responsibilities for school bus schedules, daily meals and watchful supervision and activities at home.

Hilary thrived in the environment enjoying the beach and bay out the front door and a large salt marsh area out the back, spending sunup to sundown outside, regardless of the weather. I remember holding her hand as we walked the beach in winds that literally lifted her off the sand at times. When I teased her that we might have to take cover and spend the night on the beach, she simply suggested that the bayberry groves behind the dunes where the deer slept would be a great shelter. Her amazing natural independence and resilience took strong root and continue to serve her well.

As I continued my withdrawal recovery I thought horseback riding would help, so one day Hilary and I headed down the lane from the barn together. She was riding her favorite star mare and my mount was my mule named Scout that I had bought from Herb Frantz in Waynesboro. He sold a couple every year and I had told him I was interested in one. Mules are usually dun-colored, but this particular year one was black, so I chose her. Herb and I agreed that mules are much smarter than horses. For one thing, horses will eat until they get sick or die, but a mule will walk away when it's full. One time Scout's hoof got entangled in a wire fence and, unlike a horse that would have injured itself trying to get loose, Scout waited calmly until I came to release her safely.

Anyway, Hilary and I were trotting along our crushed-shell lane and were about halfway to the main road when the girth of my saddle loosened and slid to the side with me aboard until I was hanging under Scout's belly with a death grip on the pommel. The mule kept trotting, pulling me along the crushed-clamshell surface just missing my head with her huge hoofs by inches with each step she took until she finally stopped at the railroad tracks that crossed the lane. In my pain and panic I kept praying, "Please God, don't let me die like this. Not in front of my daughter."

Hilary was petrified. By the time Scout stopped, the clothes had been ripped from my back and third degree abrasion burns covered my lower back and buttocks. Two days later as I lay with dressed wounds and flagging spirits, Jim Leaman's daughter Linda pushed her father into my room for a surprise visit. That was the best medicine ever.

A few years after I had finally kicked the painkillers, I developed a terrible headache. I took the usual cure, some Bufferin, but that day and the next morning I had no relief. Lori noticed that I just wasn't myself and finally called for an ambulance. When they arrived I told them I wanted to go to The Salisbury Hospital because I thought it was the better one, but the ambulance staff assessed my condition and said I needed immediate care and rushed me to Accomack Hospital that was an hour closer.

By the time I arrived at the emergency room I had suffered a significant stroke and developed paralysis on my right side. The doctor told Lori he had little hope – perhaps a five percent chance of my surviving and recovering. But, I made it through the critical first two weeks and was released to begin rehab to regain the use of my right side.

I was determined to handle the recovery on my own. Hilary became my therapist, walking me around the pastures. Lori tried to help me with meals, but I told her, "Nobody's going to feed me." I ended up with lots of food all over the place, but I slowly made progress. I dragged myself into our old red pickup truck and drove around in the pastures, often colliding with fences and small trees and bushes, but my skills improved every day until I could finally maneuver the roads.

My health eventually recovered much more than my marriage. We had endured years of intense controversy at the zoo, my crippling shoulder injuries, early retirement, additional medical complications and more. However, we eventually divorced and the latest chapter in my life began.

The priceless relationship with Lori's daughter Hilary that began the first day I met her in Detroit at the bridge on Pierson Lake at the Detroit Zoo continues to this day. I count that as my greatest blessing along with her children Brianna and Raylan.

Chapter 10

Corruption in the Exotic Animal World

The *zoo directors' club* is quite small. In fact, there are only around 50 accredited zoo directors in the entire country. When I was working, we all knew each other and each other's families. I was pretty much odd man out being the youngest of the bunch and having some of the most radical thoughts about cleaning up the zoo business.

The AAPZA had an ethics committee, but it was ineffective. The good old boys' network wasn't eager to give up the under-the-table dealings they had used for so long. Those somewhat shady connections were part of nearly every transaction to buy or sell the animals zoos desired for their collections. Many of the other zoo directors did a lot of foot dragging about keeping all transactions on the up and up and I was kicking up more dust than they liked. I wanted to get the kickbacks out in the open – get rid of them for good.

I once challenged the curator of Sea World in Florida on some questionable dealings he had conducted to acquire some penguins on which he was a world authority. He didn't deny my allegations but countered with, "You know, Steve, the rest of us are getting mighty tired of trying to live up to your standards." I took that as quite a compliment.

Fred Zeehandelaar mentioned earlier was the largest import/exporter of exotic animals in the United States. He was a strange little man with a heavy Dutch accent. Little bits of paper were stuck to his lips all the time from the unfiltered cigarettes or cigars he smoked constantly. His mouth was permanently circled by a chalky white rim from the Tums he practically lived on. But we got along; I liked Fred. He was one of the more reputable men I worked with. That's why he was so upset when I told him when I became director at the Detroit Zoo that I was bringing him up on ethics charges.

I went on to explain that I knew he would be cleared, but that the accusations about his receiving kickbacks were already out there anyway. I was just anxious to get his name cleared so I would be able to deal with him for Detroit Zoo business. That calmed him down a bit, and he was actually grateful to me later when his name was officially cleared.

My personal pariah was Ed Maruska. Although the Cincinnati Zoo where he was director had a pretty good reputation, to my mind Ed was the embodiment of despicable practices. We conducted an ongoing feud of head butting on nearly everything. Most of my dealings with him occurred during my time in Detroit because Cincinnati was so close.

My first encounter with him involved my attempts to establish an insect zoo at the Baltimore Zoo. Maruska had gained lots of attention for an impressive insect facility he had opened at the Cincinnati Zoo. I had some conversations with others in Cincinnati about getting some of their surplus and was told that they always had plenty. When I later asked Ed Maruska about it he said, "Oh no, we don't have any to spare." It was the first of many lies and contradictions I would discover with him.

Maruska made piles of money for the Cincinnati Zoo by selling animals to the highest bidder, regardless of where the animals ended up. At Detroit, we never did business with animal dealers. We were the only zoo in the United States to make that stand. Our surplus animals were never placed anywhere other than another accredited zoo or research institution or they were humanely euthanized.

Maruska was also the SSP Coordinator for the rhinoceros species. This gave him the control of which animals should be bred. Detroit had two rhinos at the time – one young breeding female and one very desirable young male who had great potential to enhance the zoo gene pool because he had never bred in captivity. Maruska judged that Detroit should send these two rhinos *elsewhere* to breed and replaced them with two older rhinos with very little breeding potential. The Detroit Zoo was potentially the obvious loser in this move on his part.

I took a great deal of satisfaction when, to everyone's shock, the older pair that he sent us successfully bred not long after arriving at our zoo. Ed Maruska probably got the credit for that, but we both knew he never intended that success for *our* zoo.

Maruska also milked the highly lucrative market demand for white tigers for all it was worth. They were a very popular draw. The public loved them, but they were really a mutation and had no place at zoos. The space at zoos is very limited and the animals housed in them should enhance the genetic lines, not risk weakening them. But Ed bred white tigers as fast as the cats could manage, which was even more damaging as that required so much inbreeding to keep them white. They brought phenomenal prices.

In spite of his repeated attempts to undermine my zoo, Maruska didn't hesitate to ask me for favors. On one such occasion, we had a rare birth of three Siberian lynx cubs at the Detroit Zoo. He called and requested one of the young cats to use with his education program. He knew how I felt about that, so he wasn't surprised when I refused. To me, his method of taking exotic animals for hands-on educational programs encouraged the false message that such animals can be pets. Granted the crowd loved the experience, but the animals should be the first concern.

A few weeks after I refused Maruska's request I had a call from Joyce Cohn, one of our zoo's most generous and conscientious Zoo Commission members. She called to say that she was accompanying her husband, Judge Avern Cohn (a very important Federal judge) to Cincinnati and wondered if I could arrange a private tour of the Cincinnati Zoo for her while she was there. Despite my aversion to asking Maruska for anything, I told her I would certainly do my best.

I made numerous calls to Maruska that he refused and never returned. I made my embarrassed apologies to Mrs. Cohn, but she was most courteous and explained that someone from her husband's office was able to arrange the tour for her.

She returned two weeks later with glowing reports of the Cincinnati Zoo and her wonderful personal tour – and that, by the way, she had promised the director, Ed Maruska, that the Detroit Zoo would send them one of our Siberian lynx cubs. She was very gracious when I explained the situation to her as tactfully as possible and continued my refusal to send the animal. Not many commission members in that position would have been as forgiving, but I was white hot with Maruska for attempting such a devious end run. I called to follow up on the situation and was told once again that he was unavailable. I said, "You know what, I have a lot of paperwork on my desk. I'll just hold." Three hours later, he still hadn't taken the call.

As mentioned above, I fiercely objected to Ed's program to take wild animals – trained cheetahs, tigers and the like – out to schools and other children's events. Such programs might sound like a good thing at first glance – and the children certainly loved it – but the negative result was that they then wanted wild animals as pets. Additionally, predicting when an animal matures enough to become aggressive is exceedingly difficult and therefore, potentially dangerous to an unsuspecting public.

Thane Maynard was then education curator at Cincinnati Zoo and is currently director. I respected him even though I disagreed with his participation in the visiting animals program. He used to take his six-year-old daughter to the programs with him. Sadly, a tiger turned on her at one of the shows and inflicted serious injuries. What I couldn't believe was that Thane still continued with the program.

Employee Burnout

Keeping communication, cooperation and morale positive within a zoo staff is a tall order. As I stated in "Burnout: A Case Study," a paper that I researched extensively and wrote while I was at Detroit, "The simple fact may be that, by the nature of the beast, low morale may be endemic to zoos." I polled numerous staff members of other zoos to corroborate my findings.

Perhaps communication, always difficult in any workplace, is compounded in zoos because many of the *animal* people on staff may have chosen their profession because they weren't very successful interacting as *people* people. The unconventional hours their jobs demand keep them out of sync with their families and the general public. These individuals are invaluable to zoos but can be a real challenge to relate to. They, more than most, definitely need communication and understanding from their bosses.

As discussed earlier, the necessity of euthanizing surplus animals that the staff has cared for – and in significant numbers – inflicts significant emotional stress. Additionally, the inherent abuses that exotic animals are exposed to, such as trained animal acts, traumatic shipping from place to place as either mascots or circus performers and more, often leave employees frustrated to the point of chronic depression and/or physical disorders like fatigue, cynicism, high blood pressure, stomach disorders, etc. Also, the failure of supervisors to recognize the importance of the day-to-day, hands-on workers and to acknowledge jobs well done challenges the overall morale of the zoo.

Proactive supervisors and directors can be key to alleviating and sustaining better attitudes and working environments. They should act as much as possible to limit the animal abuses in their zoo. They should share their opinions and goals with all employees on a regular basis and express mutual respect for everyone's essential role in maintaining the best zoo possible – giving as many as possible a sense of ownership in the process.

Hiring women and blacks

When I advertised a position at the zoo, I had hundreds of applicants. Those with impressive education and experience were generally too *mature* and the rest had more enthusiasm than sense along with their youth. Most of them were young men who required much more supervision than I wanted to provide.

I found that, given an equal playing field, women and blacks could often be hired for less and proved much more competent, so I'll easily admit to favoring them. Outstanding women included Kathy Latinen and Jean Brennan, the dynamic (nearly frenetic) curator of mammals I hired. She qualified to do field service in Madagascar, produced many well-received papers and eventually shared the 2007 Nobel Peace Prize for her work in conservation.

Godfrey Bourne, a brilliant black man from the academic world, was a minority curator I hired. Unfortunately, he never adapted away from the world of academia to the zoo environment. Still,

I'm glad I gave him an opportunity. To my knowledge, the only other black in a supervisory position at a large zoo back then was Lisa Stevens, head keeper at the National Zoo. I had tried unsuccessfully to hire her on numerous occasions. Zoos were simply not a part of the black culture at that time, so few chose related career paths.

Zoo Veterinarians

One of the most troubling positions to reconcile in the personnel area is relationship between the director and the zoo veterinarian. I described that situation in a paper I presented while I was at the Detroit Zoo as being "two prima donnas who unfortunately believe their own PR . . . a well-motivated zoo director attempts to hire a highly competent veterinarian, which may immediately lead to a face-off between two competent professionals."

Vets are trained to treat animal medical issues in a setting where they are in charge – a far cry from the political arena of a zoo. Zoo vets have to deal with multiple sources of information and opinions from the various animal keepers. They earn less than their fellow vets in private practice and often deal with poor equipment and strained budgets. Euthanasia, one of the least pleasant aspects of treatment, is much more prevalent in a zoo than in the private sector. Taking extraordinary measures to prolong a zoo animal's life is not as heroic as saving a family pet. Dealing with live animals is notoriously emotional and often challenges good judgment.

In dealing with my zoo vets, I always attempted to establish clearly that I was not only the boss, but that I also respected them. I would take their part whenever I could in any conflicts they had with keepers and listen thoughtfully if they disagreed with me on anything. For the most part, this strategy worked.

VIEWPOINT, Continued

Many times zoo animals suffer out of neglect; not necessarily keeper neglect, but rather institutional neglect. Often, animals reduced to mere numbers, become a low priority item. Often it appears that zoo management doesn't care or understand the real problems and concerns involved in daily animal care. Welfare issues seem to be easily ignored. How many times have you heard the phrase, "No overtime", even though you are understaffed and good, decent animal care is impossible under the circumstances. Zoos all over claim that they're low on funds, but they still have an obligation to provide for all of their animals. This includes proper housing, food, mental and physical stimulation, socialization, and an adequate number of professional zoo keepers to properly care for and maintain the animals. The priorities of the zoo keepers (usually animal care and welfare first) and the priorities of zoo management (often economic concerns first) are frequently in conflict. Zoos that claim that they don't have enough money to properly provide for their animals shouldn't have them. The USDA Animal Welfare Act provides zoos with the MINIMUM standards they must comply with in regard to facilities, space requirements, food, sanitation, veterinary care, employees, handling, and transportation. Contact your local USDA office to get a copy of the Animal Welfare Regulations, and refer to Subchapter A, Subpart F. Read it and use it; it might help in some circumstances.

What about the treatment of animals used in rides and shows? What about the handling and training of animals? These can be areas of great concern. It is sometimes difficult and often frustrating to bring animal welfare concerns to the attention of zoo management, only to see no action taken. Many keepers are afraid to do so, afraid to rock the boat or be labeled a trouble maker. That's really a shame because ultimately the animals are the ones who suffer. But, if you feel your job is at risk, it can be an intimidating prospect at best. Believe me, I know, because I was the one who brought to the attention of zoo management the beating of Dunda, the African elephant at the San Diego Wild Animal Park. I learned first-hand how difficult it can be when you speak out for animal welfare issues within the zoo.

There are places to turn, however, if you have animal welfare concerns that are not being addressed properly (or at all) within your institution. One of the places you can turn is to The HSUS. I am now working as an investigator dealing with captive wildlife issues. Because I was a keeper, I know first-hand the kind of problems you may be dealing with. I understand the setting in which you work and have seen many of the situations you are facing. I also understand the politics of zoos and the risks of going "outside" for help. But you do not necessarily have to risk your job to make a confidential report or complaint. The HSUS wants zoo animals to receive the care that the animals deserve and that zoos are obligated to provide. We want to work together with zoo keepers and other zoo staff to assure that only the highest standards of professional animal care are employed. Let's face it, we all want the same thing: the elimination of unnecessary suffering, neglect or abuse of zoo animals.

Please contact us if you have an animal welfare problem at your zoo, or know of a problem that is not being handled properly. Call (202) 452-1100. There is something you can do, and you don't have to do it alone. HSUS, 2100 L Street NW, Washington, DC 20037.

Editorial stating frustrations of animal keepers (Steve Graham)

Animal Keepers

Animal keepers might be the lowest workers on the zoo totem pole, but they are definitely the first line of relationship with the animals. With the day-to-day feeding and cleaning, they have the closest, most consistent contact with the creatures in a zoo's care. I always told keepers to spend time observing the animals while they were doing mindless jobs like cleaning water bowls. This kind of regime made for excellent keepers.

I have real disdain for zoo directors who were never keepers themselves. I honestly believe that I never asked a keeper to do anything I hadn't done myself. I think they respected that. Our relationships were based on a special bond of mutual respect.

While I was at the Detroit Zoo, I read the disturbing editorial below regarding the frustration of animal keepers in zoos.

I had to admit I couldn't really know everything that was going on at the zoo and that, by nature, we all like to believe the best about ourselves and our own with or without proof. I urged my staff to fill me in if I was deluding myself about places where the Detroit Zoo needed improvement so we could deal with any problems together. I passed the article above and attached the memo below to them and invited their feedback.

I attached this notice to the article.

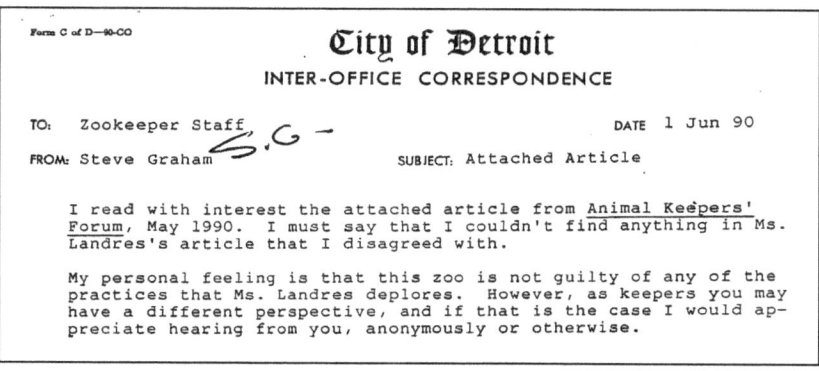

Graham's request for employee feedback (Steve Graham)

The Dark Side

By
Lisa A. Landres, Investigator
The Humane Society of the United States
Washington, DC

On 21 January, 60 Minutes featured an investigative report that dealt with the surplus animal problems faced by many zoos. The Humane Society of the United States (HSUS) felt the report was informative, but unfortunately it uncovered only the tip of the iceberg.

The surplus animal situation is best known to those keepers working around hoof stock, big cats, and the few other prolific species. These are the areas where unplanned or indiscriminate breeding often take place. Therefore, it is certainly no surprise to those working with these animals that surplus may be sold to animal dealers on a routine basis, destination unknown. The zoos apparently feel that upon transferring an animal to a licensed dealer, their responsibility ends. However, as you know, that dealer can then sell the animal to someone else. It can end up at an auction, a research facility, hunting ranch, circus, or in the hands of a private individual. Once at an exotic animal auction, the animal goes to the highest bidder, period.

This is beyond the control of the zookeeper unless a united front approaches the zoo management and proposes alternatives. Such alternatives might include chemical or surgical contraception, or merely separating males from females. One solution to the problems of exotic animal auctions and hunting ranches is to stop the problem at a major source: zoo surplus.

Now, what about the surplus animals that never leave the zoo grounds? What about all the animals, large and small, that have been pushed off into a corner behind the scenes, somewhere in your zoo? Excess animals within zoos are often condemned to live out their lives (or a large portion of them) in holding cages, meant for temporary placement only. Often, these animals are forced to live in tiny areas, frequently in isolation, often without proper shelter or adequate facilities to meet their basic needs, for months or even years on end. This is the dark side of the zoo, the part we try to forget or rationalize away, in order to keep both our sanity and our jobs. Sometimes these holding areas are so barren that we see normal animals begin to exhibit abnormal behaviors, many times leading to self-mutilation. Have you ever been so disturbed that you couldn't sleep because of some of the miserable lives animals lead right inside the zoo? Even in the best of zoos there are conditions that lead to heartache for a compassionate keeper, and suffering (mental and physical) for the excess animals.

I know this is true because I worked at the San Diego Zoo for over 10 years, and I saw surplus animals regularly living for extended periods in small, temporary holding cages. I commiserated with fellow keepers at the sad fate of many of these "excess" animals. We tried (often in vain) to get conditions changed or improved. However, the wheels of progress turn slowly, even in the bigger zoos. I met with and spoke to keepers from other zoos who expressed the same dismay and frustration as we felt. I learned that an awful lot of animals in zoos throughout the country are not being treated fairly or humanely, even within the best of zoos. I began to realize that if things like that occur in the larger zoos, they must be even worse elsewhere. I also came to realize that there are alot of fine, dedicated keepers out there who really care, and who are just as upset and frustrated as I am. I now feel that we need to work together to make progressive changes within our zoos. Our concern, first and foremost, should be for humane care and maintenance of all animals within the zoo.

I got multiple comments from my staff and tried to be as proactive in dealing with them as possible. Not all the problems could be addressed to their satisfaction, but being given the opportunity to at least be heard directly by the boss definitely improved my relationships with them.

Most good animal keepers have a close relationship with the animals they tend to every day. They weren't very pleased with me if I sometimes knew their charges better than they did. It wasn't that they were incompetent, but I think some people are born with a special sensitivity to animals – 'horse whisperers.' I believe that's another angel I have in my court.

As surprising as it might sound, animal lovers, or as zoo folks call them, "bunny huggers," aren't the best choice for animal keepers. Brad House, a vastly knowledgeable curator at first the Bronx and later the Minnesota Zoo, gave me a great tour of the Minnesota facility when it first opened. When he asked me what I thought of it, I told him I was most impressed with the quality of the animal keepers. He smiled and said, "Well, we got rid of all the animal lovers and hired animal respecters."

Dr. Barbiers had to learn the difference early on when we worked together. The zoo had a giraffe with a broken leg – an obvious case for euthanasia. However, Dr. Barbiers said she thought she could fix it. I reluctantly agreed on condition that the animal's pain was not prolonged. After two weeks with no visible sign of improvement and continued agony for the giraffe, I told Dr. Barbiers as gently as possible, "It's time to stop treatment. I think you're trying to prove you can do it, but it's not a contest. It's time to end this animal's suffering." This wasn't the first or last time I shared a different perspective than one of my zoo vets.

Currently I'm very concerned that some of the staff I worked with at the Detroit Zoo will be losing a portion of their pensions now that the city has declared bankruptcy. Many of them took such low-paying jobs because of their love of animals and the good benefits package. While I was there, they continued to work during labor strikes without pay by sneaking in the back gate that was left open for them. Detroit had a brutal climate, but they toiled through any kind of weather. I admired them above all the other workers at the zoo.

Zoo Challenges

The most daunting problem for zoos today, in my opinion, is surplus animals. This is compounded by the fact that some directors tend to be animal hoarders with a kind of collector mentality.

In the earlier years of my career, zoos were still getting some animals from the wild, but by the 1980s that was rarely the case anymore. Populations were and still are replenished from breeding within the captive population. The problem becomes keeping this ever-breeding static group adequately housed within the zoo's finite amount of space. I'm not sure about recent statistics, but in the 1980s the average zoo in North America was around 55 acres with a total in the nation of around 20,000 acres. All of the zoos in the world – best to worst – could fit within the borough of Brooklyn. These comments are taken from a wonderful book, *A Crowded Ark*, written in 1987 by Jon R. Luoma. Today's figures can only be worse.

In its monthly newsletter, the AZA lists animals that zoos have in surplus so other zoos can contact them to fill in their stock as needed. It's a good idea and works to some degree but, obviously, some animals, those with high breeding success and high population numbers, are not easy to place.

As an alternative, returning zoo-bred animals to the wild is a slim possibility at best because natural habitats have been drastically reduced and captive-born animals have limited survival skills. To my mind, attempts to return animals to the wild are extremely challenging and have a feeble chance of success except as feel good therapy for the rescuers. I've seen numerous facilities attempt such placements and recall nearly none had much success to speak of and would have been better off not trying.

Likewise, rescuing animals and returning them to the wild is rarely, if ever, a good idea. Most species that are saved are not endangered and when they are released they have to compete using far weaker survival skills for territory against the more-fit indigenous animals. Territories are always in demand and adding additional contestants into the mix helps none of the species.

The rare instances of re-introduction that are currently working are the Arabian oryx and the golden lion tamarin largely because suitable land was available for them in the wild that wasn't already populated by animals competing for the territory. These are highly unusual circumstances. The present model for reintroduction in general has a very poor record of successful placement. To continue to spend significant monies from a limited pool for such a low percentage of success is counter to serving the most animals well.

Other places offer the equivalent of limited old folk's homes for surplus animals. The Michigan Humane Society makes public pleas for money to send animals to one such facility, the Martine Collette Ranch in California. Wally Swett's business lobbied to take over chimps from Jo Fritz's refuge when it closed, and PETA's Cleveland Amory funds the Black Beauty Ranch for purported rehabilitation, to name just a few. Though animals continue to survive at such facilities, they often have less space than at the zoos and may be kept in solitary confinement to manage temperament issues.

These organizations are also guilty of speciesism – making one member of a type of animal more important than the species. Local humane societies, by necessity, euthanize countless dogs and cats to manage their populations. Why are these animals so expendable in comparison to more exotic creatures? Given a land space the size of Texas in which to place all the abandoned pets might seem a solution, but even it would fill up more quickly than ever imagined.

To my mind, the considerable funds spent for continuing to provide facilities for surplus animals could be put to so much better use for habitat protection and improvement for the animals still in the wild being threatened by loss of habitat. Such worthy organizations as The Nature Conservancy, the American Bird Conservancy and the National Audubon Society are doing credible work in this area.

Birth control is another partial solution to reducing surplus population that is being used to some degree, more in other nations than in the United States. Animals are either given injections or birth control patches or they are spayed or neutered. However, this limits the gene pool of the zoo population by excluding certain individuals from the cycle. The result is a weakening of an already at-risk species. Artificial birth control is also contrary to the natural cycles of exotic animals. They aren't like water spigots that can be turned on or off at will. In nature these animals breed on a regular basis constrained only by droughts or other natural phenomena. If animals are given hormones or removed from stock to prevent breeding, they may not be able to breed later. These measures may also compromise the complex hierarchies of group behavior in the species already compromised by being in captivity.

In my view the best, if not always the most popular solution to this dilemma is to cull the zoo stock responsibly. This takes place in the wild due to natural predators on a regular basis. Selective euthanasia in captivity is important because it allows zoos to retain the strongest of the species from a naturally selected gene pool. It also prevents surplus animals from being sold for profit to disreputable outlets where they will most probably be hunted, neglected or abused. Finally, the euthanized animals provide an excellent food source for the zoo carnivores. The fresh meat is free of any growth hormones, antibiotics or other chemicals and includes the bones and hair more similar to the animals' diet in the wild.

A CROWDED ARK
The Role of Zoos in Wildlife Conservation

Eliminating relatively healthy animals is difficult emotionally, but euthanizations performed by zoos are far more humane than those done in any slaughterhouse. In addition, such necessary steps are taken every day by local humane societies dealing with overpopulations of abandoned dogs or feral cats. If animals' lives are considered to be equally valuable, then why the repeated outcries against zoos that employ this policy, but not against humane societies? I contend the principle is the same and has even greater credence and consequence for zoos. Many professional dog breeders operate largely by these principles.

Overcrowding species in captivity is unnatural and often harmful to them. When I was taking one of my first tours of the Detroit Zoo, I noticed more than 45 Barbary sheep (aoudads) crowded into a small moated exhibit. I questioned the birth rate of the herd and was told that they hadn't had any babies in years. Weeks later I discovered the sobering truth when I saw one of the ewes give birth only to have the rest of the herd proceed to stomp it to death and mash it until it blended perfectly into the mulch of their enclosure. This was prompted by lack of space, not out of malice.

As I gained more and more experience as a zoo director, I became even surer of my views on euthanasia. By the time I took the position at the Baltimore Zoo, I determined to be proactive with the press and go public with my views so I couldn't be accused of being less than honest about such an emotional and often controversial topic. I followed the same theory when I arrived at Detroit years later but met a real hailstorm of resistance there.

Why was it so different in Detroit? Bad timing, the press-fed protest in the form of PETA and Cleveland Amory and his Fund for Animals and the sensational trial related to Mrs. Doppleberger's million-dollar law suits against me and the city mentioned earlier. I particularly recall Cleveland Amory literally pushing past me as we left the trial after the verdict was pronounced in my favor. Erik Smith, a reporter for WXYZ (an ABC affiliate), brushed him aside saying, "We want to talk to the boss first," indicating me. Amory pulled up short incensed at being upstaged when he was so fond of the usual spotlight.

In his thoughtfully crafted and painstakingly researched book, A Crowded Ark, writer Jon R. Luoma presents a compelling case for the role of modern-day zoos in wildlife conservation. He examines the history of zoos and the overwhelming challenges faced by many species in the wild that are vanishing at an alarming rate due to human incursion and disregard. But zoos' limited space and funds often dictate difficult choices. Luoma goes to great lengths to explain how the humane killing of surplus animals, though seemingly cruel to the individual, better guarantees the survival of the species – the greater good. Luoma did extensive, thoughtful research and often consulted with me and many other experienced and reliable sources for their input. His book was welcome support while I was fighting my battle about euthanizing the tigers upon my arrival at the Detroit Zoo.

A passage from A Crowded Ark reads:

. . . Only one zoo director in North America, Steve [Graham] has established a clear precedent with his public and the local news media. In 1982, Graham walked into a firestorm when he proposed killing four Siberian tigers . . . three of the tigers were old and ailing, one so crippled that it had to lean against the wall of its cage to stand up. The other had severe behavior problems. But the irony of killing endangered species was played to the hilt in the local news media. Graham, who has variously been described as outspoken, heroic, and a raving fool in the zoo world, stood his ground, insisting that euthanasia was the only moral choice. A Detroit citizen and a group of animal rights organizations sued the zoo and Graham, but the court ruled for the zoo, and the three infirm tigers were killed. The

precedent being set, in 1985 the zoo culled four more Siberian tigers, these healthy, but surplus, then two lions in 1986. There were news stories in those cases as well, and public protests, but they did not approach the intensity of the 1982 outcry, and Graham continued to stand his ground.

Wildlife Conservation

During my 20-plus years as a zoo director, the landscape changed and zoos began the process of adapting to new functions that were in many ways positive, but also frustrating in their limitations. I remember discussing this with Jon Luoma in the late 1980s when he was working on *A Crowded Ark*. He asked me about "the zoo world's general failure to practice what it preaches [regarding educating the public about wildlife preservation]."

I told him:

> *Well, yes, you're 100 percent right that we don't [adequately educate the public about conservation]. I keep saying that the only reason I'm in this business is that zoos in the United States have more than 100 million visitors every year, and that offers an unprecedented opportunity to reach people with the conservation message. But the fact is, if you hear me say that and then visit my zoo to see how well I've acted on it, you'd walk away disappointed. We haven't found ways to devote enough resources to graphics. Some of that's because once we're done with maintaining exhibits and caring for the animals, there isn't much left over. I think more of it is that we know a lot more about taking care of animals than we do about how to tell our visitors about conservation.*

Hopefully, since the 1980s and 1990s, zoos have made great strides in defining their conservation role to the public.

Naming Animals

Anthropomorphism – n. the ascribing of human motivation and human characteristics to something that is not human

Humanizing animals is a huge disservice we offer all too often to nonhuman creatures. Each species in nature has unique nobility in its own right. Attempting to morph them into pseudohumans by giving them names or assigning them human motivations demeans them.

I've been accused of taking this principle to extremes and I do plead guilty to being a purist, but I believe very strongly that we have to be careful that we aren't always making the circle come back to somebody's idea of the human being as the supreme being, the most advanced creature on earth. Maybe we are, maybe we aren't. If we were turned loose in the forest, many species would probably survive longer than we would.

Some argue that nonhuman animals have thoughts, and I would agree, but they are thinking as their species thinks, not thinking as human beings, or thinking as we recognize thinking. We can't assume animals experience emotion the way we do. Humans grin when they're happy, but a chimp grins out of abject fear. The best we can do is to observe their behavior and apply reason and past knowledge to attempt to analyze their needs when they are in our care.

Imposing our humanness on domesticated animals – farm stock and our own beloved conventional pets like cats and dogs – may have fewer negative consequences for them, but that's only because their species has adapted to close association with humans over hundreds of generations. Most species can never be domesticated. Trying to transform exotic animals into pets eventually traps these creatures in a sad and lonely void ensuring they will never be able to realize their own natural potential or remain docile to human intervention and companionship.

It's a tender trap to see a very young exotic animal, so cute and vulnerable and want to make it a part of your life. But to truly honor this is to leave it alone as much as possible. Respect its right to exist as nature intended.

Parents are often frustrated because the adorable little puppy that daughter Susie or son Sam wanted so badly and promised to take care of ends up neglected by the child. Local humane societies are challenged every day by abandoned pets and unwanted litters of unneutered feral cats and dogs. Many are euthanized on a regular basis because of lack of space and/or funds to properly care for them. The latest extensive survey made by the National Council on Pet Population Study and Policy estimates that approximately 3.7 million animals were euthanized in the nation's shelters in 2008, roughly 64 percent of the animals that entered the shelters. A similar survey hasn't been successfully conducted since then, but it is assumed the trend continues – and this only accounts for animal shelters in the United States.

This problem is magnified a hundred times or more when the pet is an exotic animal. Most local humane societies are not equipped to offer proper care to exotic species, so many exotic pets are sold to roadside zoos with substandard conditions, if they are convenient, or the animals are simply released to unsuccessfully fend for themselves. Reports of 'alligators in the sewers' or mountain lions in the northern forests are all too frequent and tragic. Pet Burmese pythons have escaped their owners and taken over as the predominant predator of the Florida Everglades.

Equally disturbing are the cases of exotic animals that were docile when young becoming aggressive and seriously harming their owners or innocent bystanders. The animals become the villains, but the real criminals are the humans that created the situation in the first place. A widely publicized example occurred in February 2009 when the pet chimpanzee attacked and mauled 55-year-old Carla Nash's face beyond recognition when she was visiting the chimp's owner.

Zoos have a responsibility to set the standard in dealing with the species they house. Educating the public about the animals is a top priority, but taking young animals to public events and extending petting zoo opportunities creates the dangerous mindset that they are pets.

Also, I contend that naming exotic animals housed in public zoos is an unwise policy. Although experts as renowned as Jane Goodall don't totally agree with me about this (she names all of the chimps in her studies), I see it as the first step in humanizing them. When the new Chimps of Harambee facility opened in Detroit in 1989, staff writer Toni Martin scripted a wonderful feature piece for the *Detroit Free Press Magazine*. The cover photo below by Pulitzer Prize-winning Manny Crisostomo is one of the finest chimpanzee photos I've ever seen, but the title that included his name, prompted a negative response from me.

My first reaction, in spite of the quality of the overall content and touching photo, was outrage because my prime directive in being interviewed for this piece was that the animals *not* be given names. After I calmed down, I conceded that the title did convey the spirit of my message – especially with the "not" underlined – but just seeing "Jo-Jo" in print set me off. (Ironically, they misspelled his name.) The fact is that giving names to the chimps or other multiple animals in a group makes it easier to distinguish them from each other in discussions. In the body of the article Martin refers to the new chimps in the exhibit as "Black Face" or "Baby" or "White Face" for the sake of clarifying which chimps she is referring to. I could better abide this because they were descriptive references, not human, names.

Graham's favorite chimp portrait – part of "no names" article
(Steve Graham)

Martin stressed the diligent efforts taken by the Detroit Zoo to choose which animals to introduce into the new facility to be successful in recreating as accurately as possible a natural society for the chimps. We tried to allow for nurturing behaviors between the young and the females and to control to some degree the issue of male dominance between "No. 1 Man" and "No. 2 Man" (as Martin dubbed them) based on past knowledge. The efforts paid off. Despite the bizarre accidents with the moated barrier and some disagreements about the placement of the pre-exhibit chimps, the Harambee chimps became a natural community.

Naming animals unquestionably creates a more intimate bond with humans. A sense of responsibility and connection comes with the process of bestowing a name. Yet some zoos continue to conduct "Name that Animal" contests to boost public participation and, hopefully, donations. The naming becomes a stumbling block if and when that 'Elsa' or 'Jo-Jo' or 'Bambi' needs to be legitimately euthanized as in the case of the baby giraffe culled at the Copenhagen Zoo. The headlines were sensational enough using terms like "butcher" and "children were witness," but because the giraffe was named Marius, the rhetoric grew even more emotional.

Surplus Animals

Every generation has the voices protesting that *no* animals should be kept in cages. The spectacle mentality and the horrid conditions of the first zoos multiple decades ago give easy credence to this response, and some just cause still exists today to sympathize with captive animals, even in the much-improved facilities offered by more progressive zoos. Historically however, many humans have also been fascinated by exotic animals and felt the need to keep these beasts where their majesty could be experienced firsthand. Additionally, exotic animals have been proof of wealth and status – of prowess in the hunt – since their discovery many eras ago.

With today's advanced technology most of the public can observe these wonderful creatures from the comfort of their homes. Film footage of dedicated nature photographers like the late Joan Root and her husband Alan, thoughtful studies like Jane Goodall's with chimpanzees, and more bring the animals close to millions without significantly disturbing the animals' freedom. Still, the desire for direct encounter continues to draw throngs of people to zoos to soak in the magnificence of the creatures.

A multitude of exotic animals already populate the world's zoos and, despite the romantic notion that would fling wide the doors of their cages and release them to their native habitat, this vision is, for the most part, impossible to achieve. Either the natural habitat they require is no longer sufficient in the world or the species has been captive so long that they've lost the survival instincts they need to live outside the zoo setting that provides for their every need.

Given that zoos *must* continue to exist, primarily for the survival of the animals they serve, the necessity of defining how this responsibility is met is critcal. The two defensible goals that modern zoos need to meet responsibly are (1) to educate human beings about the value of preserving exotic animals in their natural habitats as much as possible by displaying and defining the variety, beauty and wonders of the animal kingdom and (2) to preserve gene pools of those species destined to exist only in zoos because human beings are destroying natural habitats every year through development. Of primary concern should be accomplishing these ends with the least suffering possible to the animals given the zoos' limitations of space and means.

Former Bronx Zoo Director Bill Conway recollects seeing a harried Bronx mother dragging her children toward the zoo exit after a long day. The young ones were protesting, "Mother, we haven't seen the elephants."

She snapped, "Stop whining. You've seen elephants in books and on TV."

They continued begging. "But never so big!"

All this being said, the dilemma of how to deal with surplus animals within the finite limitations of zoos is a recurring stumbling block. We just don't have enough room to care for all of them, even with the combined efforts between accredited facilities worldwide made possible by advanced technology and communication. Too many animals, too little space.

As the earlier accounts of my zoo experience illustrate, I am a staunch proponent of euthanasia as the way to most responsibly preserve healthy gene pools of these majestic species and to minimize the suffering of aging or infirm animals. Yet these efforts are continually undermined by those who capitalize on the inherent tragedy of putting an animal down and attack the individuals who responsibly and honestly make such difficult decisions. Irresponsible, self-serving diatribes continue to force many zoo managers either to hide the fact that they euthanize *any* animals or to opt to keep the animals alive regardless of the animals' pain or the genetic jeopardy they bring to their own species.

The backlash of an unenlightened public threatens to reduce funding for their zoos and even jeopardizes their personal safety. Would-be crusaders riding to the rescue of the poor, helpless, victimized animals feel a righteous vindication spurred on by inflammatory remarks of high-profile animal rights groups like PETA and others who use arrogant rhetoric to shout down any call to debate the real issue. For example, reporter James Tozer wrote the following heavy-handed lead-in for a February 9, 2014, online news publication *The Mail* regarding the euthanizing of the young giraffe at Copenhagen Zoo. It accompanied a photo of the giraffe's still-warm body:

> "This [referencing the photo] is the horrific moment schoolchildren crowded around to watch as the body of a perfectly healthy giraffe was chopped up before being fed to the lions. Despite more than 20,000 people signing an online petition to save two-year-old Marius, staff at Copenhagen Zoo yesterday went ahead and shot the animal with a [captive] bolt pistol. Young children stood at arm's length as his carcass was skinned and dissected before the meat was thrown to the lions."

Several zoo staff members received threats via telephone and emails, according to CNN. When the petition to stop the killing failed, a new one quickly followed calling for the firing of Bengt Holst's, the Copenhagen Zoo's scientific director.

The voice of reason is eventually heard when such situations arise, but I ache for the day when the doomsday voices disappear altogether. For the day that the press refuses to print charges of "butchery" and "cruelty" against those who honestly present their difficult but utterly justified decisions. As Bengt Holst stated his case:

> We have been very steadfast because we know we've made this decision on a factual and proper basis. We can't all of a sudden change to something we know is worse because of some emotional events happening around us.
>
> It's important that we try to explain why we do it and hope people understand it. If we are serious about our breeding activities, including participation in breeding programs, then we have to follow what we know is right. And this is right.

Courageous stands against the backlash are arduous and should be applauded and supported. Happily, the EAZA (the European equivalent of the United States AZA) said it fully supported the decision of the Copenhagen Zoo. However, the AZA hedged its comments about the situation with vague statements such as "EAZA's programs and procedures vary from those of the AZA" or "the AZA Species Survival Plan [SSP mentioned earlier] program includes science-based breeding recommendations and plans for providing adequate space." These remarks are released despite the clear policy of AZA that recommends euthanizing animals in situations exactly like the one at the Copenhagen Zoo. In worst-case scenarios, obvious misinformation is dispersed, as with the Associated Press release by Malin Rising that stated, "The U.S. Association of Zoos and Aquariums said incidents such as the giraffe killing 'do not happen at AZA-accredited zoos.'" To read this knowing the truth is infuriating.

Consequently, public condemnation and attacks continue against responsible actions like those of the Copenhagen Zoo and like those I endured in Detroit when I ordered any animal euthanized. I was grateful that the local press contacted me for a response to the international drama of the Copenhagen Zoo. I had the opportunity to state publicly, yet again, the utmost importance of understanding the wisdom and courage of the director who had been victimized by the first accounts to reach the press. I applauded the actions of Bengt Holst and told Caleb Calhoun of *The Herald Mail*, Hagerstown, Maryland, in February of 2014:

> *The people knew what they were going to see. . . They had their children in front of them and they were watching what was going on; they were learning . . . there's nothing wrong with euthanizing healthy animals in order to protect the species. . . .*

Many science courses for young students involve dissecting frogs or rats as a teaching tool. Granted these animals aren't rare species, but they were living creatures, just like the young giraffe. What a wonderful learning opportunity Copenhagen Zoo was offering to those who *chose* to witness such a unique necropsy. Given the giraffe's fate, what better choice than to reap as much positive benefit from its sacrifice as possible.

I also restated my support of feeding euthanized animals to other zoo carnivores as happened with Marius when he was fed to the zoo's lions. Doing so gives them "the whole carcass meat, organs, skin, hair, bone, that they never get in a zoo hamburger …" Most infuriating for me are comments from high-profile individuals who are aware of the facts, but choose to take a stand that gives them the spotlight - persons like retired Zoo Director and TV personality Jack Hanna. The press too often uses him as a go-to for zoo-related items because of his popular appearances with a variety of adorable exotic animals on *The Tonight Show* and such. He referred to the Copenhagen Zoo's decision as "the most abominable, insensitive, ridiculous thing I've ever heard of."

I support the right of free speech, but am frustrated by the power of the media to stir up negative sentiments that so often work against reason. I shared my opinion recently at a presentation I made to the Waynesboro Rotary Club, as I will continue to do as long as I have breath. It is one of the driving forces behind my writing this book. The issue of euthanasia needs to emerge from the underground in spite of public reprisal. The light of day and open, reasoned discussion will generate support for the process and spare many animals terrible suffering.

Nicky McWerter, a reporter in Detroit, was originally opposed to my take on euthanasia. She was very popular with much of the Detroit public and had been variously my critic and supporter in the past. Her early columns reflect her disagreement with euthanasia, but when she had to have her pet cat put down, her opinion changed. She became one of my strongest supporters. Her article about this experience stemmed the tide of negative public opinion in Detroit.

My stance on euthanasia has been a long, uphill battle, even among my zoo colleagues like Bill Conway, former Director of the Bronx Zoo. Since my early years at the Salisbury Zoo we had shared lengthy conversations, for the most part friendly. He had a very distinguished manner and was extremely well spoken.

The AAZPA contacted me to make a presentation about euthanasia at one of its board meetings. Unfortunately, Bill Conway spoke before me and expounded with high-sounding rhetoric about the fallacies of euthanasia. The wind completely gone from my sails, I took the podium and simply said, "Bill, you've done again what you do so well. You've shut me up without saying one relevant word."

I was tempted to say more, but uncharacteristically, held back. I kept quiet about stories I had heard about surplus animals 'disappearing' out the back door of the Bronx Zoo. One instance related that five very old male lions had 'vanished' and days later an observer in Chicago discovered five lion skulls offered for sale by a company that butchered and sold exotic meats. The skulls most likely had been stripped clean within less than a week by dermestid beetles and brought a good price.

By the end of my tenure at Detroit, I estimate nearly 90 percent of the public in Detroit had come over to our side. Zoo attendance and Zoo Society membership had increased and my policy of merciful euthanasia continued in the open, finally without protest. Ted Reed, then director of the National Zoo, said Detroit had the "best-educated zoo public in the country." But that's long since gone and incidents like the recent one in Copenhagen point that out all too clearly. The AZA and zoo directors across the country and the world need to follow Copenhagen Zoo's example of fortitude until the practice is resolved once and for all. This book is my small, but fervent contribution to that process.

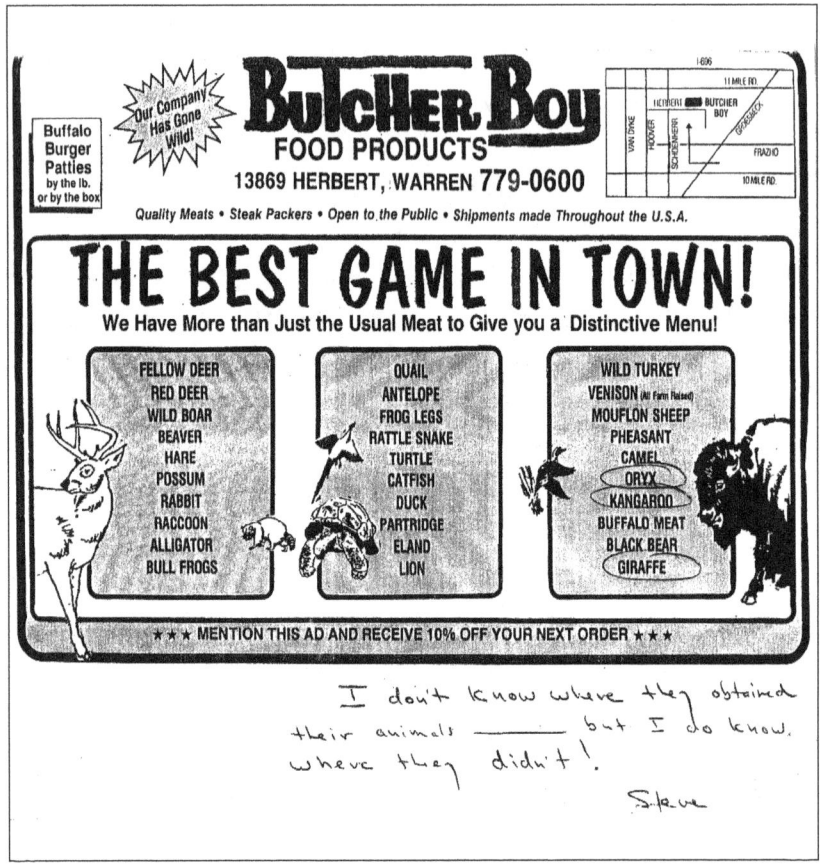

Advertisement for exotic cuts of meat from Detroit butcher Shop (Steve Graham)

One of my first experiences with major media was as a guest on TV's *20/20* in 1979. Roger Caras, my father-in-law at the time, was one of the celebrity moderators and he interviewed me about the views on the surplus animal problem and euthanasia – the very issue I had gone public with when I began my venue at the Baltimore Zoo. I had been up front with the press because I didn't want anyone to accuse me of misleading them if and when my actions became an issue. I was getting a little flak from those opposed to my stand and Roger was helping me to get a handle on it. It was nothing like I would experience years later about the same issue at the Detroit Zoo, but I appreciated the opportunity it gave me to reach a larger audience with my message.

On June 15, 1984 I took part in a debate moderated by Dennis Wholey on PBS (Public Broadcasting). The opposing side was argued by Ingrid Newkirk from PETA whose mantra was "a rat is a dog is a pony is a boy." I remember countering with "When we start sending rats to college, I'll put some faith in what Ms. Newkirk says."

This was good training for future broadcasts I would be called upon to do when my celebrity status grew at the Detroit Zoo. In September of 1988 I was interviewed by Karen Burns of *West 57th Street*, in December of 1989 with *CNN News* and in January of 1990 I was honored to be part of an exposé on *60 Minutes* about the sale of surplus zoo animals to hunting ranches, roadside zoos, and other tortuous facilities.

The glacial speed of a permanent change in public sentiment about this issue continues to torment me. I can't help but shake my head when I recall the powerful *60 Minutes* segment that so eloquently stated the case in favor of euthanasia as opposed to passing "undesirable" or ailing animals on to horrific conditions in unaccredited, ill-equipped facilities or to for-pay hunting preserves as fodder for recreational target practice. This show garnered significant support for proper zoo practice when it aired nearly *25 years ago*, but little has changed. In fact, the San Diego Zoo was exposed on the show for unscrupulous surplus animal dealings, but was repeating the same practice within weeks of the program airing. The program is still referenced when these ugly practices resurface.

I had the privilege of working with Meredith Viera who worked on the filming of *60 Minutes*, before she gained even greater fame on *The Today Show*. So important was this epic broadcast for zoos that I wrote to her.

Detroit Zoological Parks

Detroit Zoo • Belle Isle Zoo • Belle Isle Aquarium

8450 W. Ten Mile Road • P.O Box 39 • Royal Oak, Michigan 48068-0039 • (313) 398-0903

Coleman A. Young, Mayor
City of Detroit

Steve Graham, Director

23 January 1990

Ms. Meredith Viera
60 Minutes
CBS News
555 West 57th Street
New York, New York 10019

Dear Meredith:

What an auspicious beginning! Although many people may not have felt the subject matter was quite as important as most "60 Minutes" pieces, I honestly don't know how it could have been handled better.

After seeing it I couldn't help but think that it was a very sad day for zoos in this country. But sad only because if our profession chooses to address and eventually solve this unseemly problem, it will be through the intercession of "60 Minutes" rather than through the initiative of the professionals in the zoo field. As one of those professionals, I find that to be a very sad commentary.

I've worked with a lot of journalists in my time and I have never found one more committed to the truth, and at the moment I can't think of any more important attributes of a professional journalist. I look forward to working with you again.

Best personal regards,

ZOOLOGICAL PARKS DEPARTMENT

Steve

Steve Graham
Director of Zoological Parks

SG/dja

ACCREDITED BY THE AMERICAN ASSOCIATION OF ZOOLOGICAL PARKS AND AQUARIUMS

Graham's letter to Meredith Viera following *60 minutes* program (Steve Graham)

A more recent episode of *60 Minutes* that dealt with the topic aired on Nov. 30, 2016. Clarissa Ward interviewed Kevin Richardson, an animal behaviorist who has been dubbed the "Lion Whisperer." He recently relocated 26 adult lions that he had bonded with from The Lion Park, a petting zoo facility near

Johannesburg, South Africa, to a nearby game preserve rather than see them go to "canned hunts." He previously worked at The Lion Park where lions are captive bred for hands-on opportunities for paying visitors. However, when the lions grow into the predators they were born to be and prove dangerous for paying visitors, many are sold to companies that market the opportunity to shoot such exotic animals to customers for upwards of $100,000. Richardson said as he strolled freely in the preserve romping with the huge cats, "I'll admit I've made an emotional connection with the lions. I just can't turn my back on them now."

He is supported in his efforts by Chris Mercer, the head of CACH (Campaign Against Canned Hunting) who stated on the show that the canned hunting clientele aren't hunters, they're collectors. He agreed with Ms. Ward who likened these expeditions to "shooting fish in a barrel." Mercer urged anyone watching to remember that, "When you pet a lion cub, you are directly enriching canned hunts." Still such facilities are legal and flourishing.

It's sad to see how little has changed in over 25 years except the cost of basically slaughtering a helpless animal.

In recent years, cable television stations such as National Geographic and Animal Planet have offered some wonderful glimpses into the lives of animals, but I wonder if the creatures and their environment pay too high a price for the product.

The shows often glamorize going places in ATV's or on motorcycles and seriously disturbing habitat where people really don't belong. How many children watching these programs are anxious to go out and follow suit causing even more damage?

More offensive, in my view, are shows that encourage exotic pet ownership. Veterinarians featured in shows such as National Geographic's *Dr. K's Exotic Animal ER* who treat these animals are portrayed as heroes because they relieve the animals' suffering, but to what end? This only encourages the viewing public to consider exotic pet ownership themselves, the end result being a detriment to the animals that should remain undisturbed in their native environments.

The National Geographic program *Bandit Patrol* features the reintroduction of injured wildlife that have been treated and recovered into the wild. Little credence is given to the unfortunate situation faced by these creatures that then have to compete, usually unsuccessfully, with stronger, better adapted animals vying for territory and survival.

Forty years ago I spoke at a Maryland Veterinary Conference in Ocean City and urged members to take the lead in ending the wildlife trade by refusing to treat exotic animals. This was and is a difficult request to make of people who are dedicated to providing treatment to ailing animals, but the negative long-term effect of offering treatment shouldn't be denied.

National Geographic also offers *World's Weirdest*, a show that emphasizes the sensational at the expense of respect and compassion for unusual animals and situations. A nearly humorous tone accompanied the sad tale of a captive cockatoo that had plucked out nearly all of its feathers due to stress, or as the program phrased it, "boredom." Pigs that had been scarified were presented as "works of art."

Yet another television show features an older couple who maintain a roadside zoo consisting of rescued exotic animals – ones they claim "No one else wants." Again, as magnanimous as that sounds, they go on to explain their success in breeding despite having no veterinarian with them. If the animals they acquired originally were excess and unwanted, how do they justify breeding still more unless they're also servicing a market of perspective buyers to perpetuate the problem?

The Grosvenor family, wealthy Washington residents, was a steward of the original National Geographic Society. Gil Grosvenor, a friend, stepped down as chairman in 2010 ending a 122-year family commitment. The founders of the society focused on educating the public about the geography of our world and our responsibility in maintaining it. I suspect the new television programs that clearly deviate from this purpose would not please the society's forefathers.

PAWS

The dilemma of surplus exotic animals extends beyond the zoo world. Backyard breeding and the freelance exotic animal trade have boomed following two significant incidents. First was the increased use of exotic animals in the television industry with programs such as "Flipper," "Gentle Ben, "Walt Disney's Living Desert" and "Daktari" and in the motion picture industry since the mid-1960s. Second was the passage of the Endangered Species Act in 1973 that restricted hunting endangered species in the wild giving rise to hunting ranches where captive populations of exotic animals could be hunted for a fee.

Of note as well was the 1978 hunting ban in Kenya imposed by President Jomo Kenyatta. This had a negative economic impact initially, throwing many related areas into unemployment and closing the huge hunting retailer Rowland Ward Company based in Kenya. Kenyatta saw the hunters as having a negative impact on both the wildlife and the tourism industry. Within a few years tourism increased in Kenya and made up for the economic shortfall caused by the hunting ban, but many hunters sought out hunting ranches as an alternative.

Also contributing to the problem is the continued popularity of circuses, drive-through wildlife parks and unregulated exotic animal auctions selling 'pets' to enthusiasts and hobbyists. Additionally, many endangered creatures have also become pawns of the international drug trade both as unscrupulous means of transport inside the animals' bodies and as cashless, not-easily-traced monetary exchanges.

Other contributors to the problem are quasi-educational organizations that use young exotic animals for hands-on demonstration for children. Though they are very popular and instructional, many of these children then view these animals as potential pets and become potential exotic pet owners.

The animals necessary for all of the arenas listed above eventually outlive their usefulness and suffer a tragic fate.

These situations gave rise to a small group of middlemen who bartered or purchased surplus animals, first from zoos and later, as the market and demand grew, also from backyard breeders, roadside menageries and more. It has become a highly lucrative, self-perpetuating, multilayered phenomenon spawning countless cases of animal abuse and neglect. The Progressive Animal Welfare Society (PAWS – previously known as Performing Animal Welfare Society), founded in 1967 largely in response to this increased need to help the helpless animals, calls it the "cycle of hell."

Even if moves were taken to provide fewer exotic animals to such unhealthy situations, the surplus population still would be unmanageable. Sadly, such restraint is absent from the process. Hollywood breeds animals specifically for particular roles – at times utilizing multiple animals. The filming of *Babe* in 1995 required more than 900 animals, including 48 pigs for the title character of Babe alone. Though many claims were made by the film industry that *most* found happy homes later, it is highly unlikely and certainly not the usual outcome. Most film animals are used once for a specific need and then discarded in the most convenient, profitable way possible.

In addition, the American Humane Association (AHA) monitors the use of the animals only while they are on the set. Tactics used for pretraining and the conditions the animals are kept under for the majority of their association with the trainers are not covered. The USDA actually prosecuted the *owner* of an orangutan that was severely beaten during filming of a movie but off the set. The animal died soon afterward as a result of the abuse but the *trainer* who beat him is still profiting financially as a Hollywood animal trainer.

The end of the line for many of these surplus animals is the hunting ranches. The main sources for their for-pay shooting stock are zoos, Hollywood and the television industry, drive-through wildlife parks and backyard breeders. At the 2014 speech to Rotarians, I shared this. One of their younger members was an avid hunter and said that he had a membership in a hunting ranch, but assumed the animals had been imported from the wild. When he heard the facts, he was very taken aback. I like to think he withdrew from his association with the facility soon after that.

What started in the early 1970s quickly grew legs until the "Texotic" hunting ranches soon spread beyond Texas into virtually every state in the union. The HSUS (Humane Society of the United States) has identified many zoos that have sold to such establishments including five that are accredited – the National Zoo, Lincoln Park Zoo, St. Louis Zoo, Houston Zoo and the San Diego Zoo. Today there are more black buck antelope in Texas than in their native India.

Earl Tatum was an animal dealer featured on the *60 Minutes* segment in 1990 for purchasing surplus animals from the San Diego Wild Animal Park and delivering them to hunting ranches or other deplorable destinations. He was of the same ilk as the infamous Hunt Brothers, animal dealers mentioned earlier. He often worked with an equally questionable person named Leon Leopard. I ran into him during my career far too many times.

While I was director at Salisbury Zoo, I went to a hunting ranch I had seen advertised in Pennsylvania under the guise that I was a potential customer. I was first escorted to a lounge/game room and shown some small cages with two lions and one tiger and told they could be had for $1,000 each. That meant I could shoot them in the cage, not even in some makeshift outside shooting gallery.

Then the owner drove me in a pickup truck loaded with feed to a fire tower in the nearby woods. As we stood in the top of the tower, the animals came to feed and he listed the prices for them. He explained that whatever I killed would be processed within an hour and I could claim the head and the hide. I'm sure they had a good market for the meat as well.

I said thanks but no thanks and quickly left.

Roadside zoos are monitored only by the weak AWA (Animal Welfare Act) and the USDA has a history of being ineffective in taking action against those who are not in compliance. The eternal *why* is often unanswered. Catoctin Mountain Zoo is a prime example and there are thousands more like it in the nation and the world. Drive-through wildlife parks initially appear to offer a more desirable setting for their animals, but the increased opportunity for breeding among the animals creates even more surplus stock to be disposed of.

Exotic Pets

The list of animals coveted by exotic pet fans is shocking – tigers, bears, lions, bobcats, cougars, lynx, chimps, orangutans, monkeys, alpacas, baby elephants and more. Even worse, some of the most popular are the oddities like albinos, the results of genetic inbreeding and therefore weaker and more vulnerable, but deliberately bred for their market value. Exotic pet owners are attracted to unique varieties which are generally the result of weaker recessive gene mutations such as white tigers. These 'freaks' are bred deliberately and threaten to weaken multiple bloodlines. I recall turning down repeated offers for thousands of dollars from such animal dealers for an albino snapping turtle that a kid had found at a ballfield and given to the Detroit Zoo where it still resides.

When these cute exotic babies grow into their more dangerous or uncontrollable adult years, they're dumped – sometimes simply abandoned – by their owners or merely escape their crude enclosures.

Most notorious are owners of venomous snakes – for them, the more deadly, the more macho. Each snake species has a unique antivenin required to treat bites. Potential victims are children in apartment complexes where the snakes often escape. Local hospitals are helpless to administer the correct treatment without knowing what kind of snakebite it is. I got a call from a hospital in Detroit to supply antivenin to the victim of a very rare venomous snakebite who owned multiple exotic deadly poisonous snakes and had suffered numerous bites. His chances of survival were slim to none. I had to refuse because I had only one dose and needed to keep it for my own staff.

Unfortunately, lobbying continues in Washington against the limiting of any aspect of the exotic pet trade. Primary is the Pet Industry Joint Advisory Council (PIJAC). Although its website reads very positively, mentioning the group's association with the USDA and the AWA (Animal Welfare Act), neither of them has been effective or efficient enforcing their regulations – more emphasis is placed on "protecting the right to own a pet."

As the website goes on to read, "Pet sale bans and limits on the types of pets people may own can cripple legitimate businesses. . ." First, their definition of "legitimate" businesses would be questionable. But more important are the exotic animals that would be crippled by the attempts at domestication that PIJAC supports.

One of the most horrifying incidents associated with private ownership of exotic animals occurred in March 2012 in Zanesville, Ohio when a depressed man named Terry Thompson released his private collection of 18 tigers, 17 lions, 8 bears, 3 cougars, 2 wolves, a baboon and a macaque before committing suicide. Authorities felt they had no choice but to shoot the free-roaming animals before they injured anyone.

While I was at the Detroit Zoo I served as head of the surplus committee of AAZPA. They had the ridiculous rule then that allowed accredited animal dealers to buy but not sell at animal auctions. I heard a rumor that my friend Karl Mogenson was selling animals at auctions – a clear violation of his AAZPA accreditation, so I went to one in Texas that had been widely advertised. I caught sight of him there unloading animals for sale – evidence to confront him with later. He was subsequently expelled from AAZPA.

The venue was a large arena filled with any and all variety of pathetically displayed species – giraffes, hippos, monkeys and more. I tried to stay undercover taking a seat by myself high in one of the bleacher stands. Unhappily, the auctioneer spied me from the podium and indicated my location to the crowd. He then asked me to stand saying, "This gentleman doesn't think you should be allowed to buy and sell these animals." A hail of boos and worse followed along with lots of angry expressions and gestures. I felt very alone in the heart of Texas hunting ranch territory and was glad to get out of there alive.

Roadside zoos and animal research facilities that are damaged by weather events such as floods and wind result in dangerous animals escaping into the local areas where they breed to dangerous proportions. Florida is especially affected by this as many such facilities prefer the more tropical climate. A recent example is the proliferation of non-native lionfish with their hundreds of deadly poisonous tentacles flourishing in the coastal waters of the state. These millions of lethal fish can be traced back to six females of the species that escaped into the wild during area floods.

Exotic Animal Internet Trade

Human vanity and insensitivity often inflict obscene damage on exotic animals. Beyond the folly of exotic pet ownership are the lure of exotic objects coveted by egocentric collectors – elephant legs for trashcans, crocodile skin bath mats and more. Until recently such trade flourished in select markets and pet stores, but the Internet has opened up a global network less hampered by borders where customs officials continue to combat this illegal smuggling. The new market of individual buyers streamlines the illegal imports by avoiding large scale shipments of rare snakes, lizards, birds, etc. that border agents can more easily discover than single a African wild cat or baby monkey masquerading as a domestic pet or child. The penalties are smaller, too when smuggling a single specimen.

British photographer and filmmaker Adam Lach at Napo Images recently came face to face with the ugliness of this market at a photo shoot at an airport in Warsaw, Poland that displayed specimens collected over the years in the middle of the departures area to raise awareness of the problem. He coined his project "Human Tsunami." His distress is amplified by the reality that anyone with an Internet connection can visit the traffickers' websites. Says Lach, "The buyers' only limitation is language. One who knows languages can buy anything."

What is needed is a heightening of conscience and morality regarding our treatment of animals. This, unfortunately, is impossible to legislate. The public must be educated about our profound relationship with the planet and its animals. My fervent hope is that zoos will step up to help to meet this challenge.

Regulatory Agencies

The USDA is mandated to inspect animal care facilities at least twice a year, but inspectors can show up unannounced as often as they want. The concept, as usual, is good, but once politics/government is involved, the reality falls far short of the intent. For example, when I was at the Salisbury Zoo I was making rounds with the USDA inspector. We came to the Delmarva fox squirrel enclosure. The creatures resemble gray squirrels on steroids. I asked the inspector why he didn't have a sheet for them as he did for the other species and he said, "We only make up sheets for the mammals."

Puzzled, I asked, "Then why is it the squirrels don't have one?"

"They live in trees," he explained.

'Seriously?' I thought. As you can imagine, I stopped asking questions after that and hoped the zoo would pass his 'learned' inspection – which it always did.

While I was in Detroit I was often at odds with the Michigan Humane Society that was headed by David Wills who had been recommended to the position by then HSUS (Humane Society of the United States) president, John Hoyt. Although Wills was well liked by the Detroit public and talented at cultivating the press, he often faltered. One popular radio show personality received a call while on the air describing how he had just witnessed David Wills rescuing an injured dog from a busy highway risking his own safety. Problem was the radio show host recognized the voice – it belonged to David Wills.

Michigan Humane Society had confiscated a 100-plus pound abused chimp from a traveling show. He had been prompted into tantrums by high pressure hoses to 'entertain' the public. Confiscation was a positive move, but no one at the society could get near enough to the animal to even feed him, much less minister to him. They finally called me for help.

As the staff watched, I started talking 'chimp talk' softly to him and then asked for a ladder so I could get closer to the raised platform the cage was sitting on. I was trying to stay calm, so I lit a cigarette. The chimp immediately started shaking his hand – he wanted one too. I gave him one and continued the soft chimp talk until he reached out through the bars and began grooming the hair on my arm.

Wills was dumbfounded, but we both knew he was furious with jealousy because he was not good with animals. In fact, he soon left the Michigan Humane Society amid accusations that he had embezzled lots of money.

Surprisingly, Wills was then hired (again with Hoyt's backing) as vice-president by the HSUS. Hoyt's influence is the only explanation I can come up with to explain how Wills got the job – that and his copacetic relationship with Al Neuharth of *USA Today* who might have spoken in his behalf as well. Ironically, John Hoyt, a former minister, was eventually discovered to have sold his house to HSUS for a highly inflated price, but retained the right to live there for free. Even more allegations against the two began to surface after this.

The ultimate irony is that after I retired I got a letter from Hoyt and Wills offering me a place on the HSUS staff as zoo representative. I had to laugh out loud. Although they were offering a tempting salary, I wouldn't have taken the job for ten times the offer.

Still, I admire the bulk of the work the HSUS does, most notably the money the organization raises for humane causes and its working for the protection of farm and domestic animals.

I was director of the Salisbury Humane Society during my tenure there with the zoo. Years later, after I had retired, I heard that the current director of Salisbury's humane society had been fired. I called to offer my help and was asked to serve as interim director. After I reluctantly agreed, a local reporter wrote a wonderful editorial that mentioned that if he were in a foxhole, he would choose me to be with him – one of my greatest compliments. I worked three days a week for some months until the board hired an applicant from HSUS. Her best credential, in my opinion, was that she had been crucial in getting David Wills fired from the HSUS years earlier.

The AZA is responsible for setting many of the regulations for accreditation and various policies for zoos in the United States. Although founded in 1924, it gained more autonomy and came into prominence early in my zoo career. I began working with it in the early 1970s when it set up shop in Oglebay Park, West Virginia.

One of the early directors, Bob Wagner, was a man I very much admired. As in all agencies, politics is a necessary evil and almost always an issue. As the organization grew, some members of the board felt perhaps Bob had not kept pace, was maybe not quite sophisticated enough, and they brought in a new executive director over him. I was infuriated and immediately sent them my letter of resignation. This created two problems. First, I was giving up some major influence in the organization. I gained accreditation status for five zoos in my career, more than anyone before or since, and because Detroit had three separate venues (the Detroit Zoo, the Belle Isle Aquarium and the Belle Isle Zoo), I had three votes, one more than any other member of the group. Second, regulations state that all directors of accredited zoos are *required* to be members of AZA. Still, I stood my ground, even asking that my dues for the current year be prorated and I be reimbursed the difference. I never got the money, but the resignation stood and I retained my position as director of the Detroit Zoo in spite of the AZA membership requirement.

In many ways, I respect the positive differences AZA has made for zoos, but I'm still troubled by their lack of backbone in facing the public strongly on issues such as euthanasia, where the organization fails to live up to what is stated in their written policy.

Controversial topics are too often downplayed to the public if there is any threat of initial criticism.

Thus, my campaign for the animals continues.

Chapter 11

Coming "Home"

Thomas Wolfe's third novel *You Can't Go Home Again* relates the folly of attempting to return to times and places past, but I don't know that I agree. Despite the shadows of my youth, I had many lingering visions of the angels who steered me through my checkered early years that drew me *home*. In some ways, I've been fortunate to reclaim my roots with a new clarity of mind and gratitude.

My marriage to Lori endured multiple challenges including years of intense controversy at the zoo, my crippling shoulder injuries, early retirement, additional medical complication. After leaving the Detroit Zoo we lived in Pungoteague, Virginia for nearly ten years. Lori supported me through many trials – physical and mental – but we eventually came to a parting of the ways. As part of the divorce settlement, she got the farm, so I was pretty much footloose for a time.

As at odds as I was with my family at times growing up, it was the last surviving aunts and my aging family on The Hill that brought me back in 2008 to a small brick house on Mentzer Gap Road in Waynesboro, Pennsylvania – the place of my youth, of my rebellion, of my faltering and, if not for the many angels there who helped me, of a time in my life I might have never survived. Perhaps I could repay some of the debt, reclaim some belonging.

My Aunt Alma Graham Senkbeil, my father's only sister, widowed and childless, was nearing the end of her days alone in a small apartment. I reconnected with her and did what I could to make her final days the best they could be. After visiting one assisted living facility after another, she finally settled on Providence Place, a beautiful complex in Chambersburg, Pennsylvania. My sister and niece had visited her one afternoon and called to say how happy Aunt Alma was. She had actually danced for them during their time together. The next day, she died. She had lived there for only 60 days.

My mother's youngest sister, Alice McCoy, and I had always been close. She was only 15 years older than me. When she was young, she was convinced that my mother gave birth to me so she would have a live doll to play with. Aunt Alice, widowed, was living alone in a small house on King Street.

As Aunt Alice's battle against Alzheimer's worsened, so did her safety at home. I found her one day with a bottle of Wesson Oil about to explode on a lighted stove. She became so combative that I called 911. When the ambulance staff attempted to get her into a wheelchair for transport to the hospital, she actually cold-cocked one of the workers. After successful treatment, she was released to Hearthstone Retirement Home near downtown Waynesboro where her care was stellar. The staff called me quite often with updates and I was able to stop by on a regular basis. In late 2013 she was hospitalized after suffering a severe seizure. I managed to secure her care at Mennohaven, an outstanding nursing care facility in Chambersburg, Pennsylvania, where she spent the final days of her life. A volunteer held her hand almost constantly in my absence and was with my aunt when she died.

Blanche Washington, my black mother on The Hill, had lost her husband Charles some years earlier. He left her relatively secure financially, but her attorney and old family friend knew he could call me if she ever needed any help. Her niece Dedra was like a sister to me. She and her son Cory lived with Blanche. Dedra was a wonderful lady who made up hundreds of charity baskets at Christmas every year among other things. She fell victim to breast cancer not long after Blanche suffered an episode, probably a stroke, and was hospitalized at Quincy Nursing Home. She passed away within months and Dedra soon thereafter.

After a few years on Mentzer Gap Road, pretty much a backcountry speedway, I moved to a farm in Sabillasville, Maryland. The quiet and solitude of the mountains are just what I need though I travel nearly every day to Waynesboro. My usual destination Monday through Friday is The Parlor House Restaurant where I have brunch/lunch and connect with friends, one of whom is Ed Miller, ironically once one of my father's best friends. It's great to reminisce as we plan interesting field trips like tracking down the original Mason-Dixon stone markers in the area. With all of my health issues, I sometimes feel like I fit right in regardless of the 20 years head start on life some of them have on me.

I've also paired my continuing love of auctions with an interest in local history. My main focus has been with Renfrew Museum and Park and Renfrew Institute for Cultural and Environmental Studies, both once near and dear to my mother's heart. They are on an idyllic 107 acres of land just east of town offering various meticulously restored buildings including a limestone manor built by Daniel Royer in 1812, a reconstructed Pennsylvania bank barn and a magical four-square garden. There are picnic grounds, the bubbling branch of the East Antietam Creek, woodland trails and a special welcoming aura all its own. Along with the recreation of the Pennsylvania German lifestyle of the period, enhanced by outstanding ongoing educational programs about the culture and environment offered by Renfrew Institute, this special place has most certainly earned the fitting title of 'the jewel of Waynesboro.'

Though I mentioned them earlier in the book, I feel the need to recognize briefly my most important angels:

My grandparents and mother – for nurturing me through my formative early years and softening as much as possible the alienation between me and my father

Blanche and Charles Washington – for gently teaching me essential values through their outstanding examples of overcoming prejudice and achieving as much excellence as possible

Miss Marcella Waltz and Miss Armatha Newman – the constants of my youth

Jim Leaman – valued teacher, father figure and the strongest man of knowledge and manner I've ever known

Diz Freeman and Bill Levick – whose gas station offered me refuge, a job, compassion and trust

Charley Mentzer – the good, good cop who watched out for me in spite of myself

Eldon Joiner and Glenn Fry – mentors of respect and understanding who gave me chances I probably didn't deserve but certainly needed

Nancy Blank – my supervisor in Frederick at community action (O.E.O.) who both reigned me in and gave me the lead that kept me going when college failed me

Msgr. Robert Kline – my guide to the college of knowledge, a farewell to pot and an enduring sense of self-confidence

Mike Scherer – my link to the alcoholic rehabilitation scholarship that saved my college career

Laura McCray and Joan Lister – pillars of support at Salisbury Zoo in so many ways

Coleman Young – an inspiration in every way for his service to his own against great odds and his support and respect for me

Joyce Cohn and Audrey Rose – a source of support and inspiration through the challenges at Detroit

Dr. Lionel Swann – a civil rights warrior with a presence that filled the room

Kathy (Latinen) DonCarlos – my keystone at Detroit moving from concessions to curator of mammals on her excellent merit – my greatest mentor

Doris Applebaum – a tireless wordsmith and record keeper, she embodies goodness, diligence and humility

Amy Gibson – my closest friend and confident for more than a decade who has kept me afloat in body and soul

Final Words

Certainly everyone has a story to tell – *many* special stories about their unique life experiences. I feel fortunate to have gotten to this point and challenged, as well, to somehow summarize what I hope this book might accomplish beyond my own self-satisfaction in having completed it. I believe the answer is twofold.

On a personal level, the narrative recaptures pivotal moments in my past and, more importantly, acknowledges the host of generous caring people who enabled me to live what I hope has been a meaningful life.

On a public level, it honors the animals – the creatures that enrich all of our lives and literally saved mine. We must provide for and protect these animals or all of our lives will be diminished by losing them. This was a challenge I confronted as meaningfully as possible throughout my 20-plus year career as a zoo director and as a private citizen before and since.

The many special experiences I had, especially in the zoo arena, inspired me to accept this responsibility. The extraordinary people I met who were generous in their support – sharing their knowledge, funding, friendship, experiences, and more – remain my heroes to this day. I've learned so much, but most imnportantly I've learned how *little* we really know about these creatures with whom we share the earth.

I continue to struggle with where I stand on zoos today. Do the ends justify the means? Can the benefits we derive from holding these animals in captivity justify the pain and sacrifice they suffer as a result? Try as we may, an elephant can't walk 40 miles a day in captivity. A polar bear can't swim more than 24 hours continuously to reach an ice floe. Cheetahs are reduced to greyhound status chasing a fake rabbit around a track to replicate their natural environment.

It's difficult to forget the grossly obese gorilla in a cage at Detroit with no chance for any exercise. The intensely direct stare of the orangutan in Baltimore as if he was trying to tell me something about his need – all animals' need – to be free. Is this, and more, worth the experience and understanding we, as humans, gain by relating to them face-to-face in zoos and animal parks?

Is it any wonder some of these captive animals, like Shamu the orca or an occasional rogue elephant or lion, reach their limit of endurance and turn on their handlers? We can't even consistently predict when individuals of our own species will snap, so the challenge of doing so with animals is overwhelming.

Hopefully, something I've related that has touched me will translate to my readers and inspire them to become involved in any and all areas available to them that advocate for and protect the animals. If you are fortunate enough to have discretionary funds, consider contributing to conservation and animal support organizations. They currently occupy a very small slice of the charitable giving pie overall.

Visit your local zoo or animal facility. Learn about it. Support it. Improve it, if you can. The greater the public understanding of what goes on, the more likely things will change for the better.

Honor *all* animals – in zoos, on farms, in homes – everywhere you can. Consider how much richer our lives are because of our associations with them. Repay them with the care and respect they so deserve.

Think. Start a dialogue. Don't just accept everything you're told. As a child of the 60s I learned to question everything – to use the brain we've been given and question convention. This goes way beyond zoos . . . but it's a place to start.

Steve Graham's Credentials

Education

1964   –   Graduate of Waynesboro Area Senior High School, Waynesboro, PA

1971   –   B.S. Psychology, Mount Saint Mary's College, Emmitsburg MD

1975   –   Laboratory Course in Ornithology, Cornell University

1979   –   American Association of Zoological Parks and Aquariums Professional Management School

1989   –   Safari in Rwanda

1988   –   Safari in Tanzania

1984   –   Safaris in Zambia, Zimbabwe and Botswana

1977   –   80, 1983, 1985, 1987 – 90 – Safaris in Kenya

Professional Experience

1972 – 77 – Director, Salisbury Zoo

One of the first ten zoos accredited in the U.S.

First zoo in the world to complete its inventory on the International Species Information System (ISIS)

Only zoo in the state to receive number-one status by the Humane Society of the United States

First guidebook for this zoo

First docent organization for this zoo

First major fundraiser for this zoo for the jaguar exhibit

1977 – 78 – Associate/Acting Director, Baltimore Zoo

1978 – 82 – Director, Baltimore Zoo

Accredited for first time

First moated exhibit in the zoo's 105-year history

Major renovation to two existing historical buildings on zoo grounds

$4 million animal hospital

1982 – 92 – Director, Detroit Zoological Parks Department

Detroit Zoo, Belle Isle Zoo and Belle Isle Aquarium all accredited for the first time

$12 million front entrance renovation

$2 million Elephant House renovation

$600,000 Siamang Exhibit

$800,000 Snow Leopard Exhibit

$600,000 Penguinarium renovation

$8 million Chimpanzee Habitat

$1.5 million Lion House renovation

$1.5 million Tiger House renovation

$360,000 educational graphics improvements

50% increase in operating budget

First capital improvement in 15 years

> Detroit Zoological Society membership increased from 2,500 to more than 18,000

1991	–	Retired
1999–2000	–	Interim Executive Director, Wicomico County Humane Society
2001	–	Interim Executive Director, SPCA of the Eastern Shore

Major Lectures

Johns Hopkins University

Michigan State University

Salisbury State University

University of Michigan

University of Pennsylvania

Publications

"The Use of Mirrors in Imprinting Chicks" – Presented at the Northeast Regional Conference, American Association of Zoo Keepers, June 25, 1971. Published *American Association of Zoo Keepers Journal*, 1971. Reprinted in *International Zoo Keepers Journal*, Vol. 103, February 1972.

"The First Record of Caretta caretta caretta Nesting on Maryland Beach" – *Bulletin of the Maryland Herpetological Society*, Vol. 9, No. 2, June 1973. Resulted in this species placement on the Maryland Endangered Species List.

"Zoo Pets" – Presented at the American Association of Zoological Parks and Aquariums (AAZPA) Northeastern Regional Conference, May 1973.

Salisbury Zoo Guidebook, May 1974 – editor

"Observations on Maras at the Salisbury Zoo" – *The Keeper*, Vol. 1, 1975.

"Low Budget Educational Items for Zoos" – *AAZPA Proceedings*, 1975 – 76.

"Some Ethical Considerations for Zoo and Aquarium Professionals" – *AAZPA Proceedings* 1978.

Amiable Little Beasts, co-authored with Roger Caras, Macmillan Books, December 1980.

"Zoo Director: Animals vs. Business" – *AAZPA Proceedings*, 1981.

"Veterinarians: Vexation to Veneration" – *AAZPA Proceedings*, 1982.

"Case Reports and Experience" (accompanied presentation on "Surplus Animal Management: Problems and Options") *AAZPA Proceedings*, 1983.

"Burnout: A Case Study" – presented at AAZPA Annual Conference, 1984.

"Animals: Means or End?" – *AAZPA Great Lakes Regional Proceedings*, 1986.

"Zookeeper Training: A Personal History" – *AAZPA Great Lakes Regional Proceedings*, 1986.

"The Changing Role of Animal Dealers" – Presented at AAPZA Annual Conference, 1987.

"Renovation of the Penguinarium at the Detroit Zoo" – *International Zoo Yearbook*, The Zoological Society of London, 1987, 26: (125-132).

Awards

Distinguished Alumni Award, National Alumni Association, Mount Saint Mary's College, 1979.

Who's Who in America, 1982 – 90.

U.S. Television, Best Entertainment Promotion, Detroit Zoo – "Zoo Stars," 1983.

Management Development School, Fifth Year Instructor's Award, AAPZA, 1984.

J. Barrett Award, Metropolitan Detroit Convention & Visitors Bureau, 1987.

Men of Achievement, International Biographical Centre, 1989

Professional Associations

American Association of Zoological Parks and Aquariums
Professional Fellow Member – 1971 – 1991

Past Chairman   — Long Range Plan for Great Lakes Region
    Speaker's Bureau Committee
    Animal Welfare Committee

Past Vice Chairman — Board of Regents' Professional Management School, including five years teaching experience

Past Member   — Legislation Committee
    Education Committee
    Keeper Committee
    Surplus Committee

Member of Accreditation Team for Binder Park Zoo, Hershey Zoo, National Zoo,

Roger Williams Park Zoo, Toronto Zoo, Van Saun Park Zoo

American Association of Museums, Contributing Trustee

American Ornithologists' Union

Canadian Association of Zoological Parks and Aquariums

The Coolidge Center for Environmental Leadership

Committee to Preserve Assateague Island, Inc.

East African Teaching Zoo

Gainesville, Florida, Advisory Board

International Crane Foundation

International Snow Leopard Trust

International Union for Conservation of Nature and Natural Resources, Species Survival Commission and Asian Elephant Specialist Group

International Wild Waterfowl Association

Michigan Citizens' Advisory Committee on Endangered Species

National Audubon Society

National Chimpanzee Breeding & Research Program Advisory Committee

The Nature Conservancy

Santa Fe Teaching Zoo

Society for Conservation Biology

The Society for Wildlife Art of the Nations

Vulture Study Group / Africa

Whooping Crane Conservation Association

Current Memberships in Professional Organizations

Barrier Island Center, business member

The Carter Center

Chesapeake Bay Foundation

Citizens for a Better Eastern Shore

Martin Luther King Memorial Charter Subscriber

NAACP gold life membership

The Nature Conservancy

Renfrew Institute for Cultural and Environmental Studies

Southern Poverty Law Center

Wall of Tolerance Honoree Leadership Council (SLC)

We Decide

Past Memberships in Professional Organizations

Arizona Primate Foundation, advisory board

Baltimore Attractions Association, president

Chesapeake Audubon Society

Detroit Aquarium Advisory Committee

Food Bank of Southeastern Virginia, past board member

Food Bank of the Eastern Shore, past chairman

Holy Land Conservation Fund, Board of Directors

Institute of Museum Services, grant reader

Johns Hopkins University, adjunct professor

Judicial Conference of the United States Sixth Circuit Committee on the Bicentennial of the Constitution, committee member

Maple Shade Residential Homes, Inc. (juvenile halfway house), executive board

Maryland State Trapping Board, humane representative

Michigan Wildlife Festival, 1988, honorary chairman

Michigan Wildlife Festival, 1990, co-chairman

SPCA of the Eastern Shore, Inc., past president

Substance Abuse Awareness Month (S.E. Michigan), 1986 honorary chairman

Virginia Foundation for Natural Resources, board of trustees

Ward Wildfowl Foundation, advisory board

Wayne State University, Department of Biological Science, adjunct assistant professor

Wicomico Environmental Trust, chairman

Wicomico Humane Society, president

www.ingramcontent.com/pod-product-compliance
Lightning Source LLC
Chambersburg PA
CBHW071556080526
44588CB00010B/921